Hermann, Missouri

One of the Prettiest Towns in America

PHOTOGRAPHY BY

William Fields

Tony Carosella

AP

Acclaim Press™

MORLEY, MISSOURI

Acclaim Press
— Your Next Great Book —
P.O. Box 238
Morley, MO 63767
(573) 472-9800
www.acclaimpress.com

Publishing Consultant: Keith Ellebrecht
Editor: Charles A. Francis
Book Design: Rodney Atchley
Cover Design: M. Frene Melton
Front cover photograph: Festhalle I (Fields)
Back cover photograph: Sky Rockets in the Night (Carosella)

ISBN: 978-1-942613-19-0 / 1-942613-19-9
Library of Congress Control Number: 2015914203

Second Print: 2021
Printed in the United States of America
10 9 8 7 6 5 4 3 2

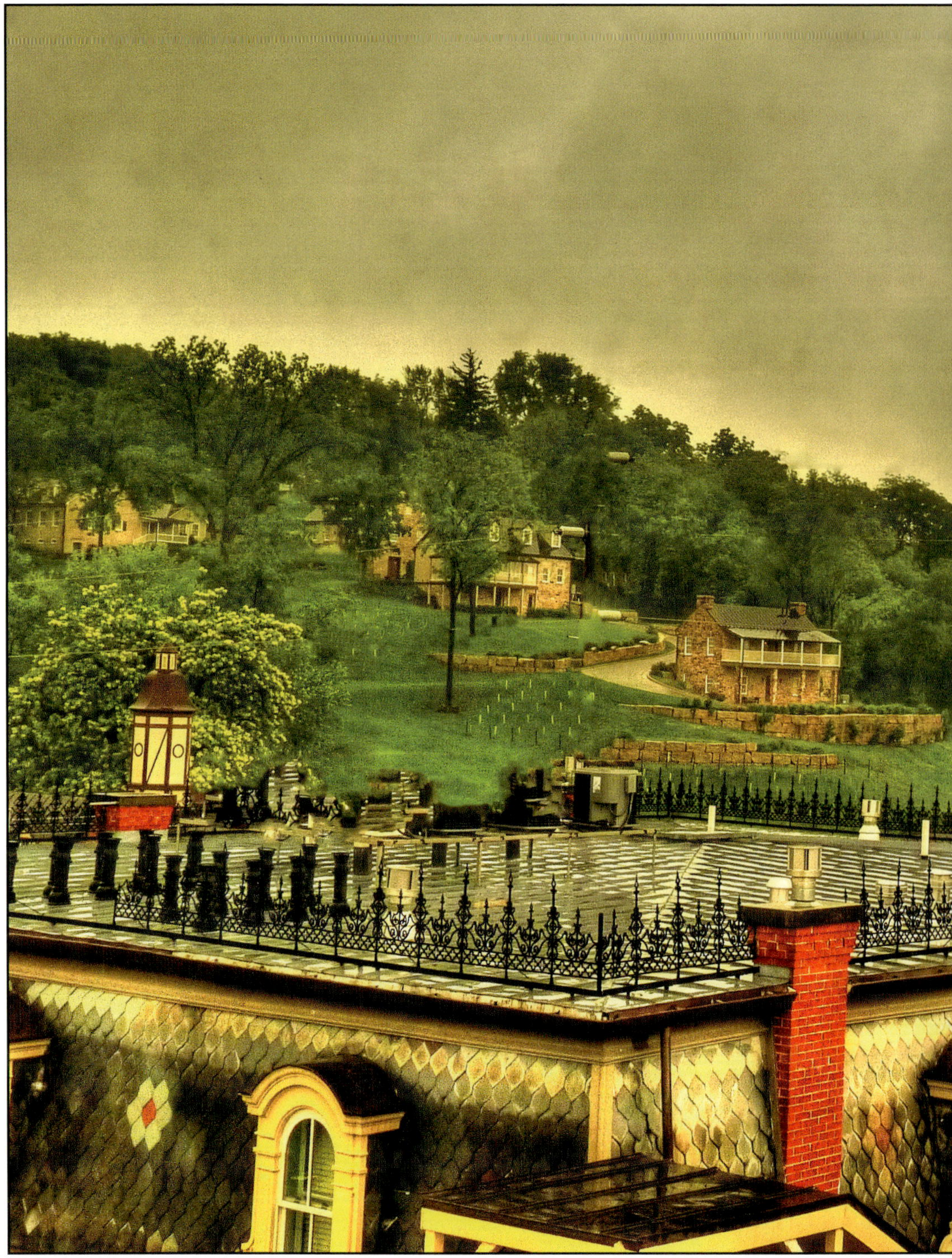

Star Mill Over Rooftops
William Fields

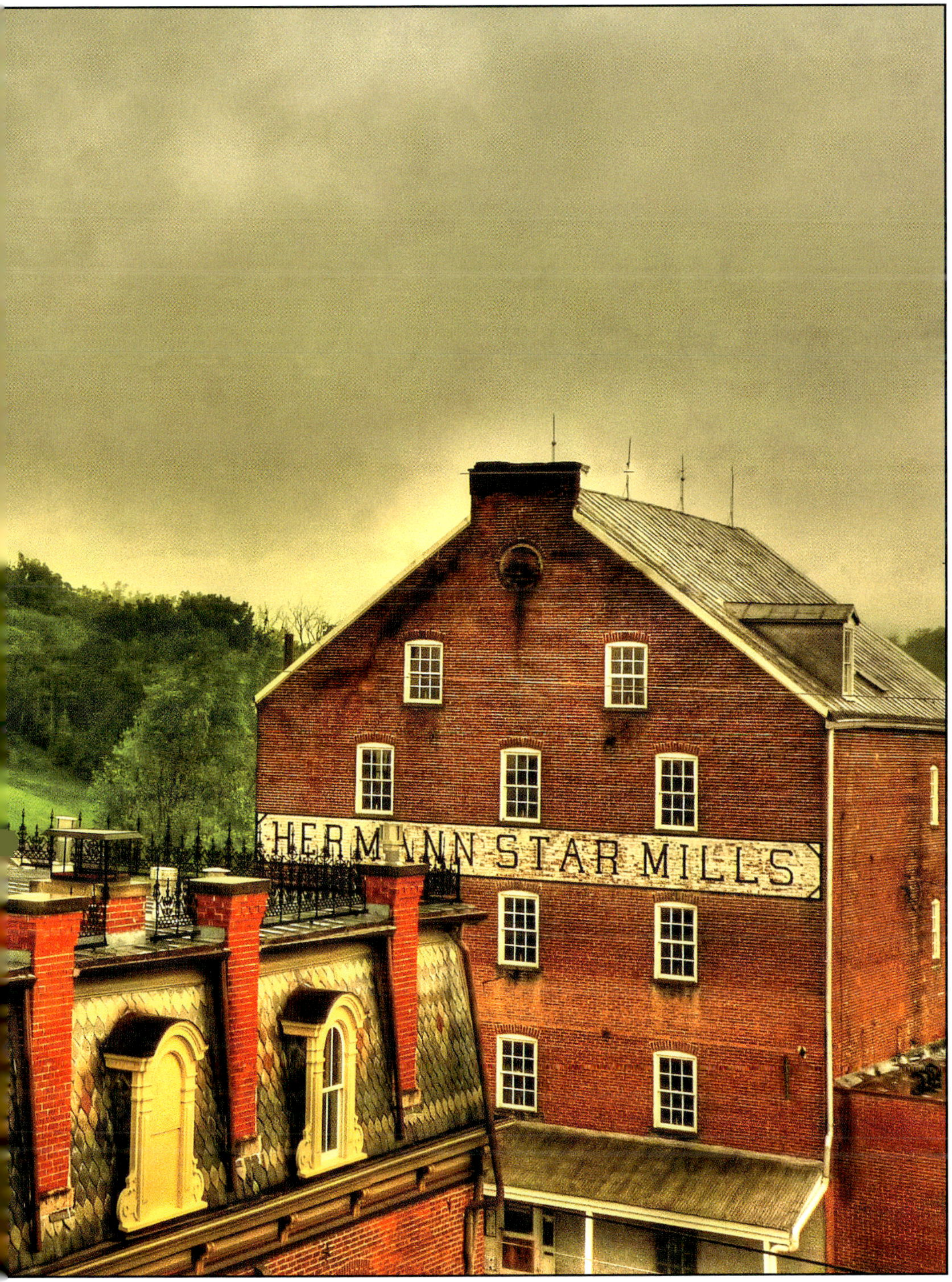

Contents

Foreword

The German Settlement Society was formed in Philadelphia by a group of people who had a dream of creating a settlement where they could preserve their German heritage. The fulfillment of that dream began in 1837 when they came to the land along the Missouri River that was to become Hermann.

In 1970 we took our family to a Maifest in Hermann and discovered that settlement. We had been to Germany a number of times and suddenly here in our own backyard we discovered a little bit of Germany along the Missouri River. That was the beginning of what would become a long and exciting journey.

The first building that we restored was the Reiff House Hotel that had been scheduled for demolition. When we finished that project, we wondered how well we had preserved the dream of the Reiff family. As we continued to restore historic buildings, we found that we asked ourselves that question at the end of every project. Did we capture the dream of the original builder of that building? We hope that we have.

The beautiful art photography, by William Fields and Tony Carosella, attests to the success of the work of many people to preserve these dreams. We consider the citizens of Hermann today to be true members of the German Settlement Society. Did the members of the original settlement society ever dream that the town they founded would be named, "The Prettiest Town in America"? We think so!

Mary and Jim Dierberg

Introduction

Hermann, Missouri has been deemed one of the prettiest towns in America. It has been chosen by travelers and travel writers. It is the choice of retirees driving recreational vehicles and motorcycles. Butchers, bakers and shoemakers choose this lovely town by the Missouri River as a place to stop and drink in the charm and beauty or to settle down and make a life.

The French and the Spanish came here in times gone by. Meriwether Lewis and William Clark came through what is now Hermann on their way with the Corps of Discovery. Later the German Settlement Society came. The texture and the flavor of the town was largely designed by those settlers.

In more recent times, other nationalities and ethnicities have come and made their homes here by the "Big Muddy" river; on its hillsides; in the forests and in the fields.

They each had their reasons but they all had one common purpose in mind. They came because this is a beautiful place. There is little crime. The air and the water are good. There is a spirit of community and a sense of something like a tribal connection here that we all share. No one had to tell us that Hermann is the prettiest town. We all knew it as soon as we saw it.

To say that we are biased would be an understatement. To say that we are blessed would be stating the obvious. After all, haven't we chosen Hermann too?

William Fields and Tony Carosella
October 1st, 2015

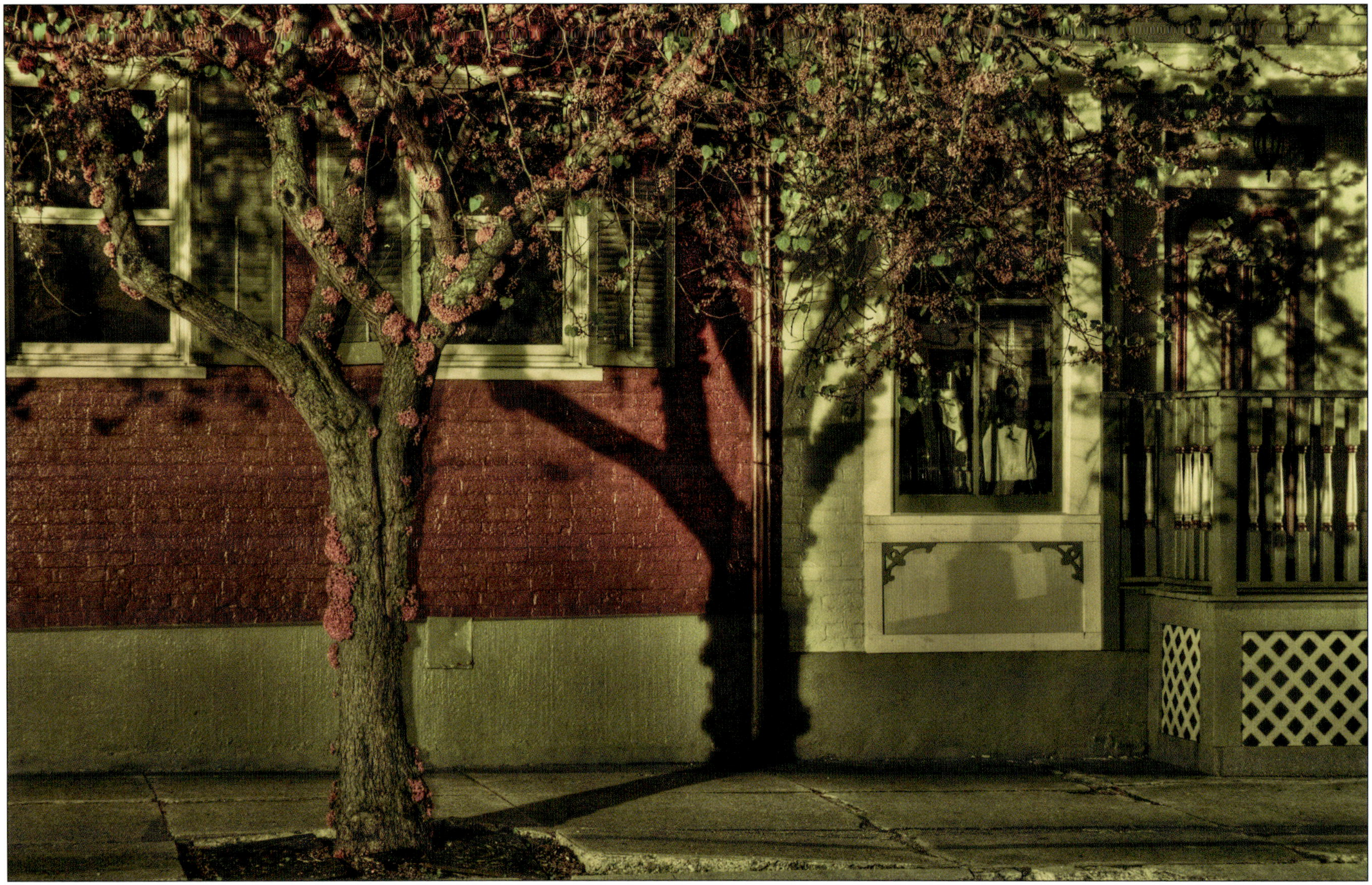

Schiller Street Redbud

William Fields

"The Axis of the earth sticks out visibly
through the centre of each and every town ..."
– Oliver Wendell Holmes

The Land

"Land and water are not really separate things,
but they are separate words,
and we perceive through words."
– David Rains Wallace
The Untamed Garden and Other Personal Essays

"The land belongs to the future; that's the way it seems to me. How many of the names on the county clerk's plat will be there in fifty years? I might as well try to will the sunset over there to my brother's children. We come and go, but the land is always here. And the people who love it and understand it are the people who own it—for a little while."
– Willa Cather
O Pioneers!

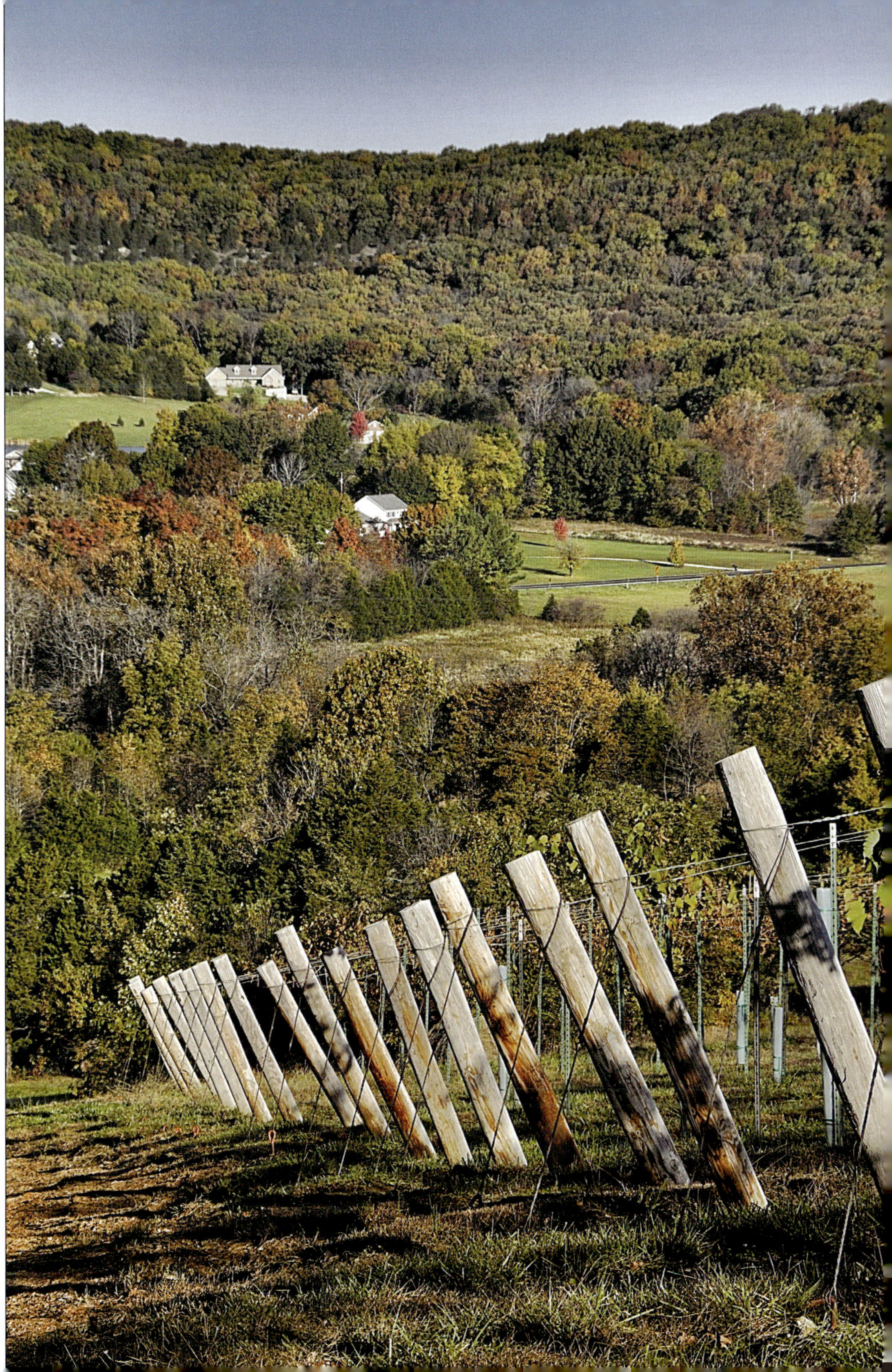

Bracing the Rows
Tony Carosella

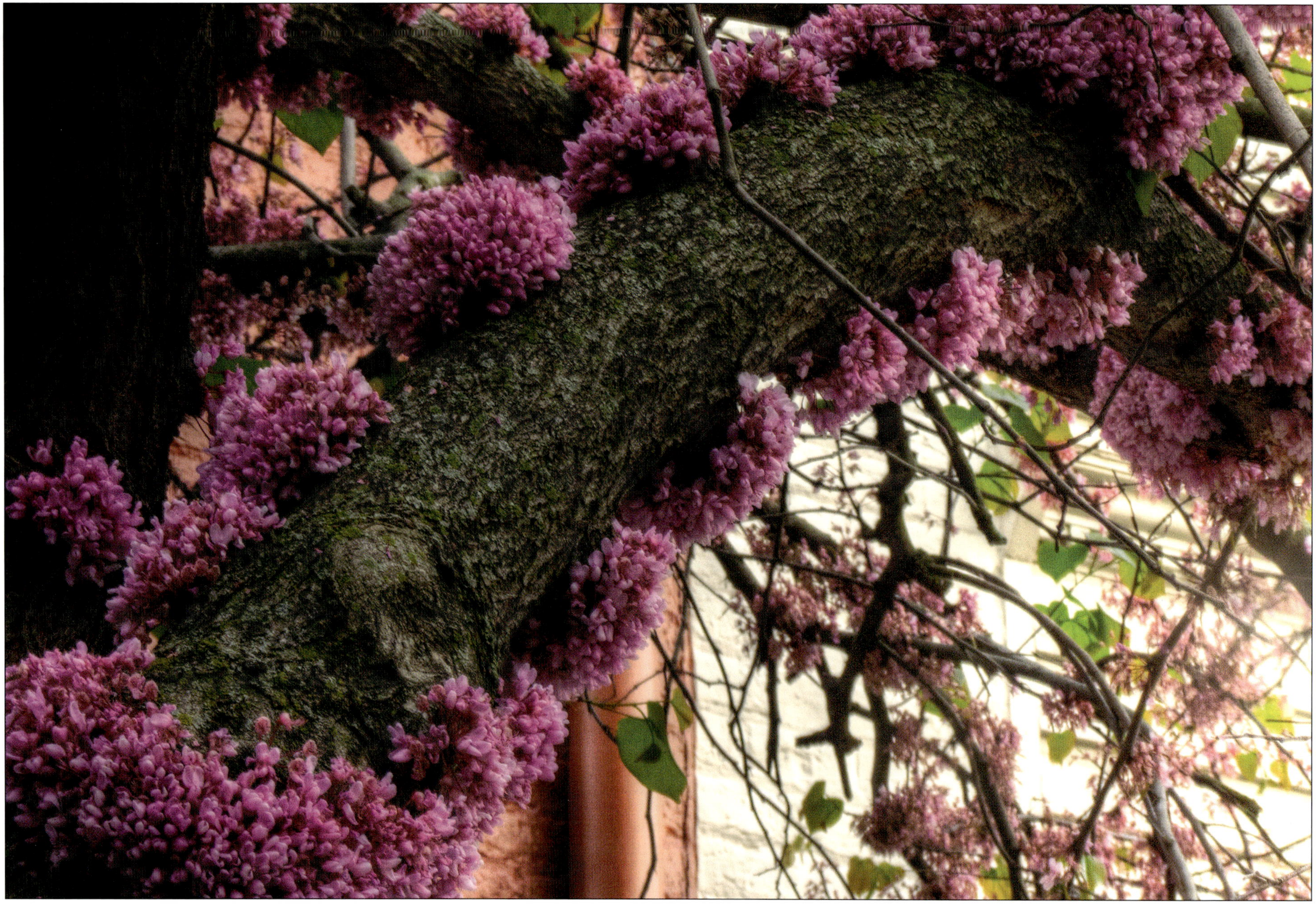

Alpha-Redbud Festoon

William Fields

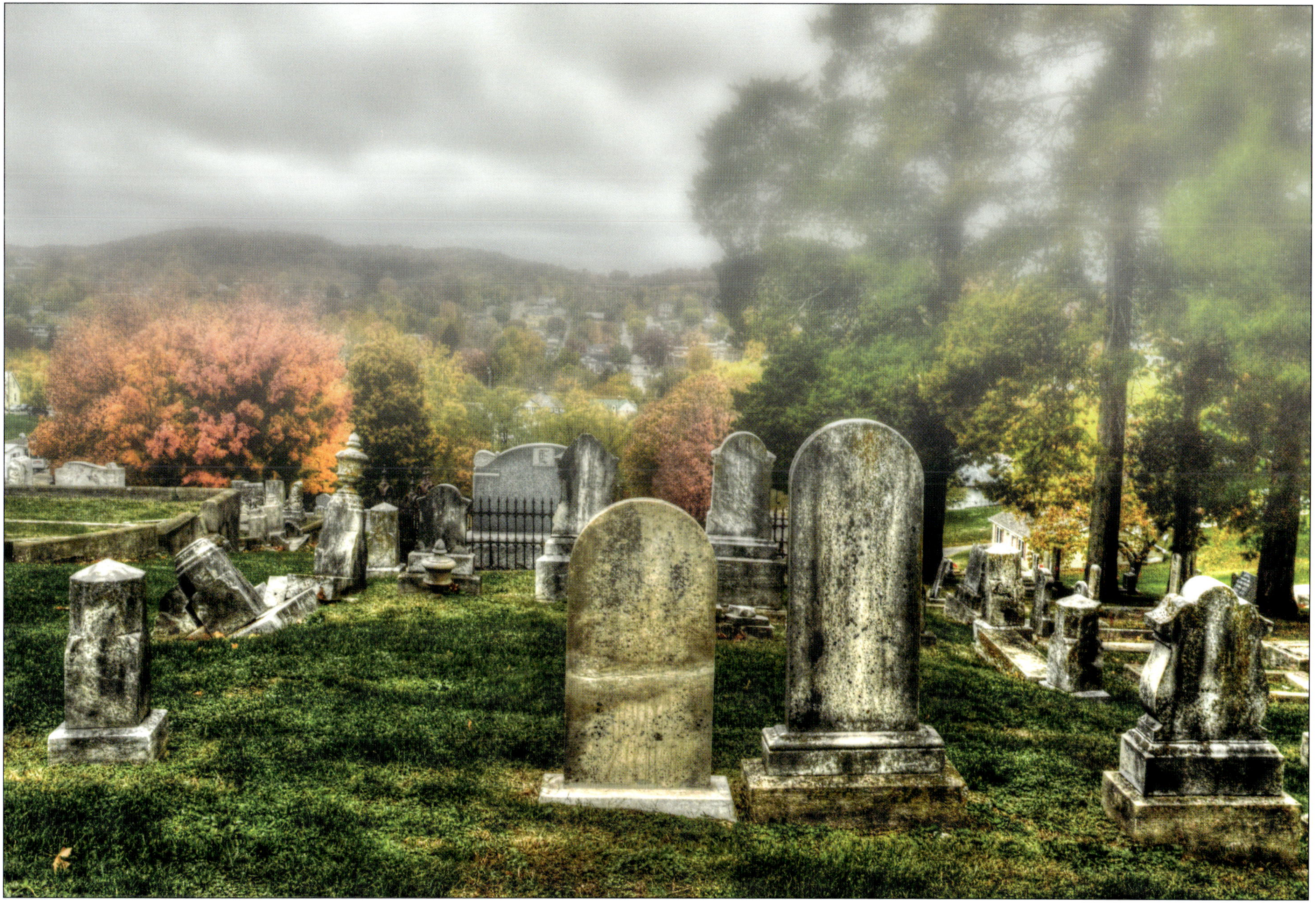

Omega-Cemetery Hill
William Fields

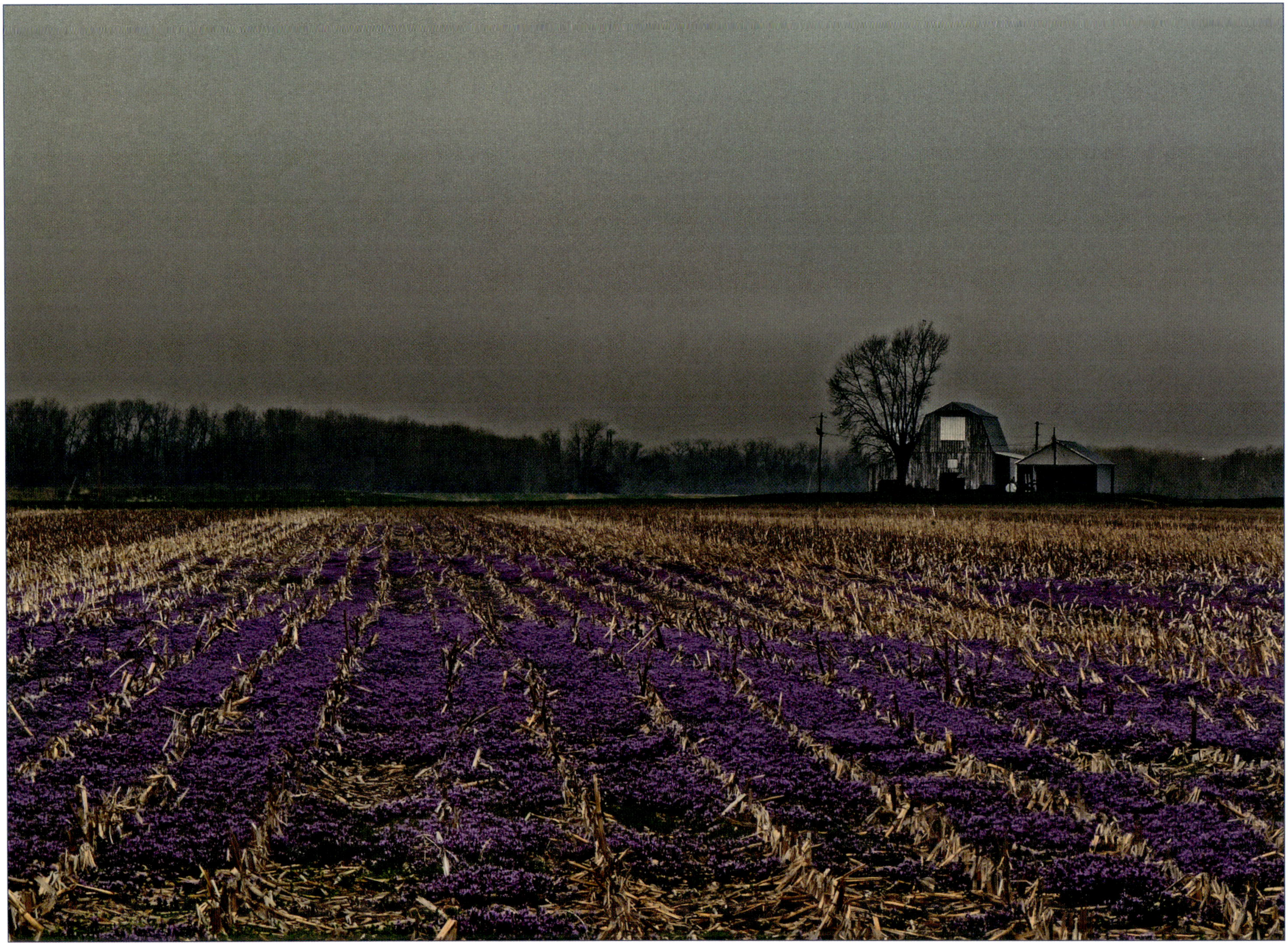

Henbit
William Fields

"The seasons on the land change our world
in so many ways."
– William Fields

"Aim for the moon. If you miss,
you may hit a star."
– W. Clement Stone

"The day, water, sun, moon, night – I do not have
to purchase these things with money."
– Plautus

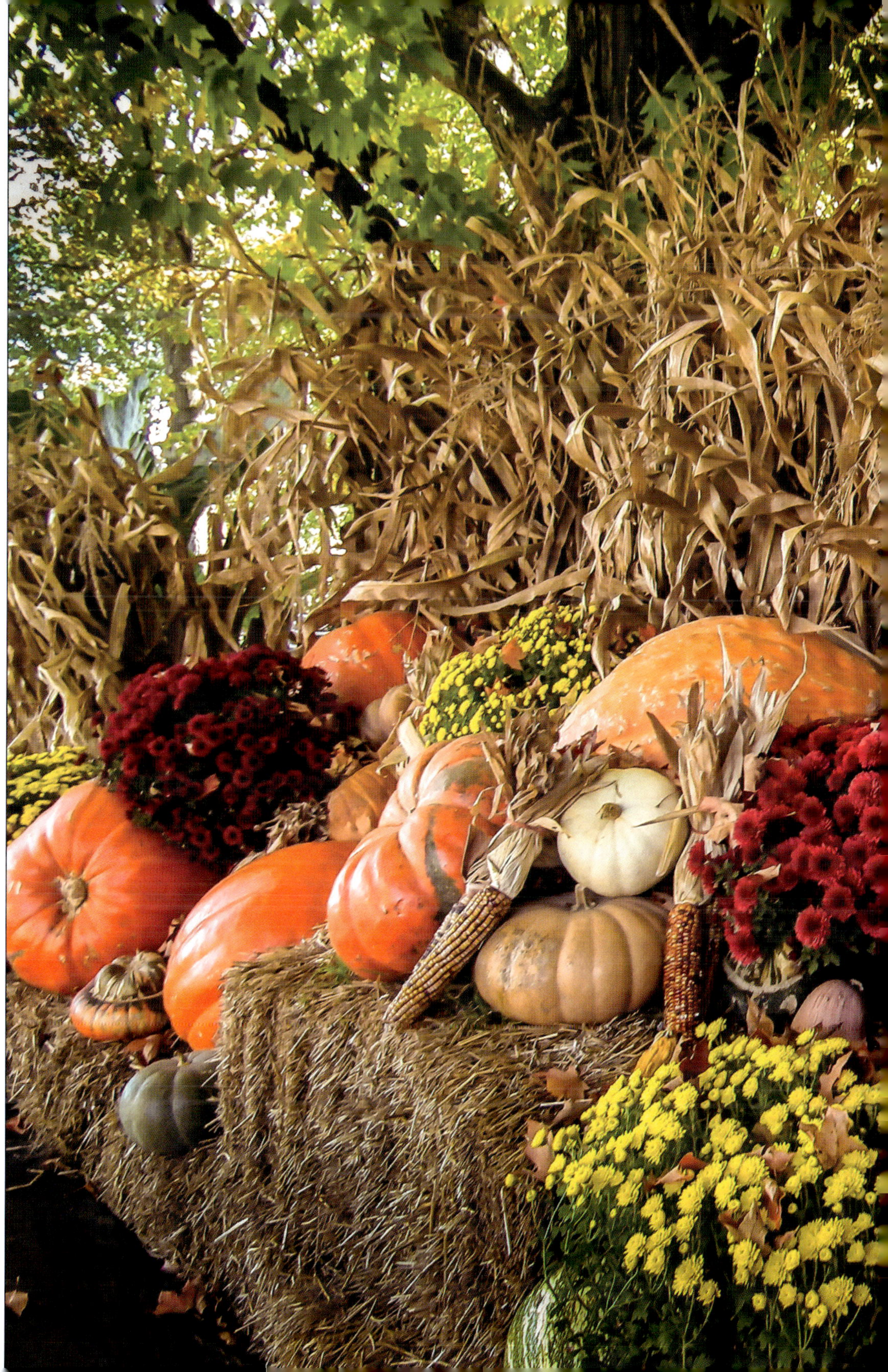

Stone Hill Bounty
Tony Carosella

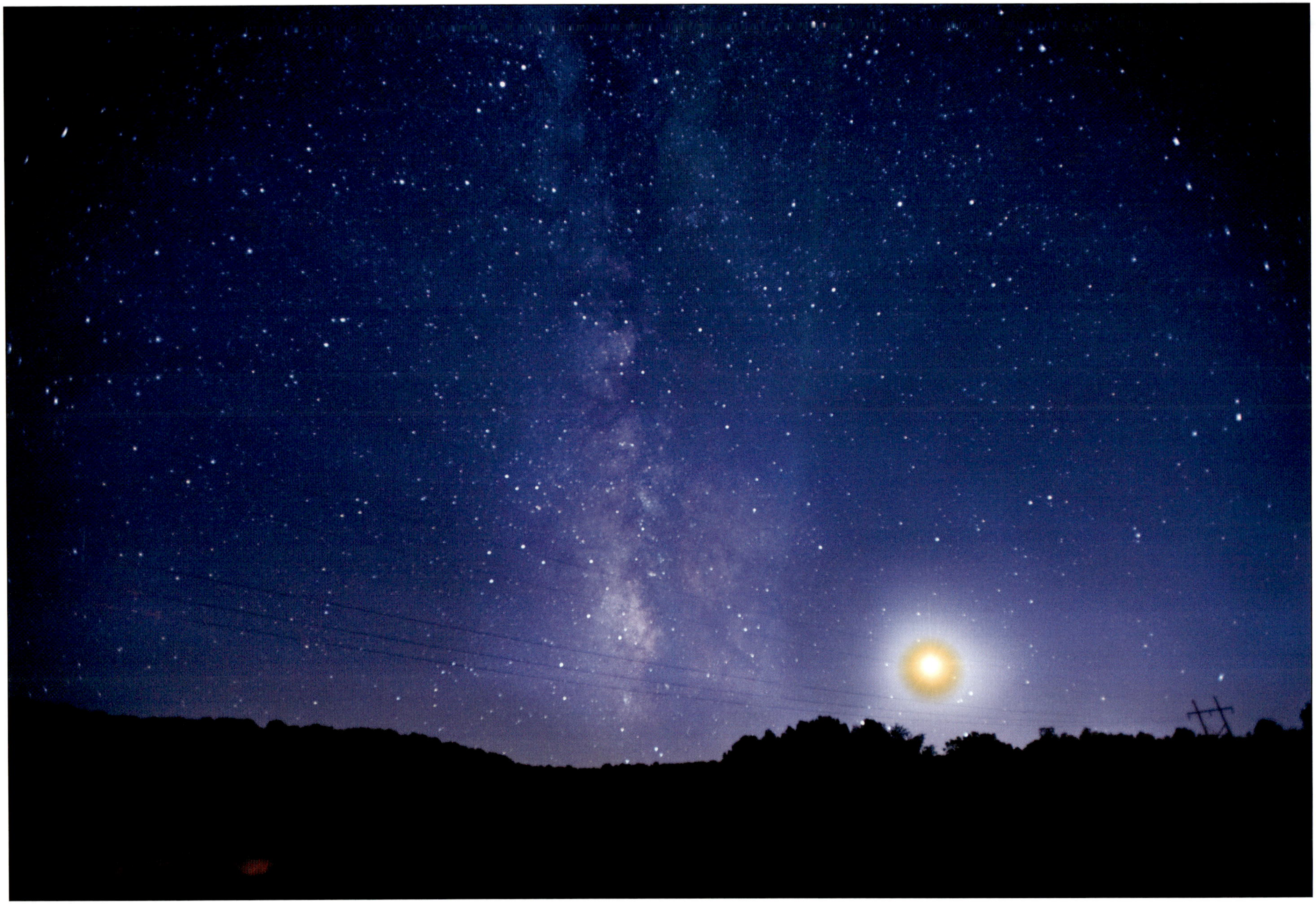

Over the Power Lines
William Fields

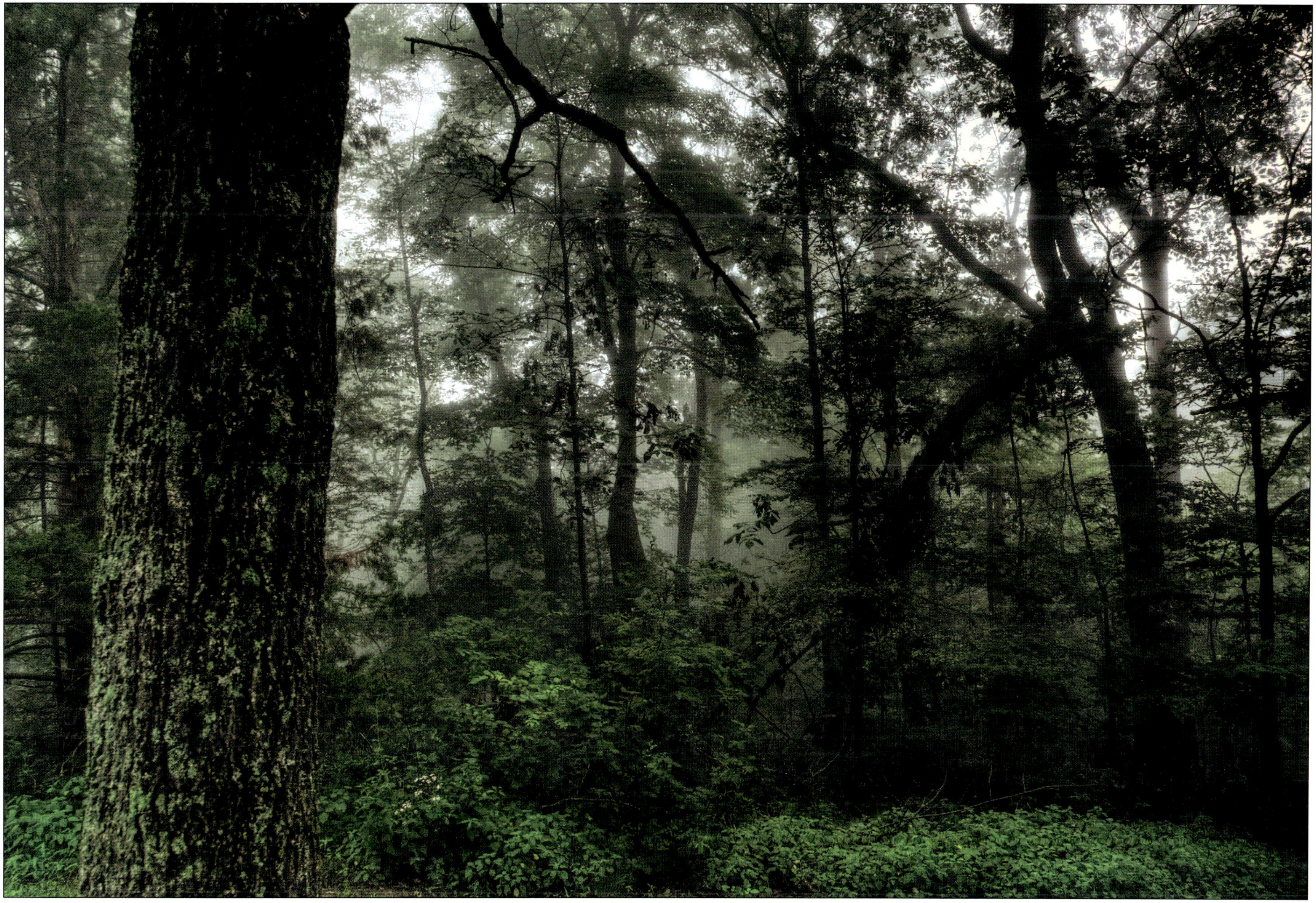

Misty Forest, Summer
William Fields

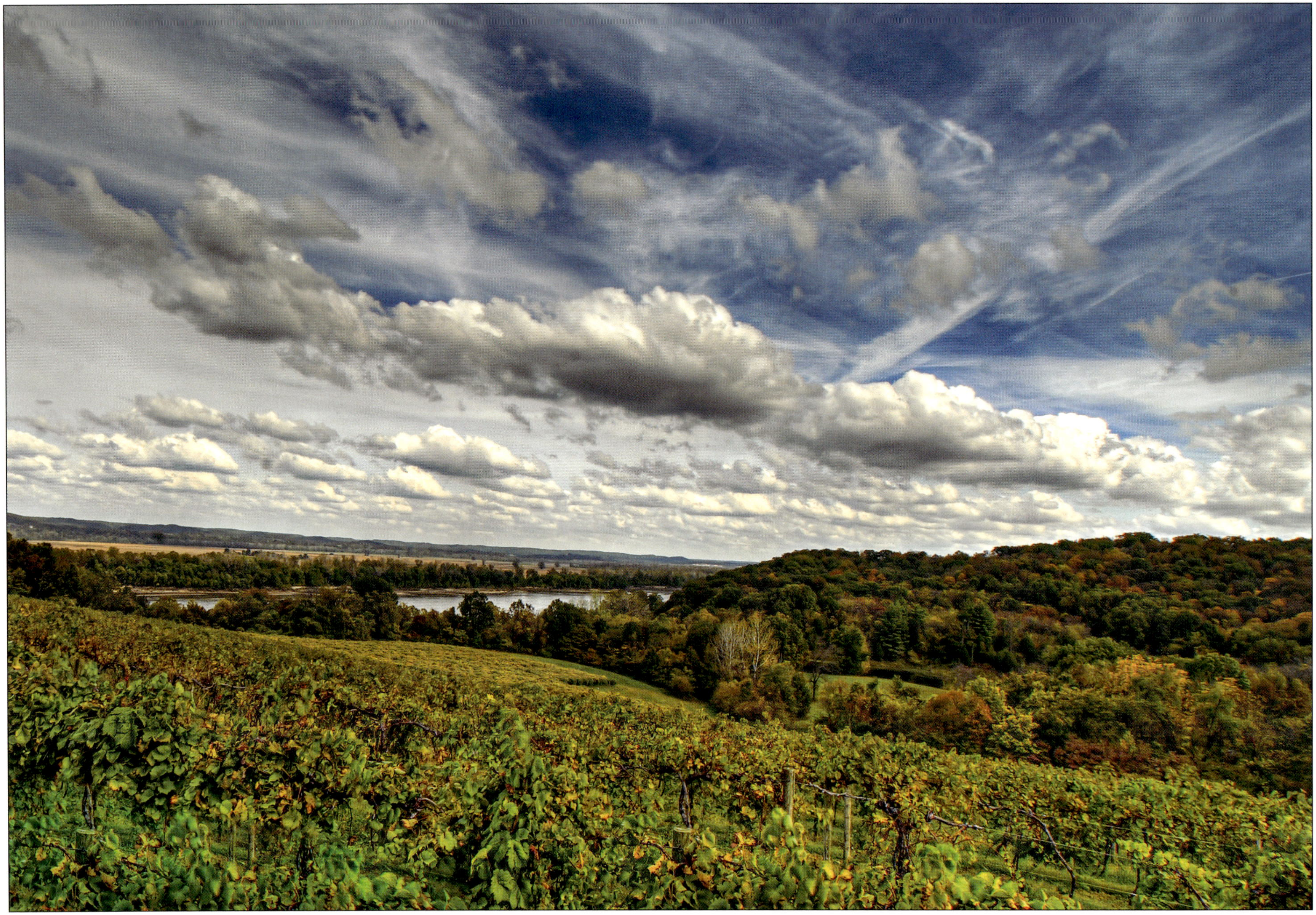

Vineyard View
Tony Carosella

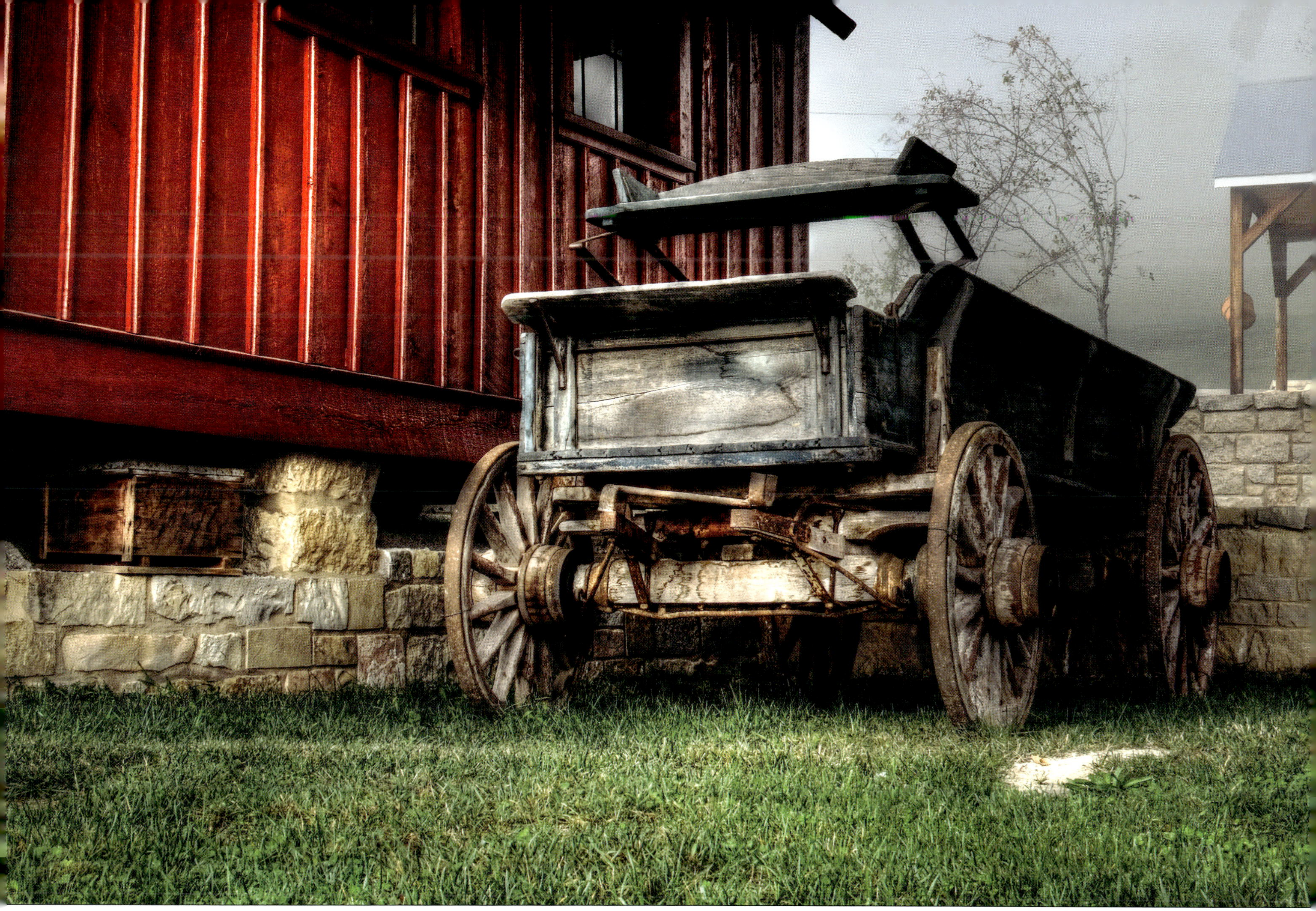

Hermann Farm Buckboard

William Fields

Grandmother's Grace

William Fields

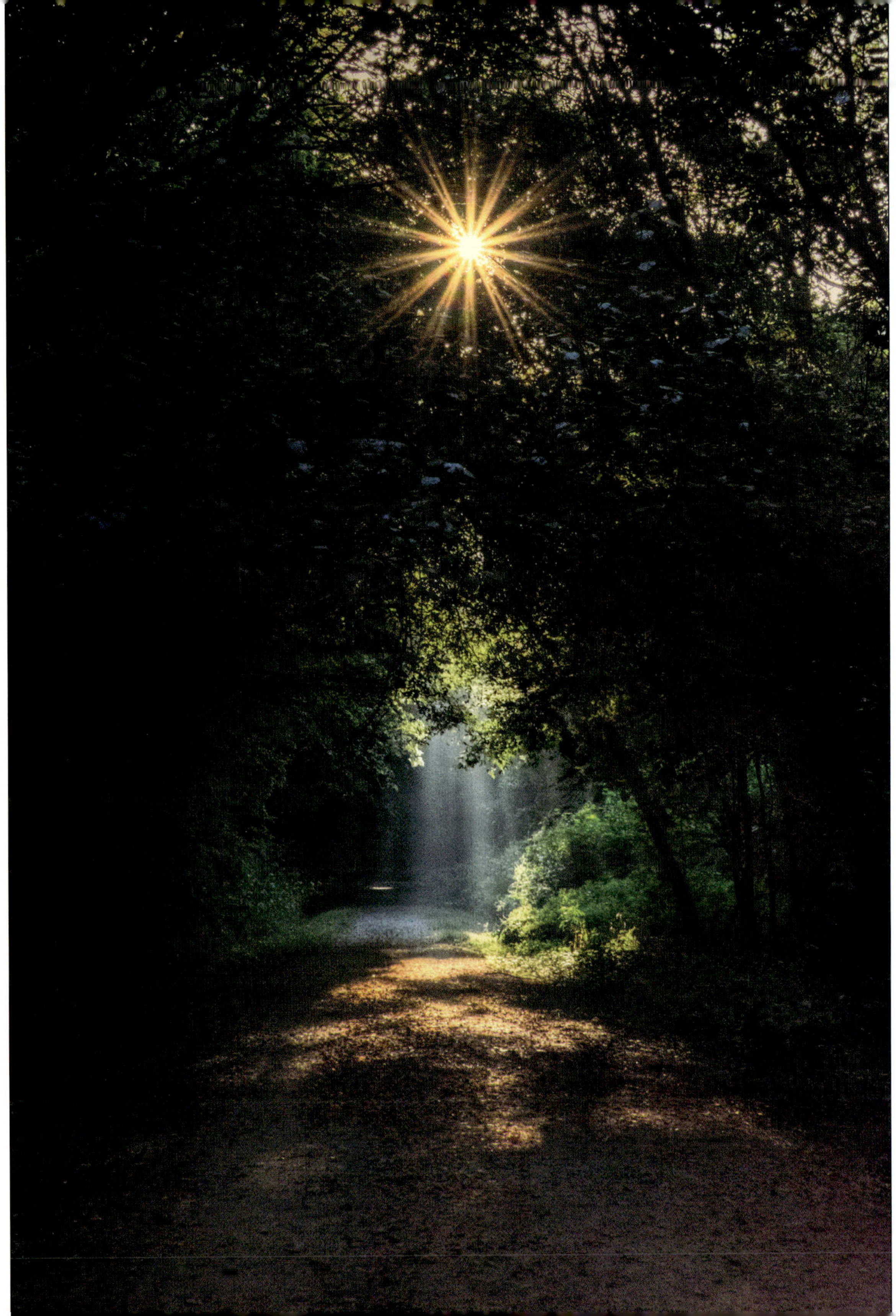

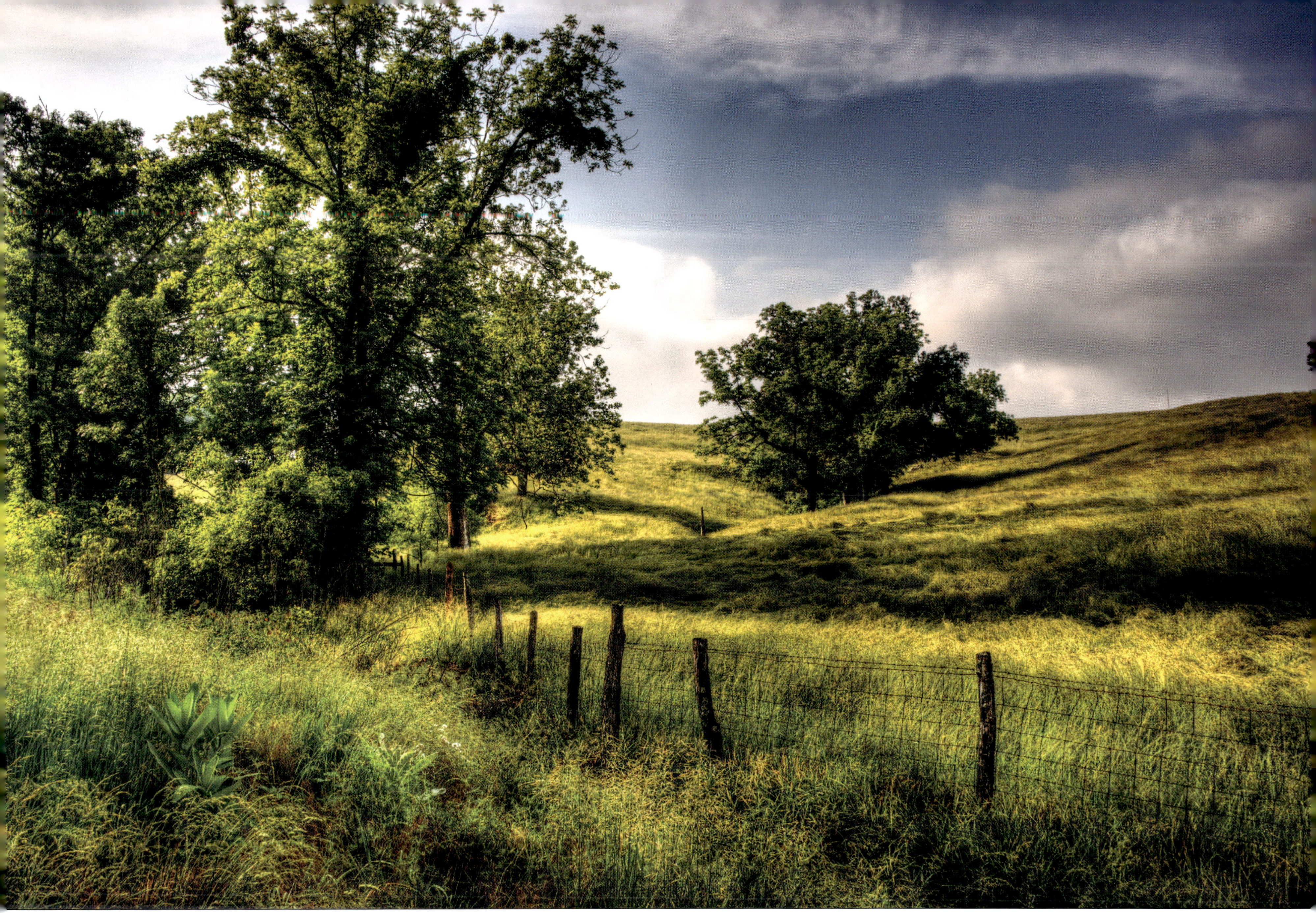

Heck's Farm
William Fields

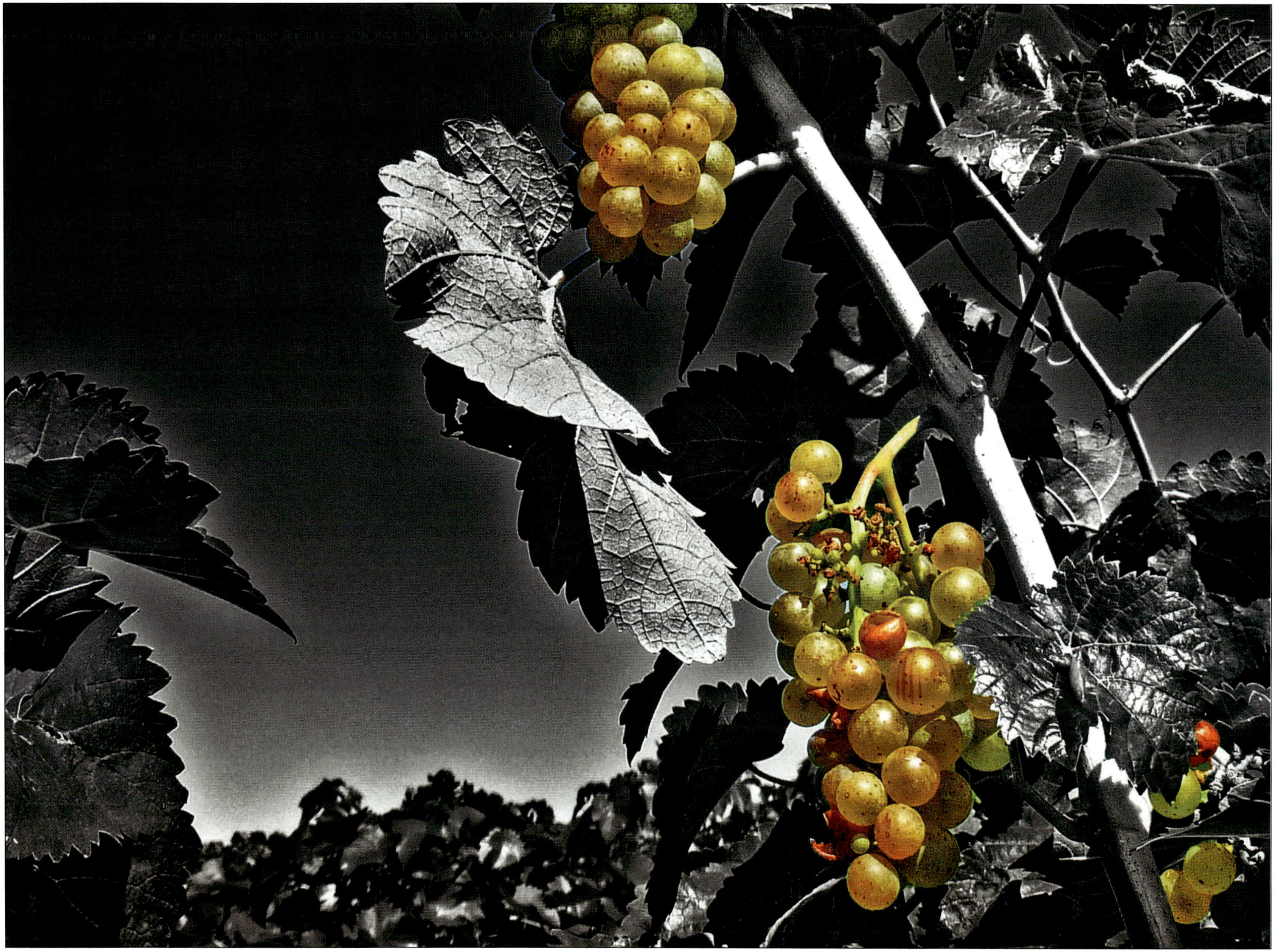

Arc of Vignole
William Fields

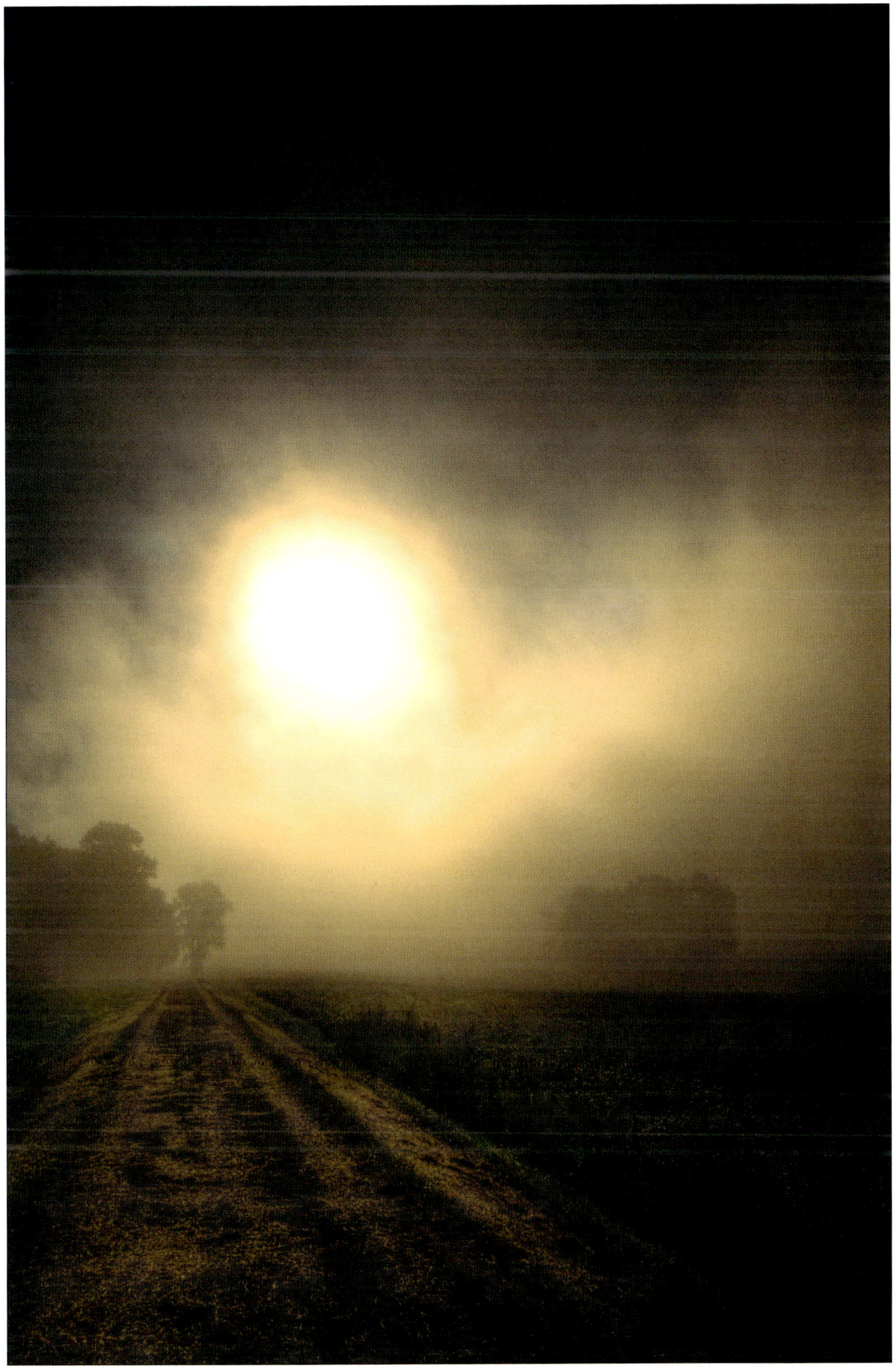

A Mist in the Bottoms
William Fields

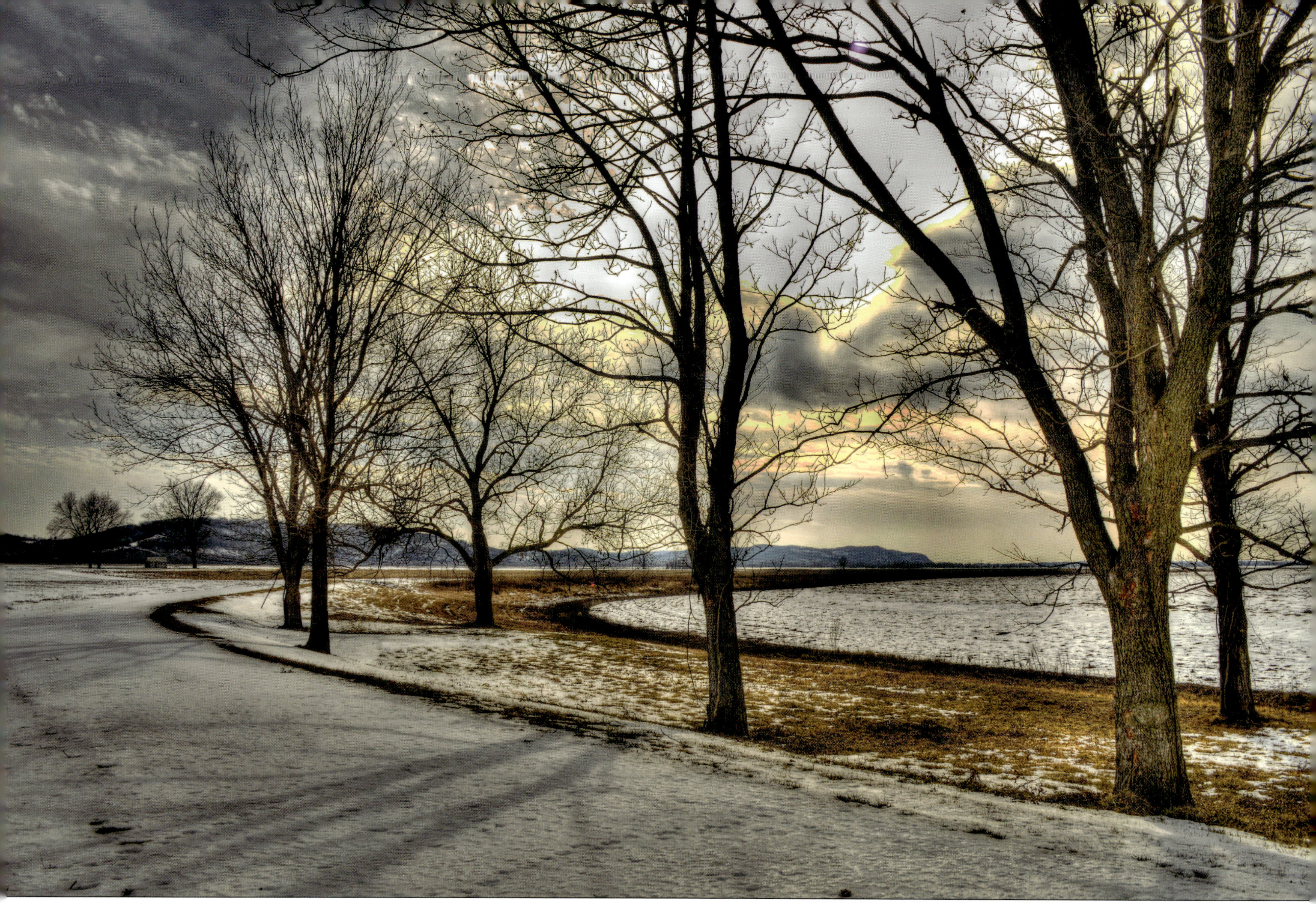

Along an Avenue of Trees
William Fields

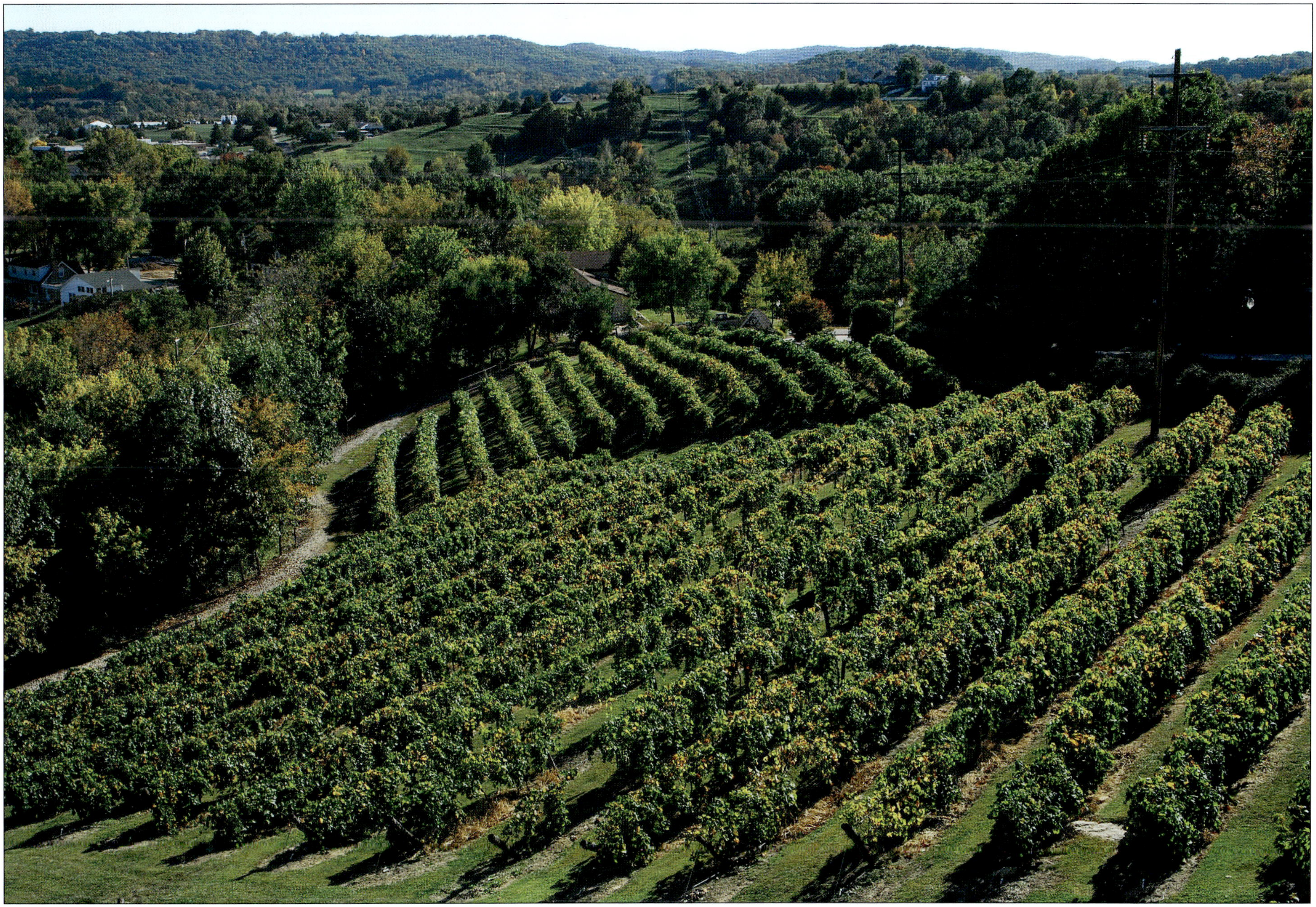

Hermann Hill Vineyard

Tony Carosella

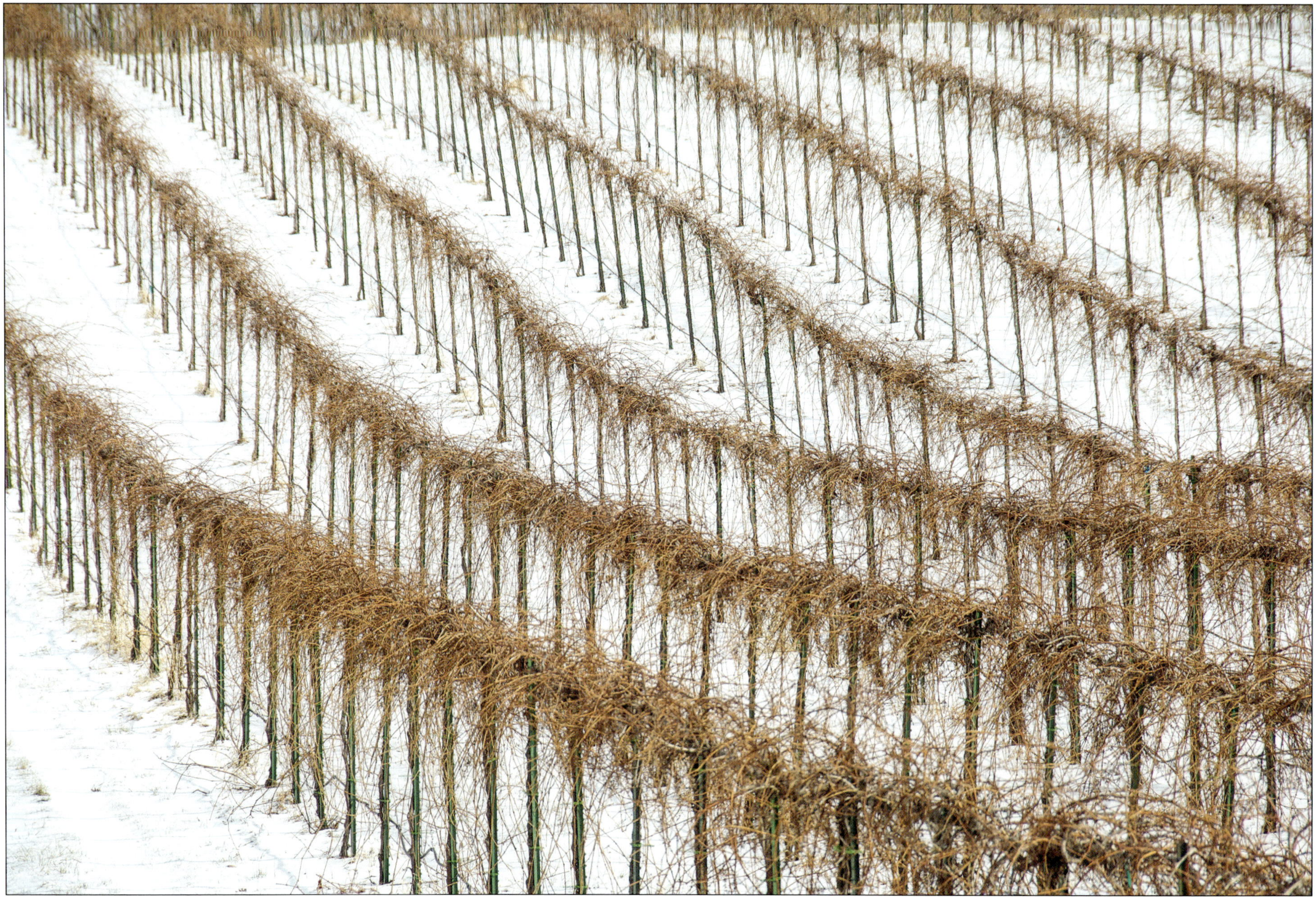

Winter Vines

Tony Carosella

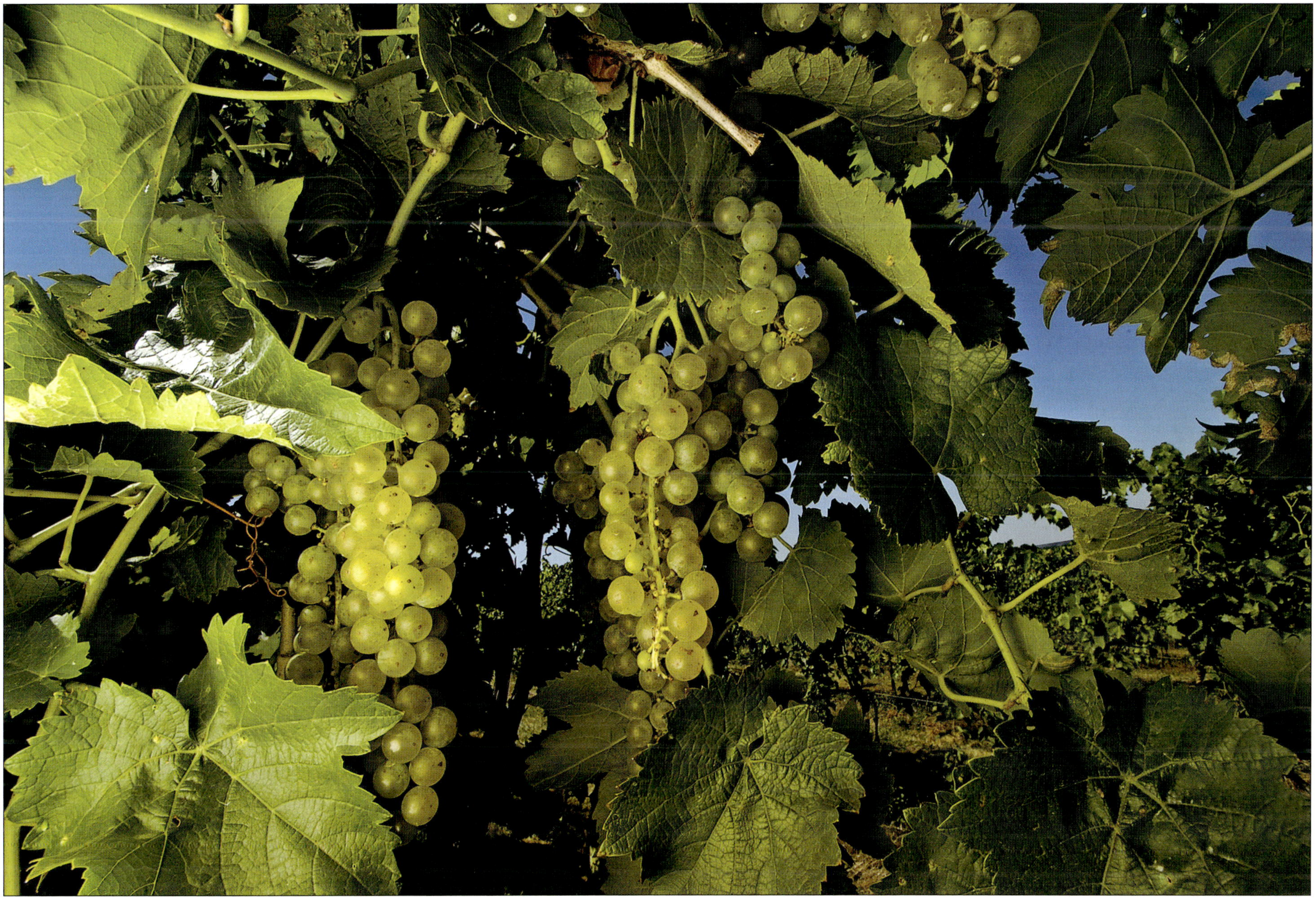

Vidal Grapes

Tony Carosella

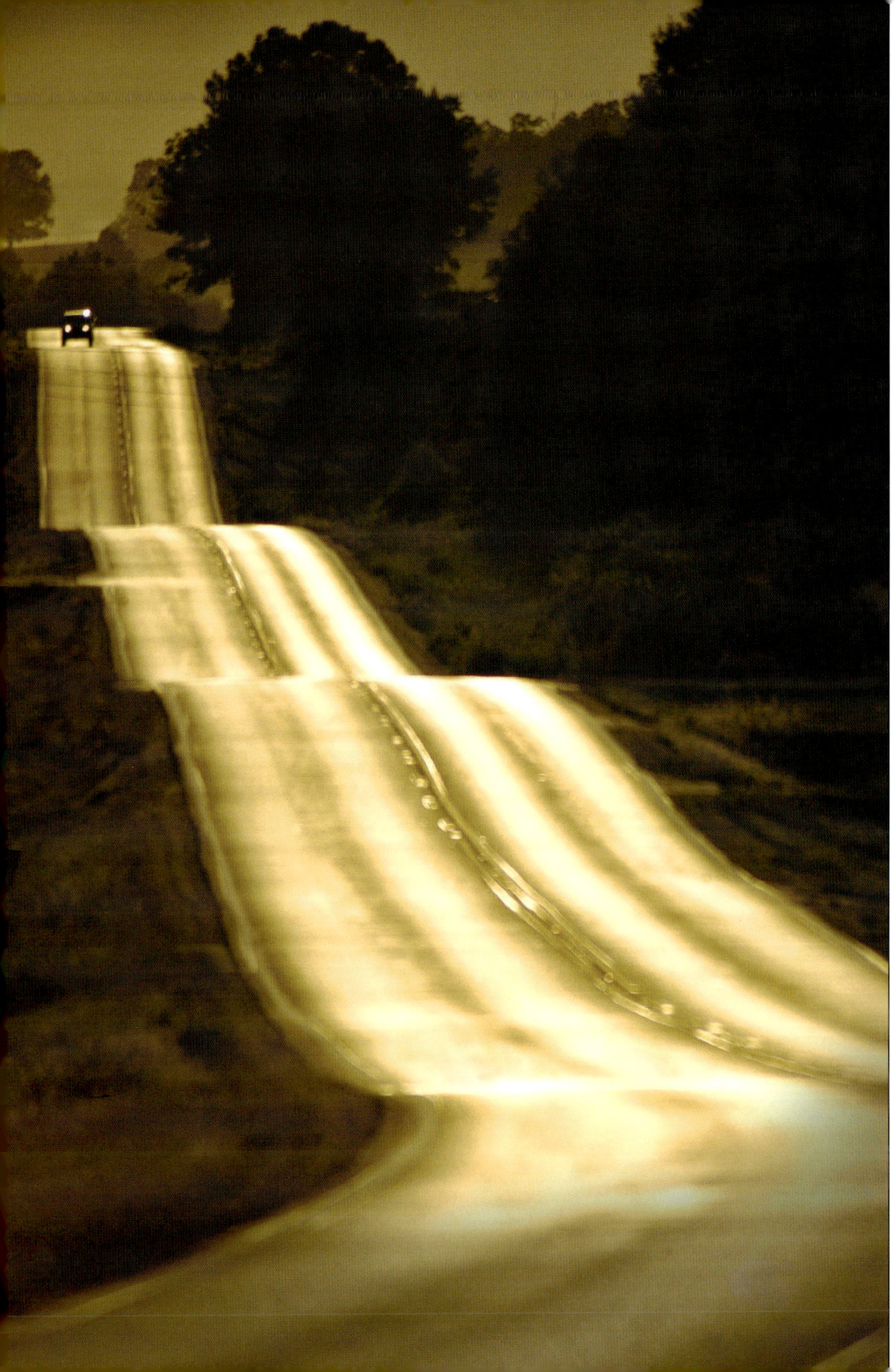

"Roads are no place for naïve
chickens dreaming of nirvana."
– Shalom Auslander
Hope: A Tragedy

"We need the tonic of wildness … at the same time that we are earnest to explore and learn all things, we require that all things be mysterious and unexplorable, that land and sea be indefinitely wild, unsurveyed and unfathomed by us because unfathomable. We can never have enough of nature."
– Henry David Thoreau
Walden: Or, Life in the Woods

Ribbon of Highway

Tony Carosella

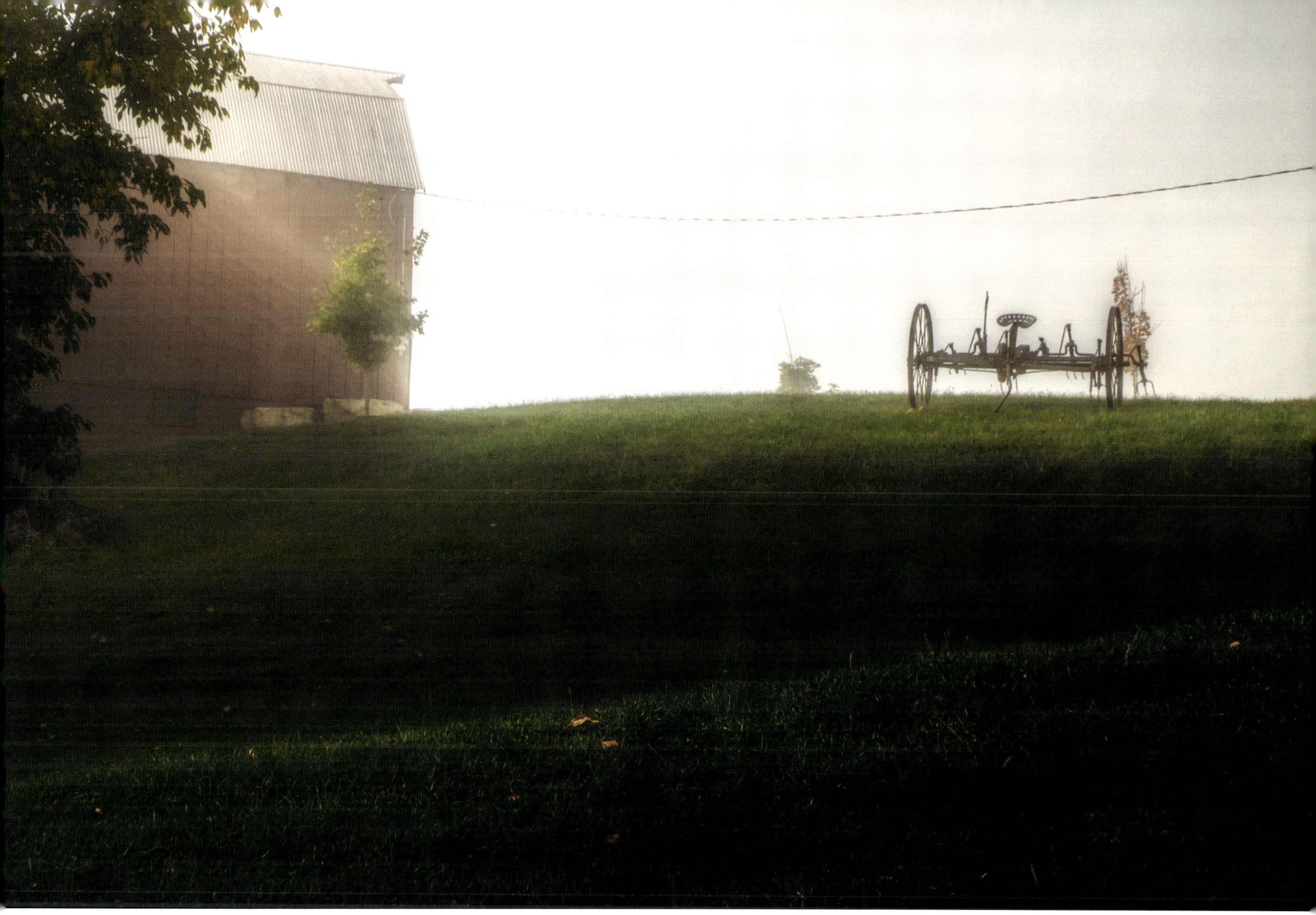

Mists of Time
William Fields

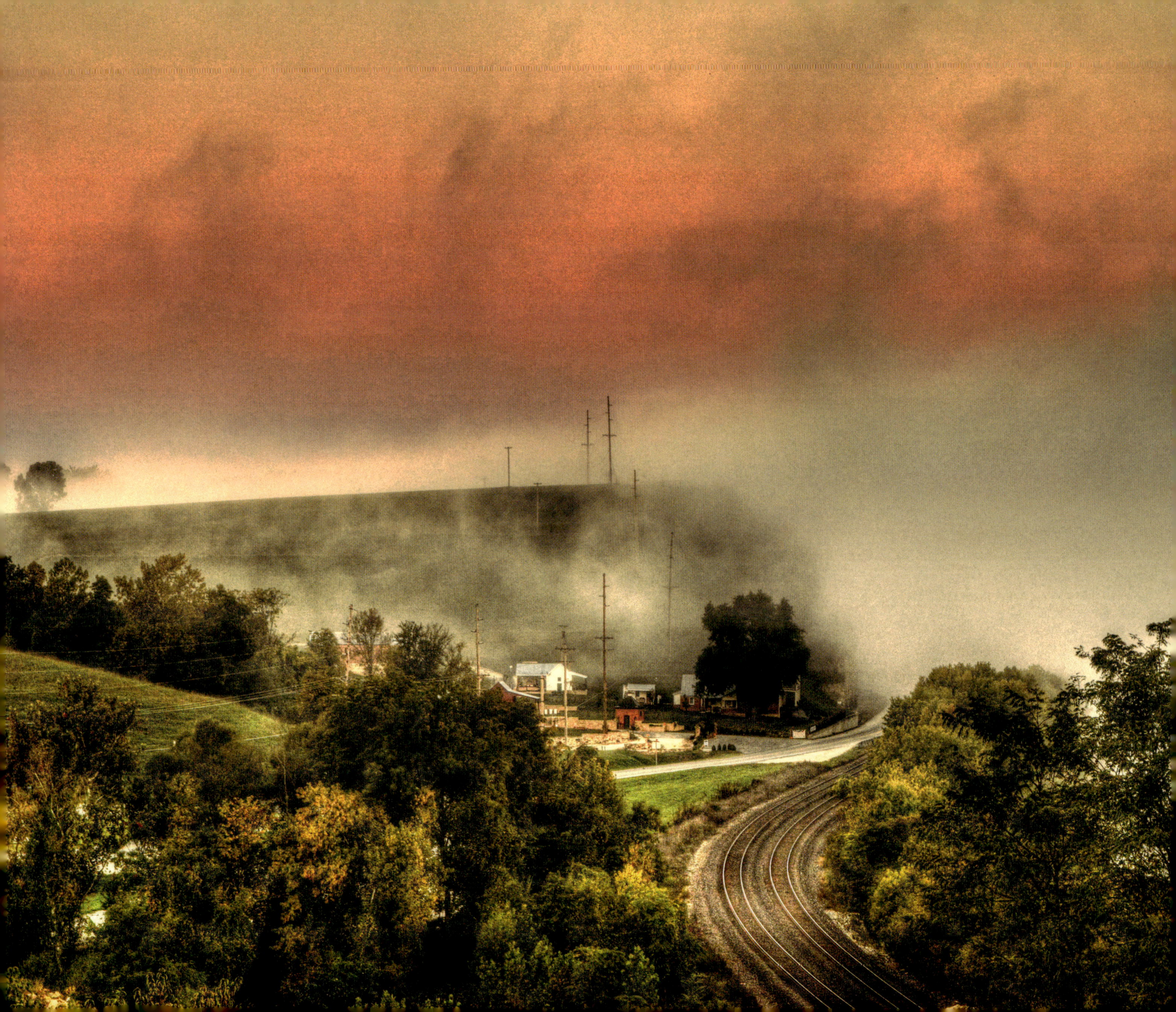

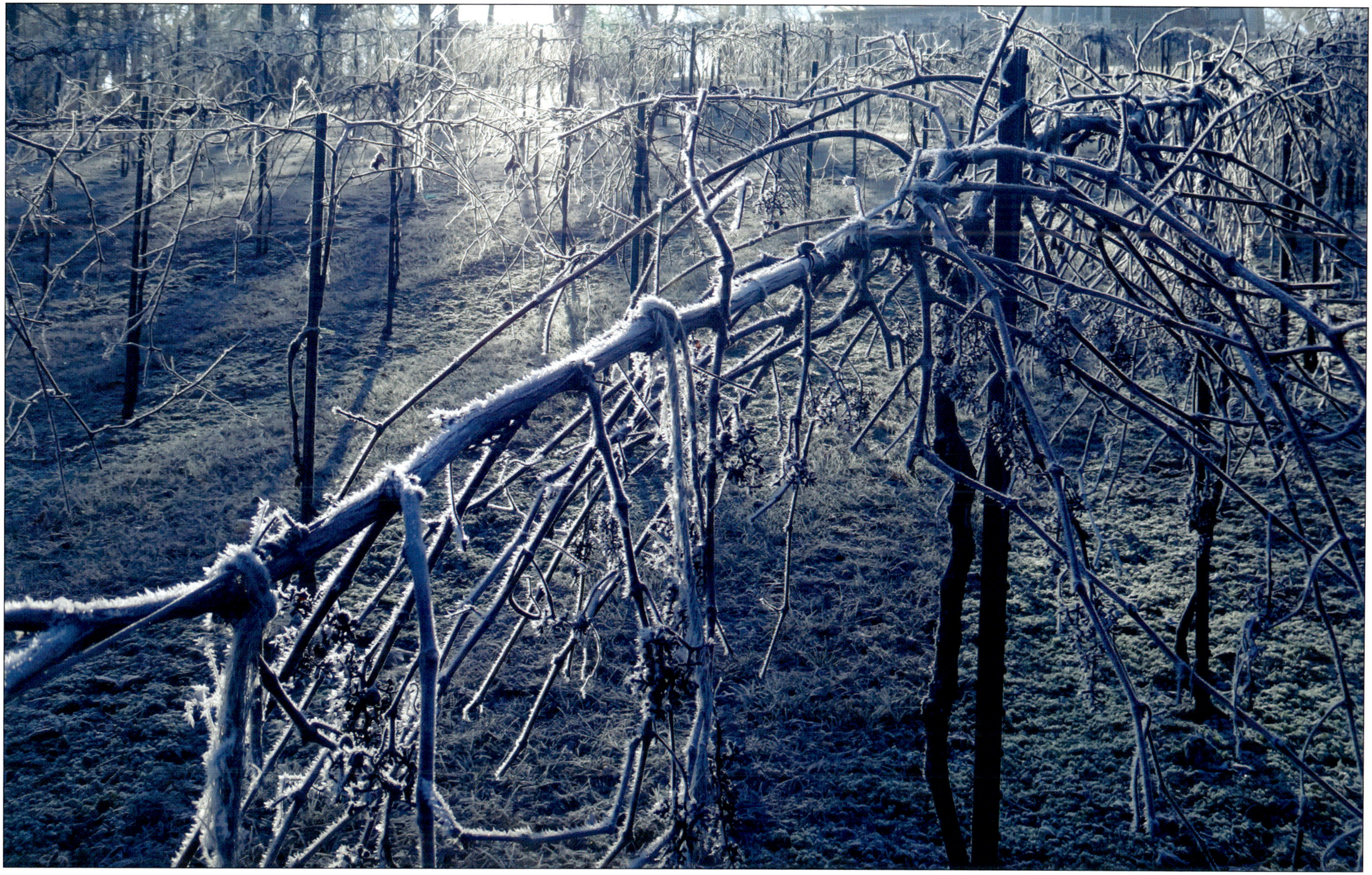

Frosted Vines
Tony Carosella

She'll Be Comin' Round the Mountain
William Fields

A Mere Strand of a Web

William Fields

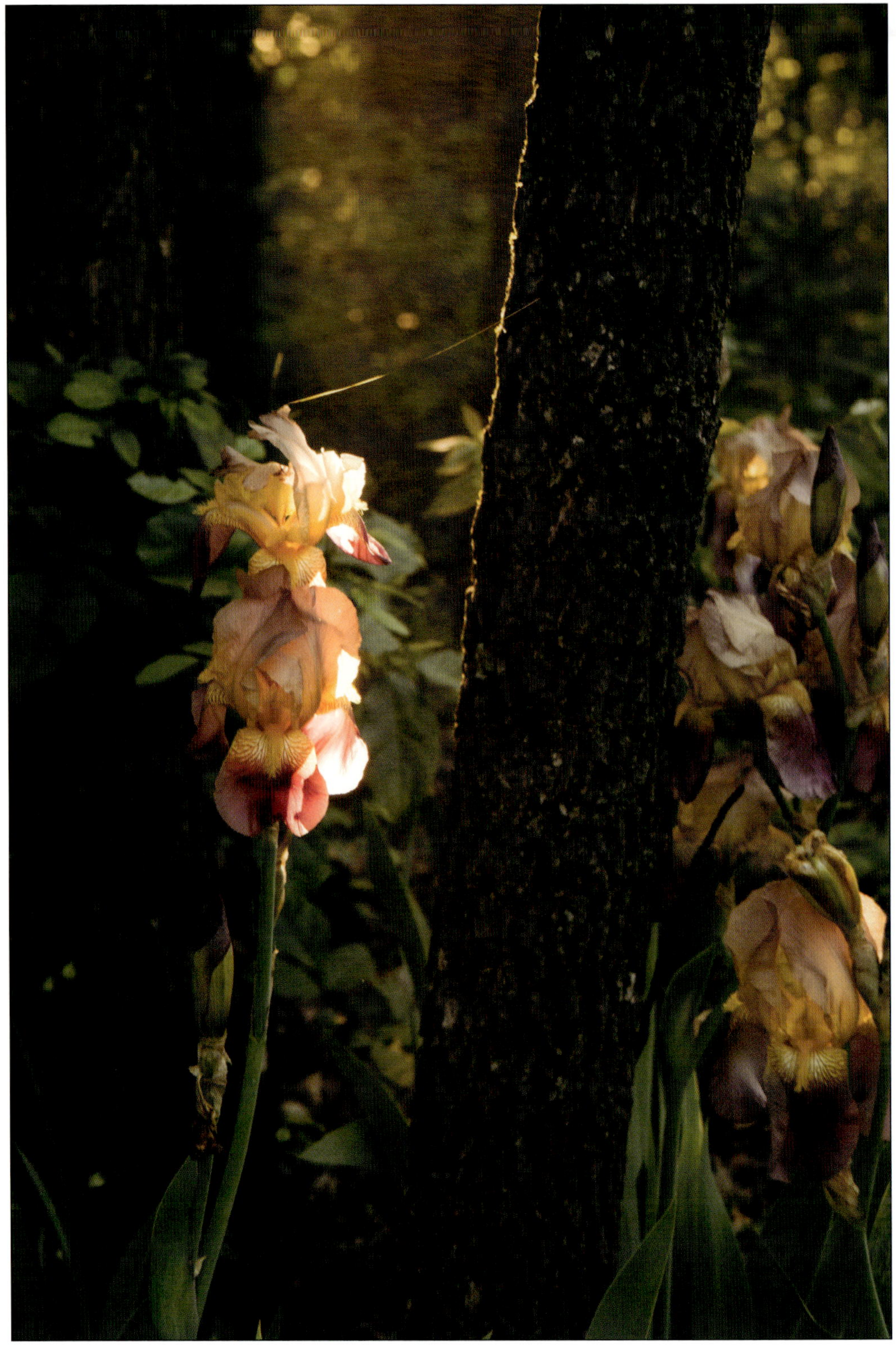

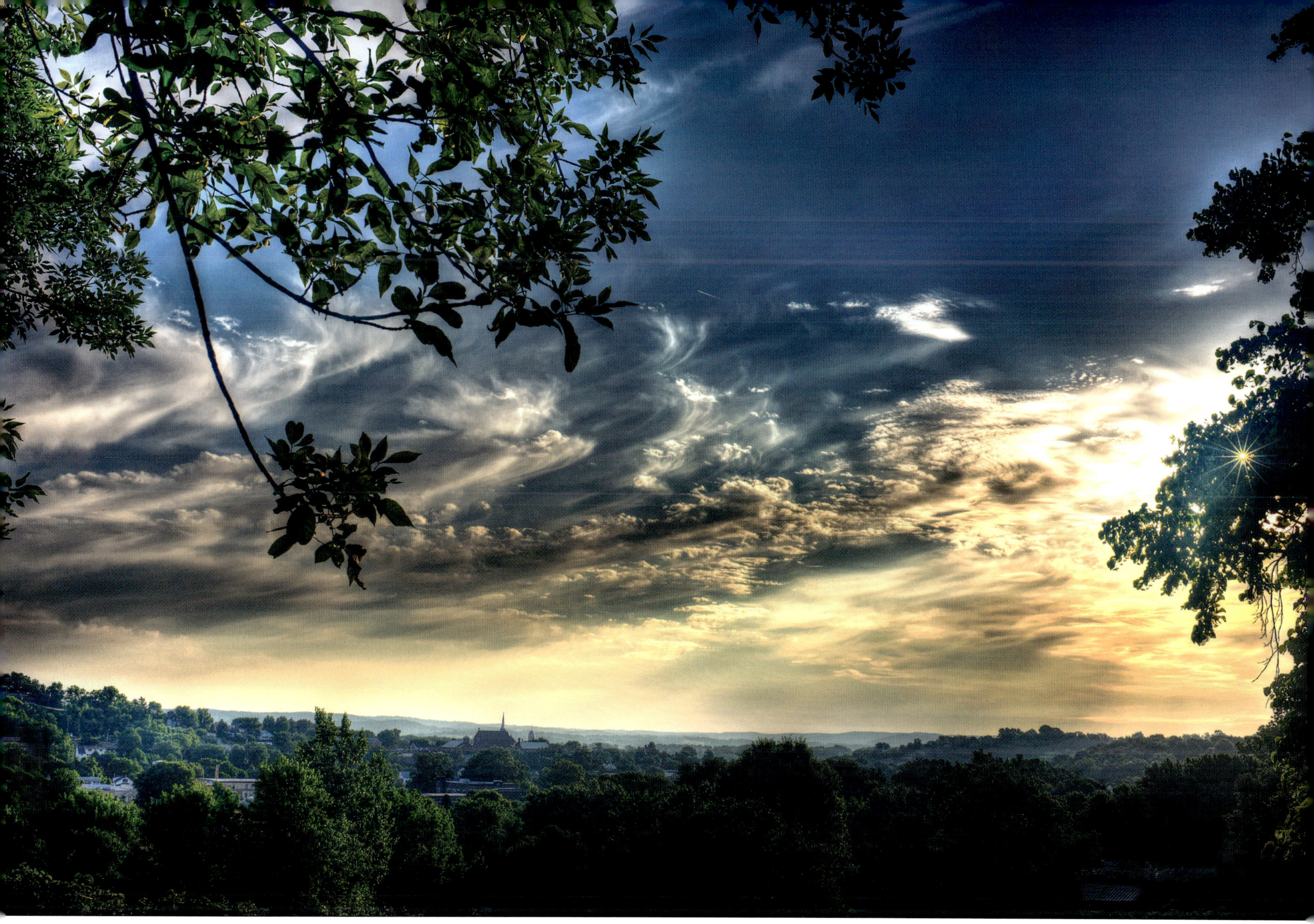

Peaceful Dawn
William Fields

Veterans of Ancient Storms II

William Fields

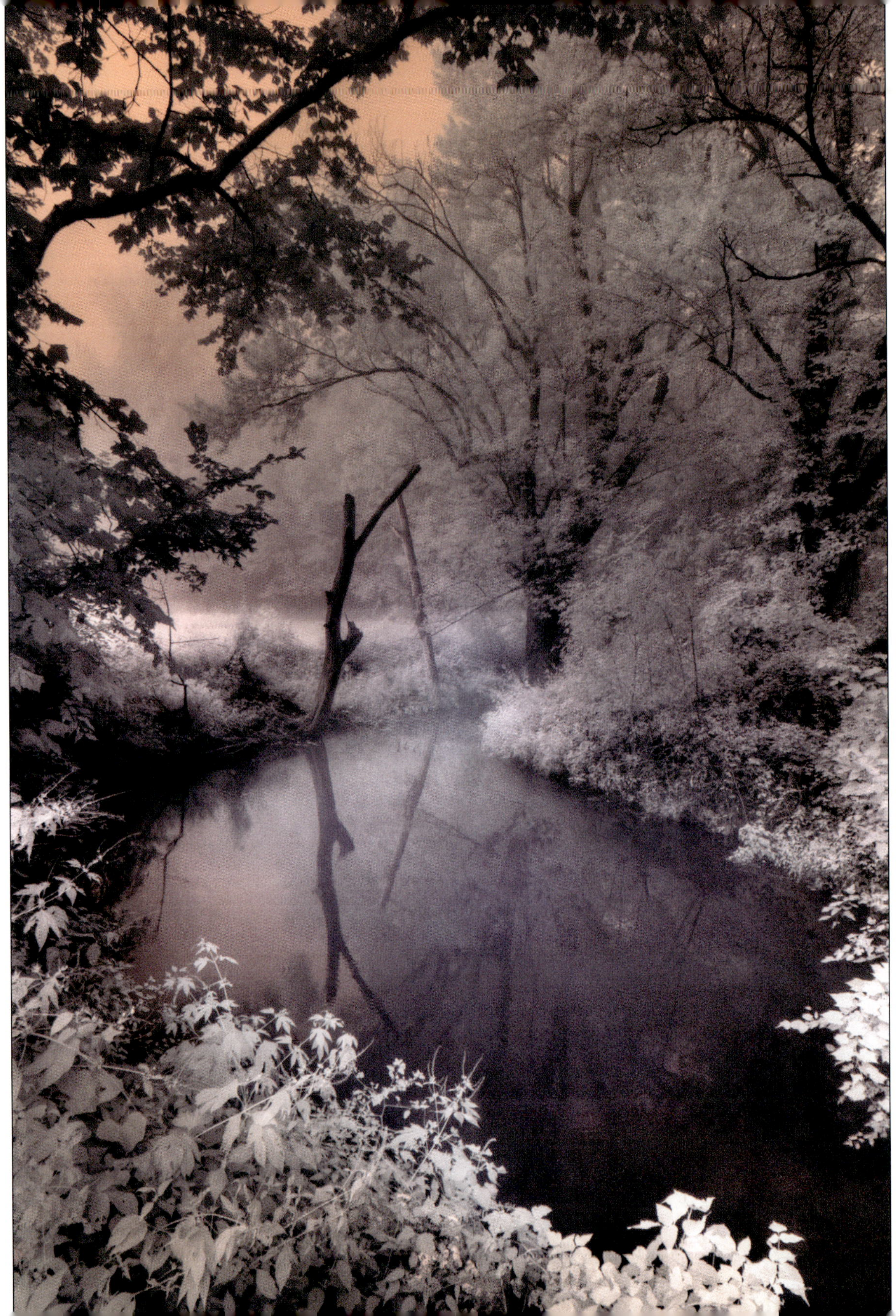

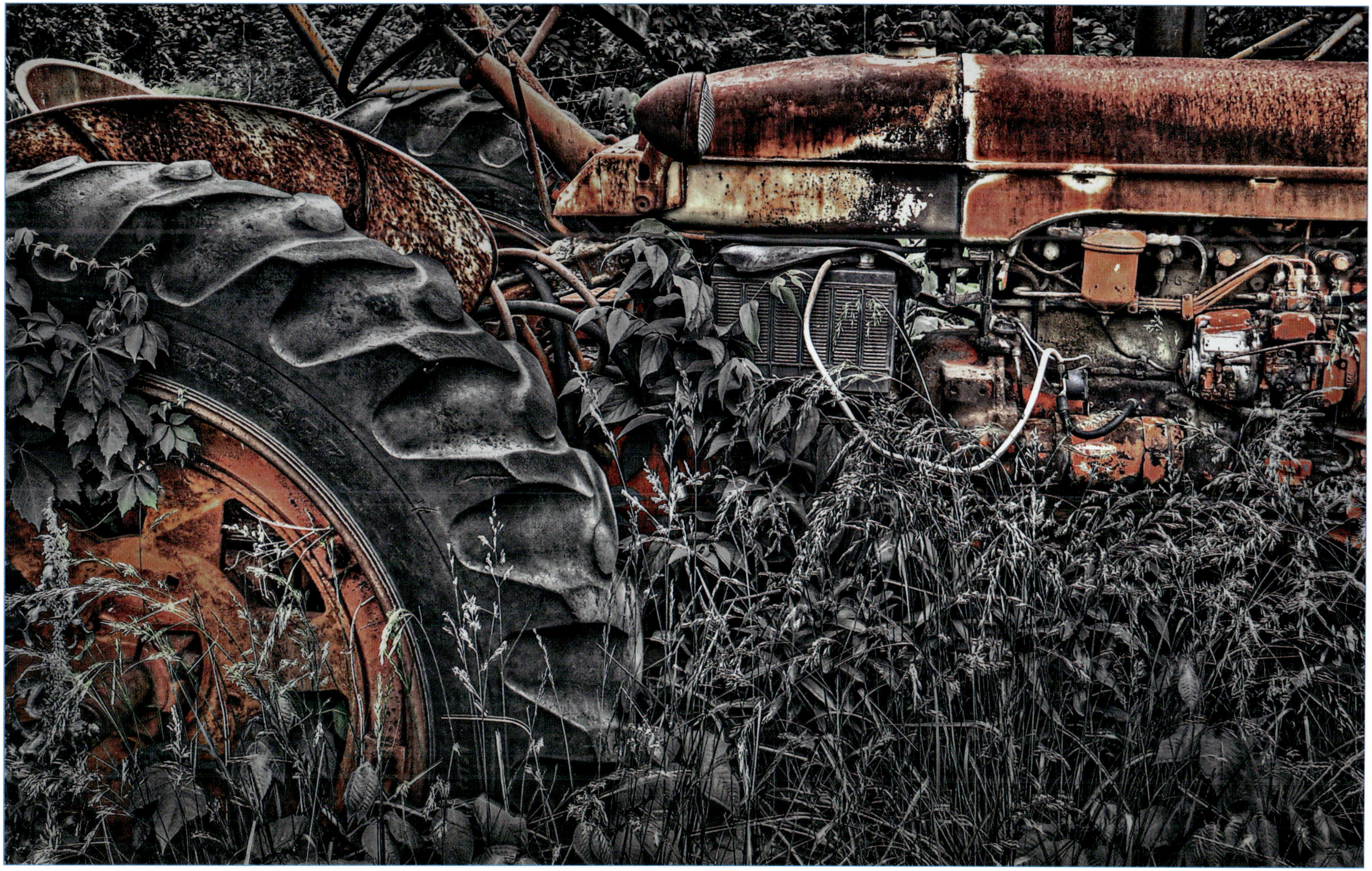

Old Bay Tractor
Tony Carosella

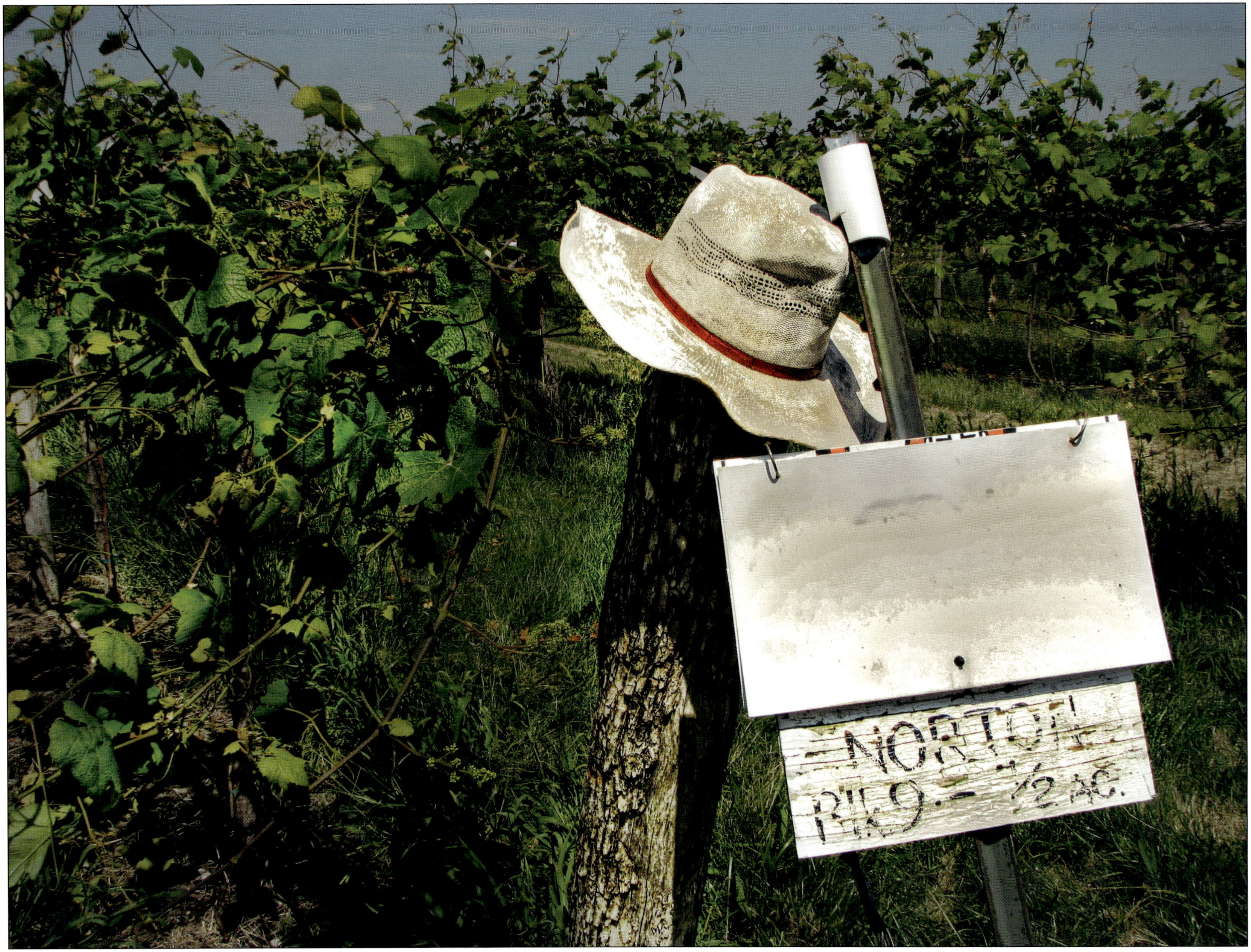

Walt's Hat
William Fields

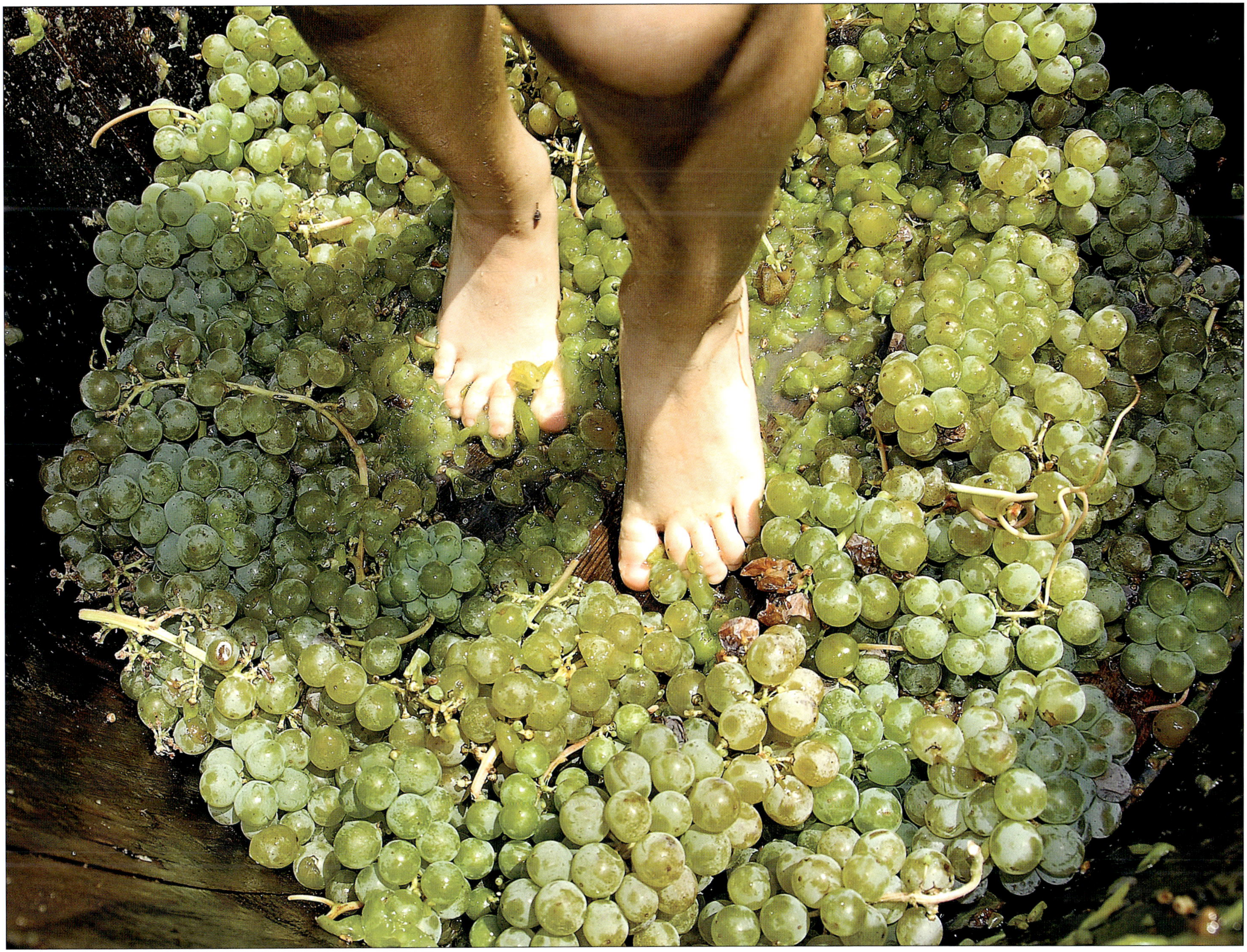

Grape Stomp
Tony Carosella

Hermann Hill Vineyard II

Tony Carosella

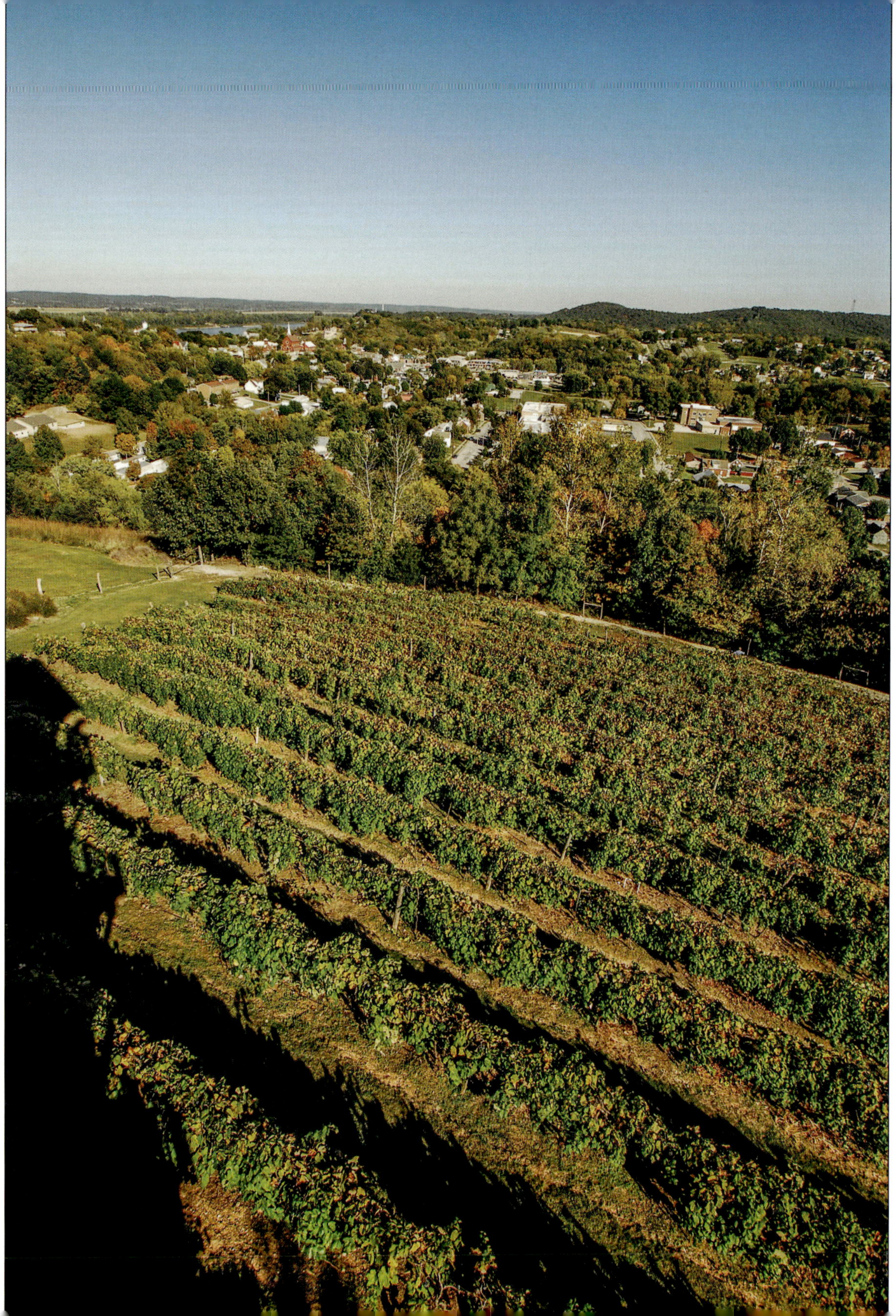

The River

"The Missouri is, perhaps, different in appearance and character from all other rivers in the world; there is a terror in its manner which is sensibly felt, the moment we enter its muddy waters from the Mississippi."
– George Catlin

"The River is so integral to our community that it almost seems to have a spirit of its own. It is a highway of commerce. We fish on it. We hunt, we wile away the hours doing nothing. Sometimes we just look at it. More often than any other endeavor, I just look at this river and dream."
– William Fields

The Eight-O-Five
William Fields

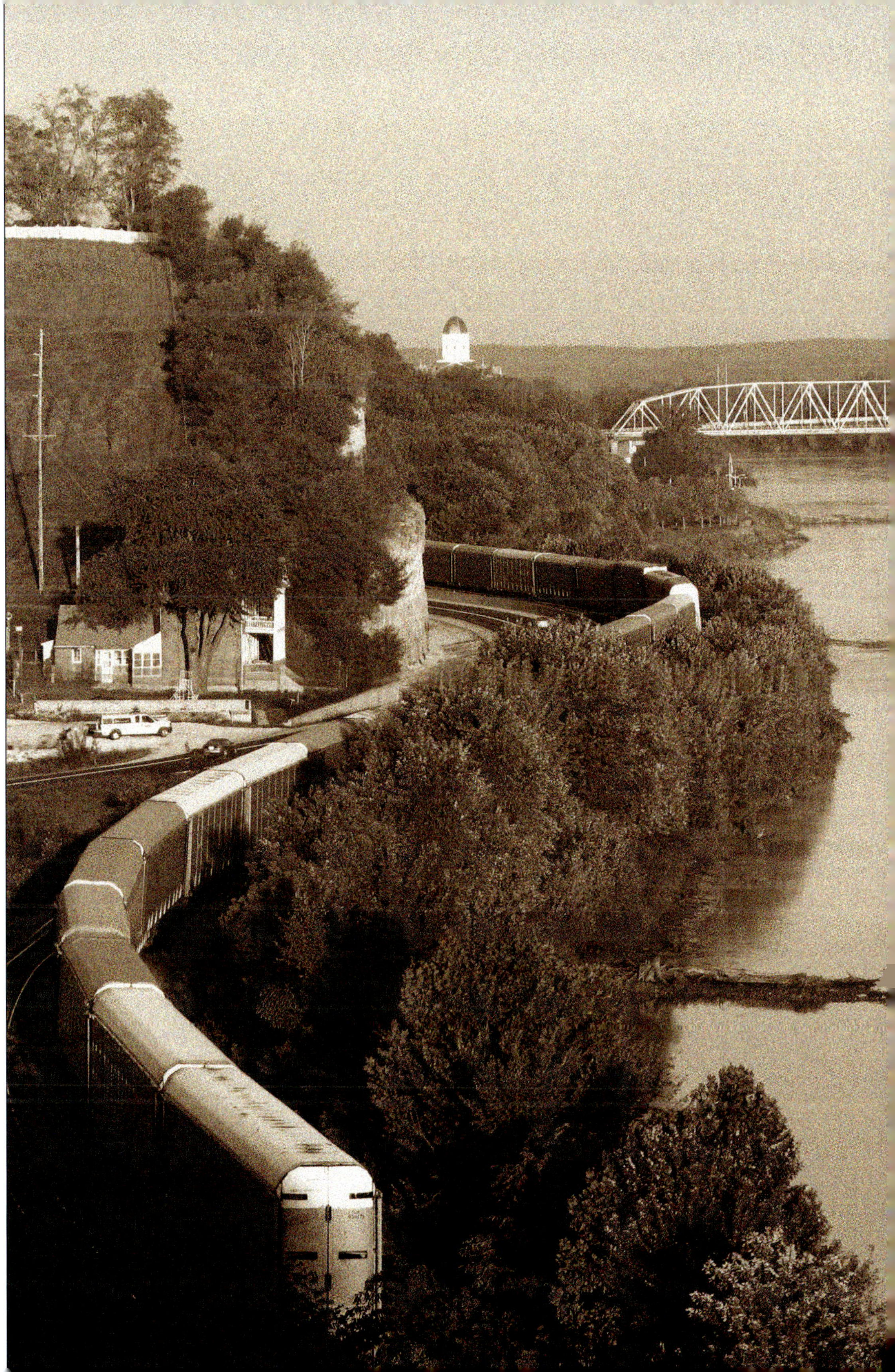

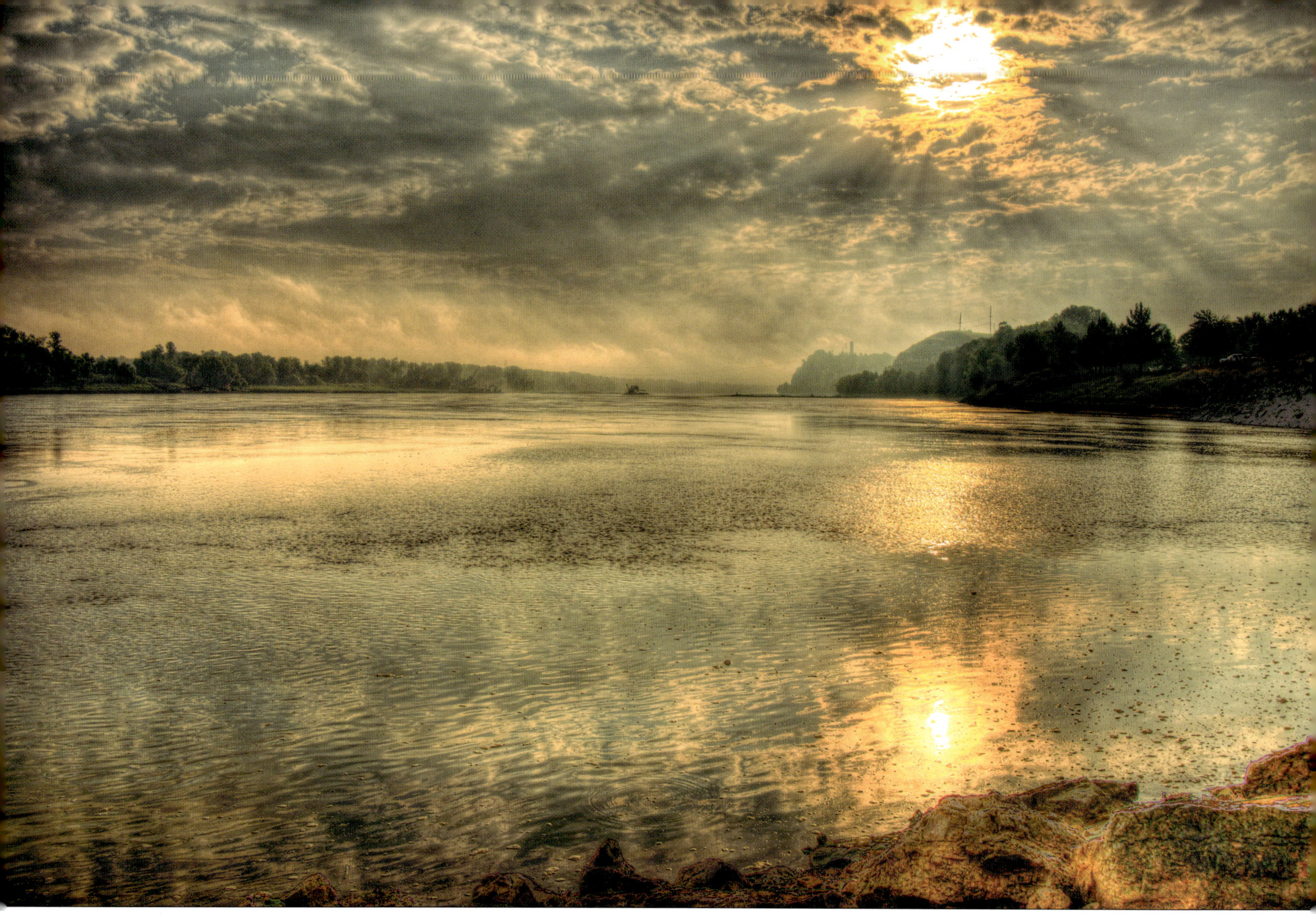

Big Muddy Morn
William Fields

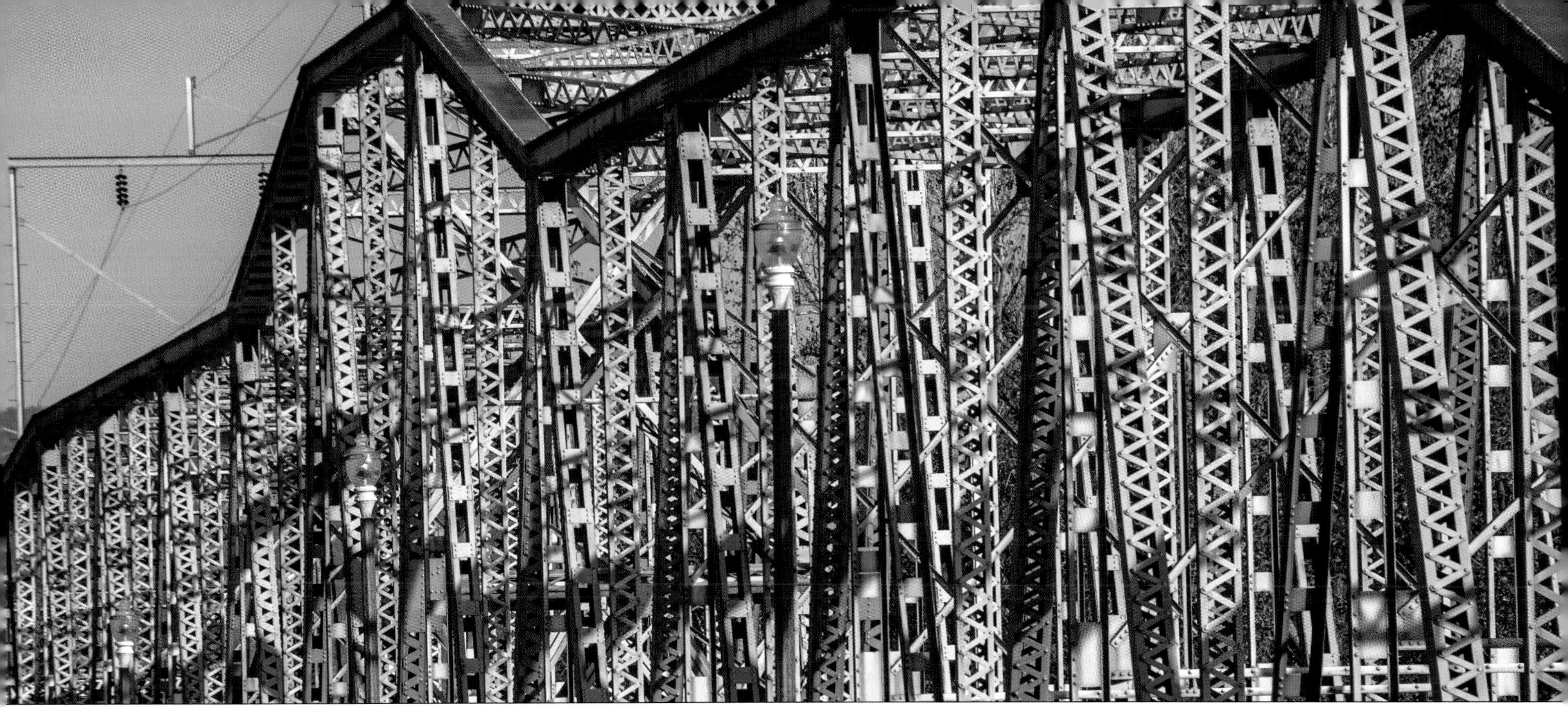

First Bridge
Tony Carosella

The story of Hermann can't be told without discussion of the Missouri River. Early settlers, modern geographers, historians and school kids will tell you that the longest river in the United States is the Mississippi. There are those among us who refute that wisdom. The Mississippi is a narrow, clear water creek until it merges with the mighty Missouri at Saint Louis. In truth, it is the Missouri that flows down out of the Rockies in Montana and across the Great Plains. It is the mighty Missouri that is called the 'Big Muddy' for all that way. When the great river is met by the Mississippi at Saint Louis it makes a bend and continues on down to the Gulf of Mexico near New Orleans. Western explorers thought in terms of straight lines and so erred in their assumptions. Hermann was built on the banks of the Missouri. The river is entwined in its growth and commerce in much the same way the great water is embraced by the land.

– William Fields

"Water is the driving force of all nature."

– Leonardo da Vinci

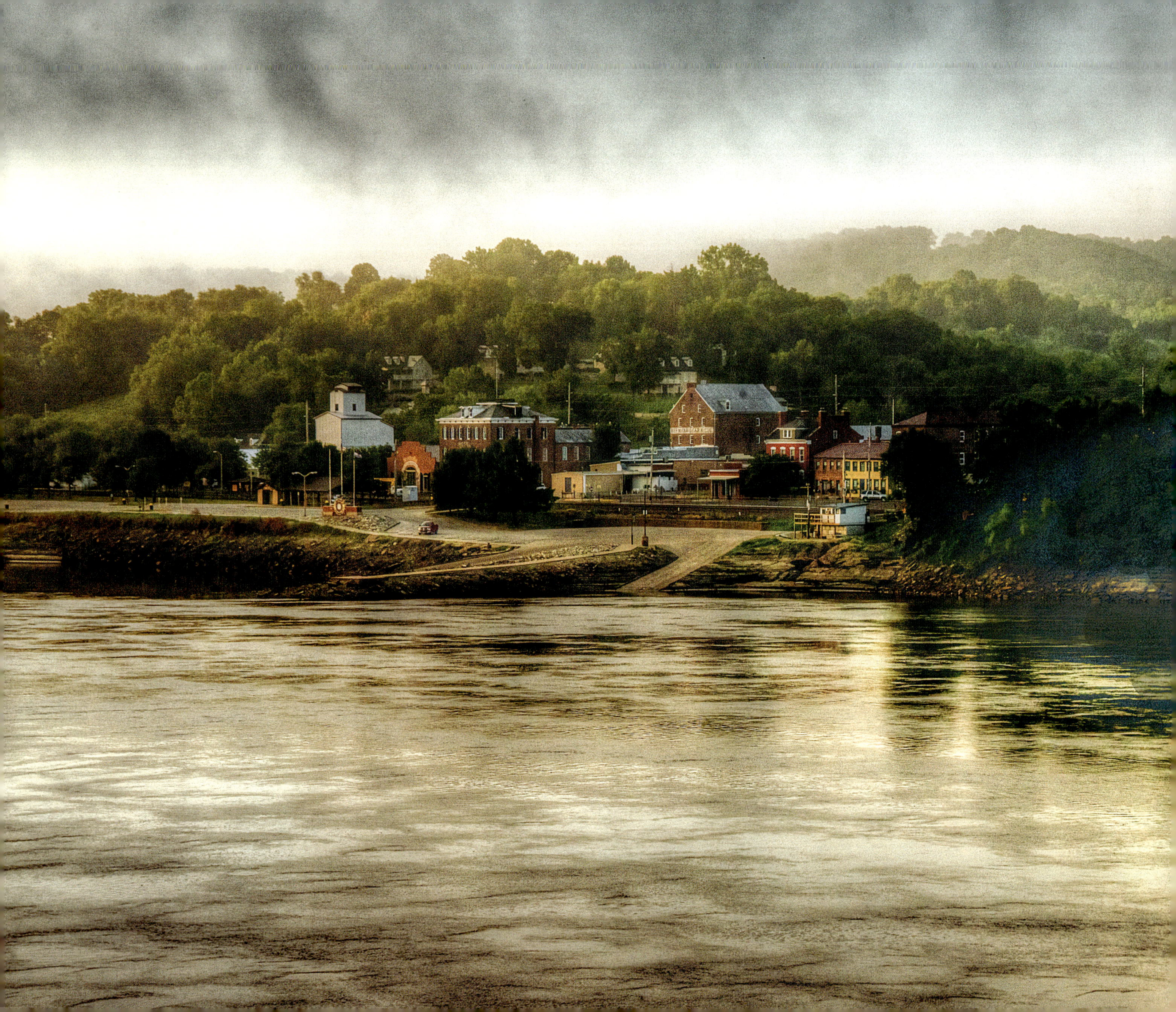

Hermann on the Missouri IV
William Fields

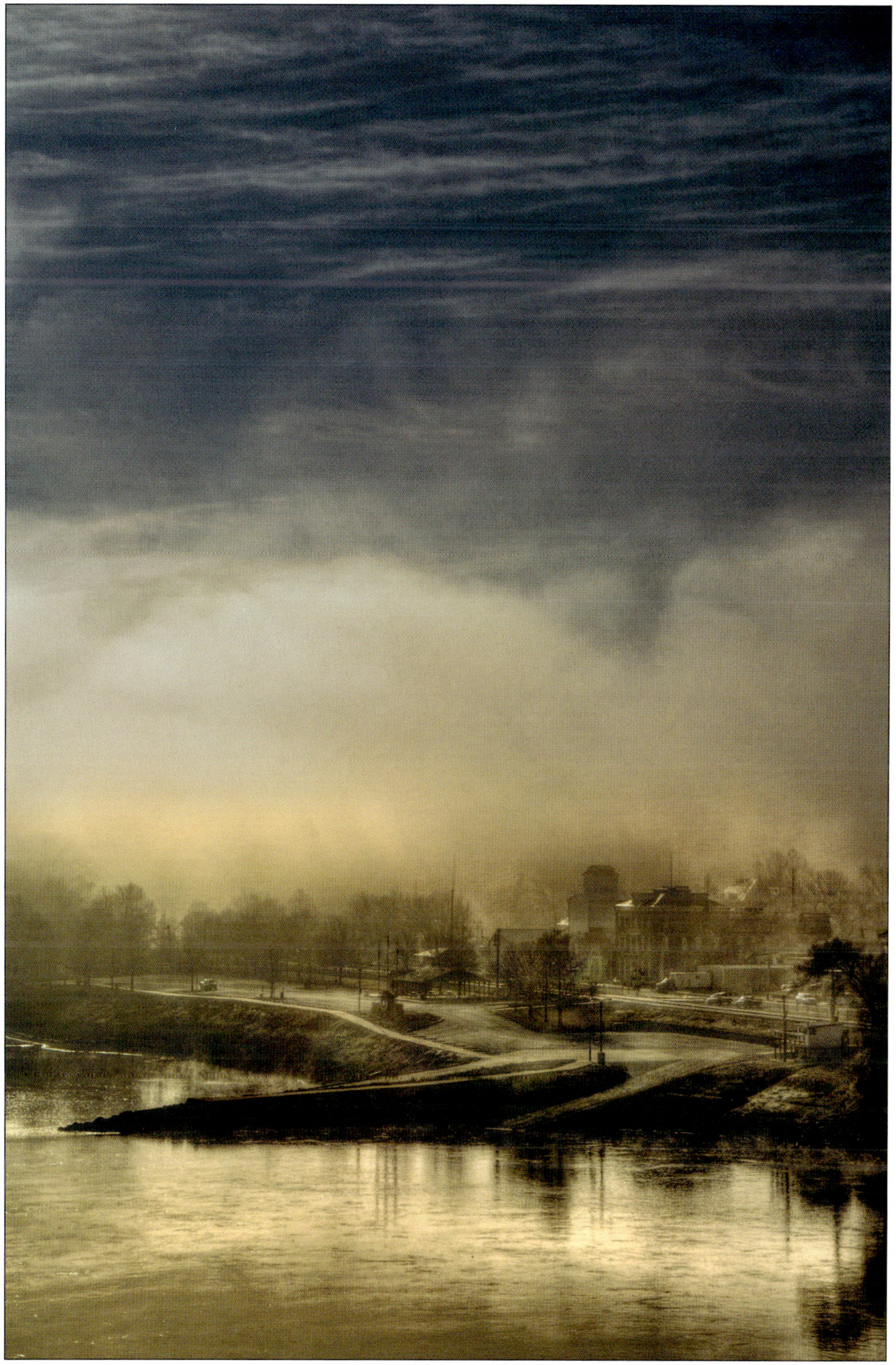

Hermann on the Missouri
William Fields

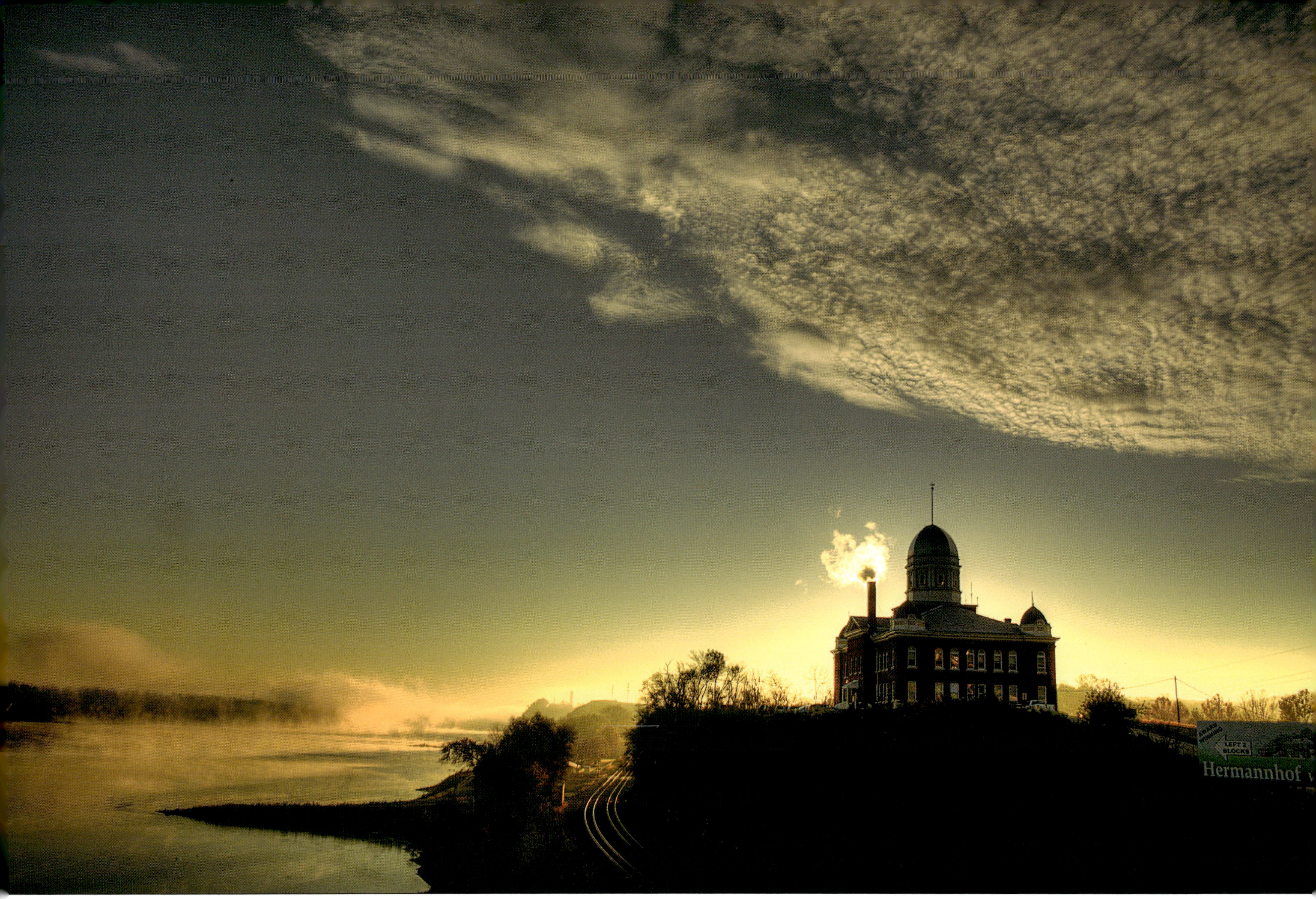

Courthouse Smokestack

William Fields

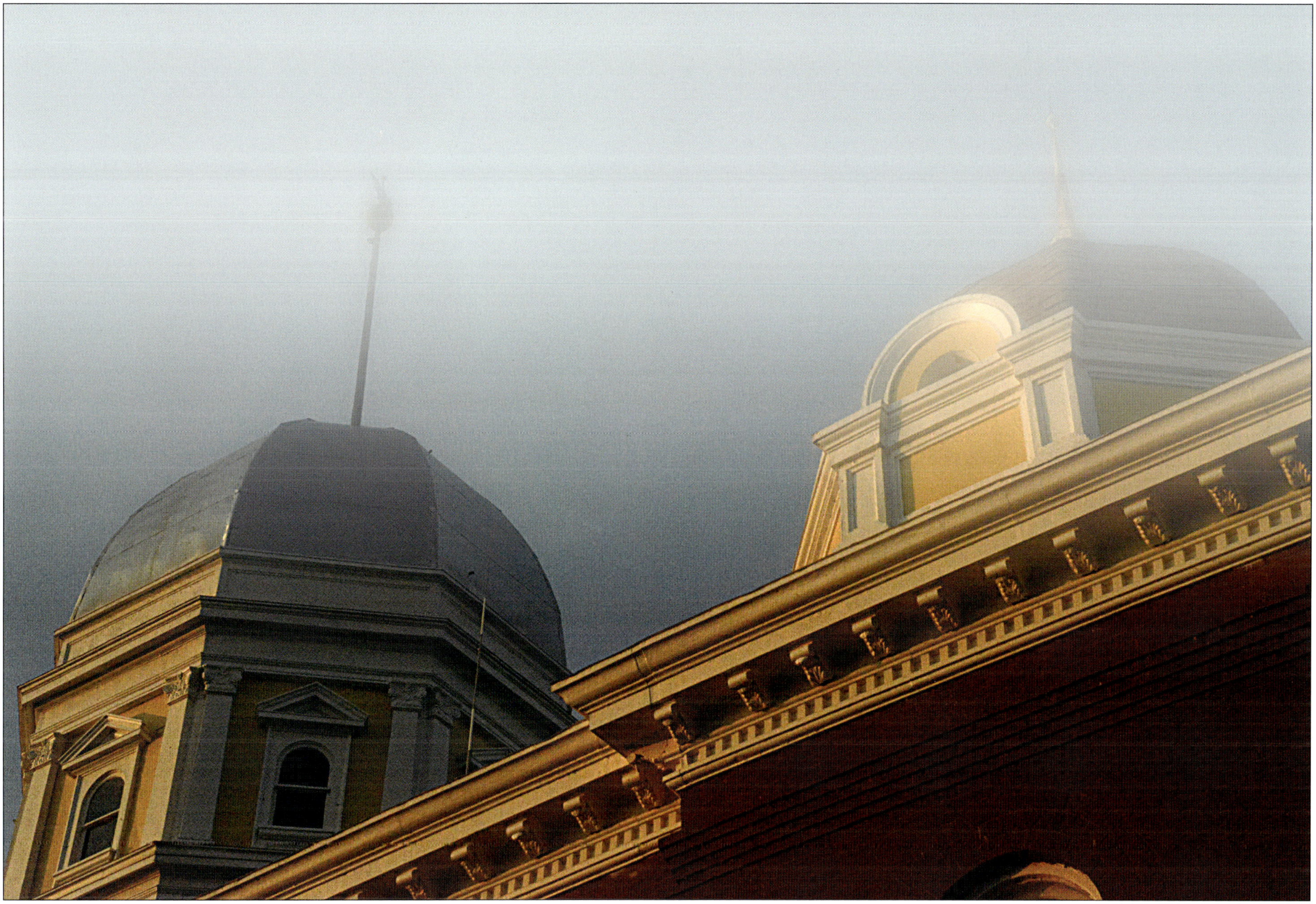

Courthouse Dawn in Fog
William Fields

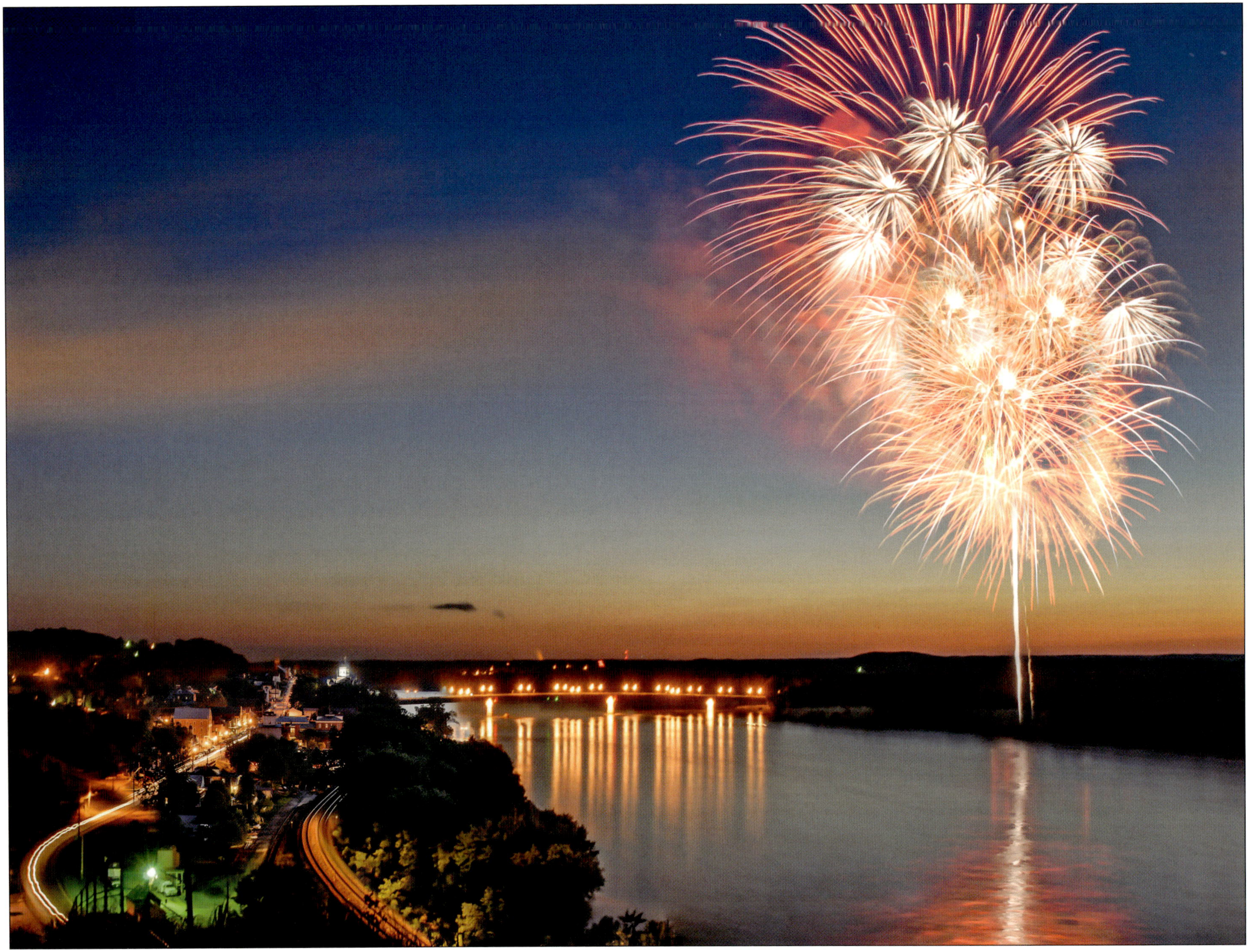

Sky Rockets in the Night
Tony Carosella

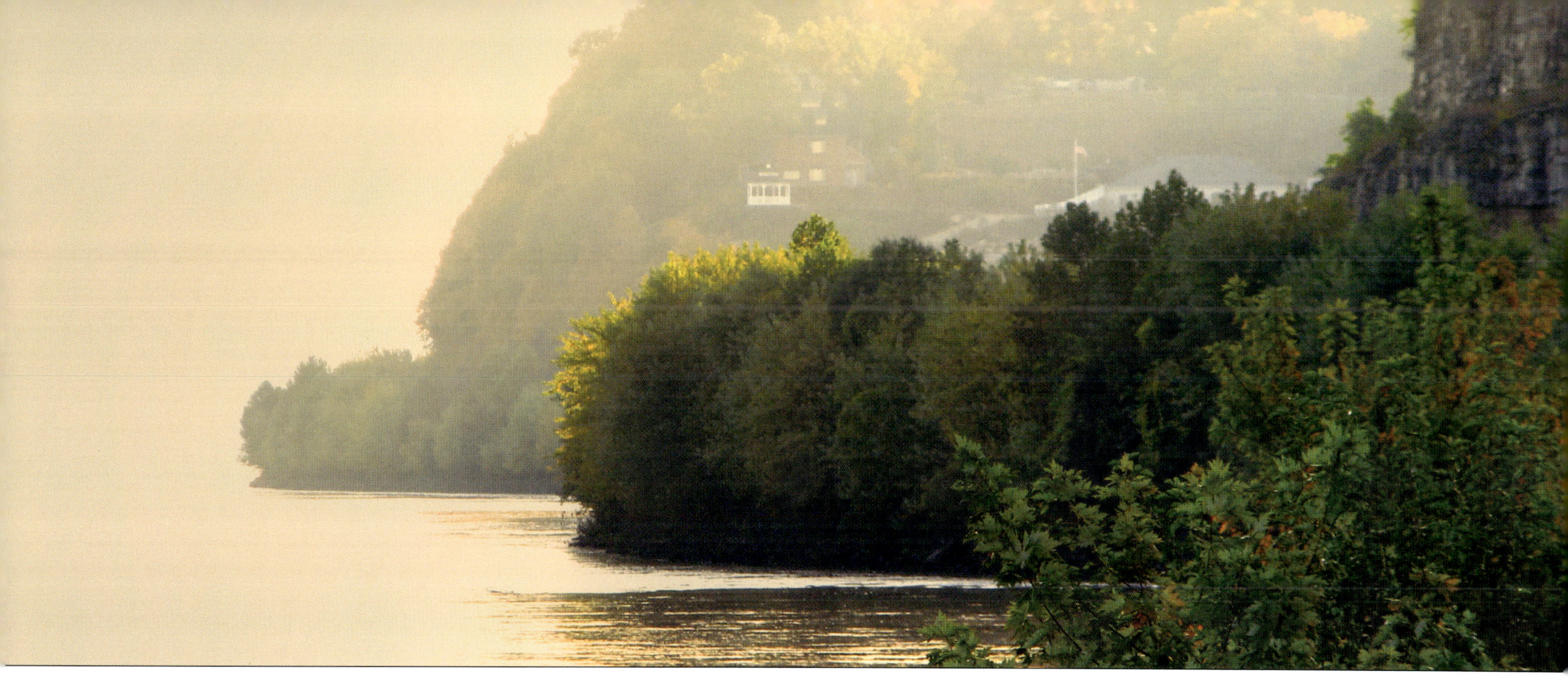

Islands in the Stream

William Fields

"We must begin thinking like a river if we are to leave a legacy of beauty and life for future generations."
– David Brower

"A river seems a magic thing. A magic, moving, living part of the very earth itself."
– Laura Gilpin

"The river is everywhere."
– Hermann Hesse, *Siddhartha*

"Oh, Eeyore, you are wet!" said Piglet, feeling him. Eeyore shook himself, and asked somebody to explain to Piglet what happened when you had been inside a river for quite a long time."
– A.A. Milne, *Winnie-the-Pooh*

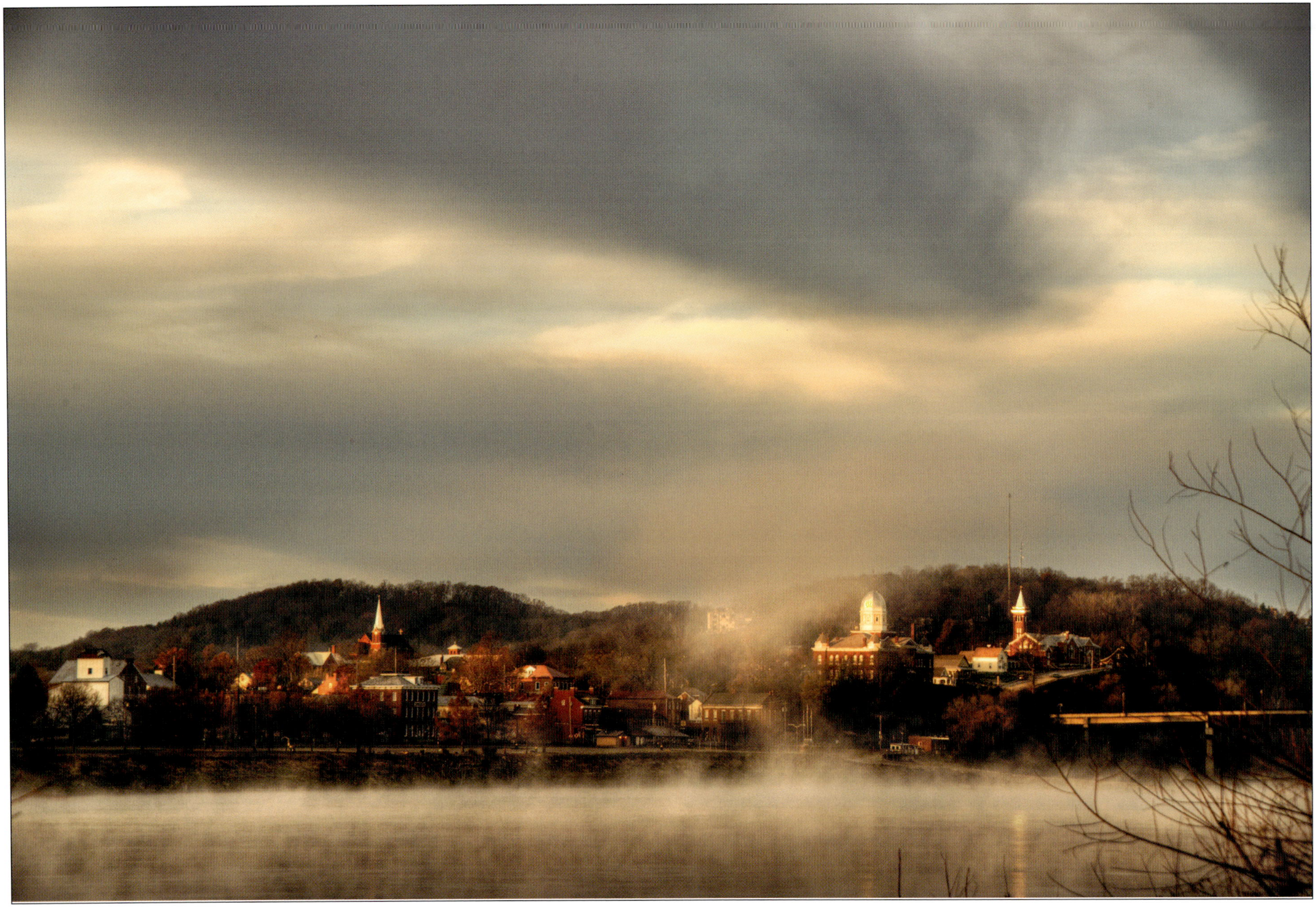

Hermann Rising from the Mists
William Fields

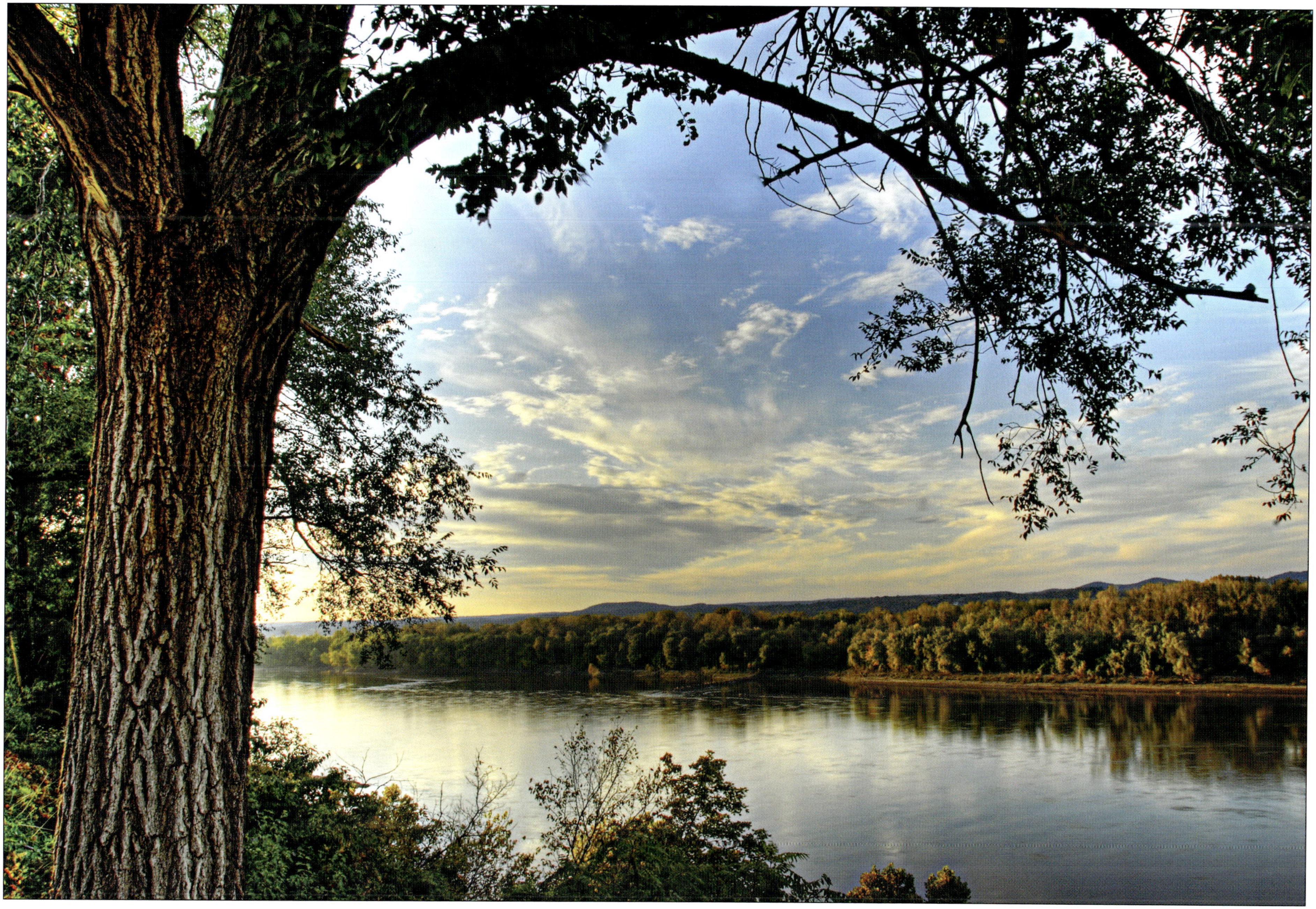

Missouri Pastoral
Tony Carosella

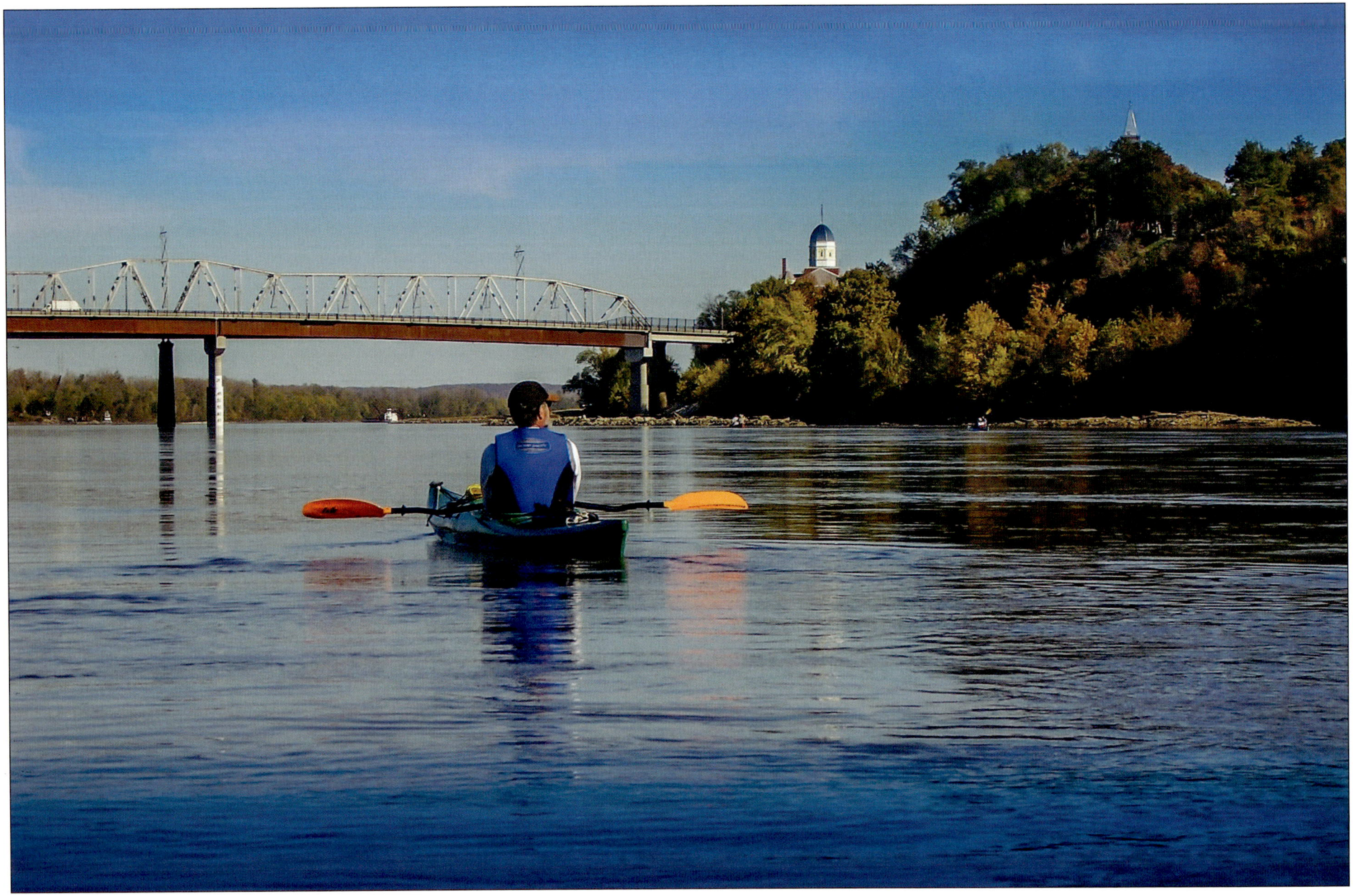

Gary's Paddle

Tony Carosella

"Eventually, all things merge into one, and a river runs through it. The river was cut by the world's great flood and runs over rocks from the basement of time. On some of the rocks are timeless raindrops. Under the rocks are the words, and some of the words are theirs. I am haunted by waters."

– Norman Maclean

A River Runs Through It and Other Stories

River Sunset

Tony Carosella

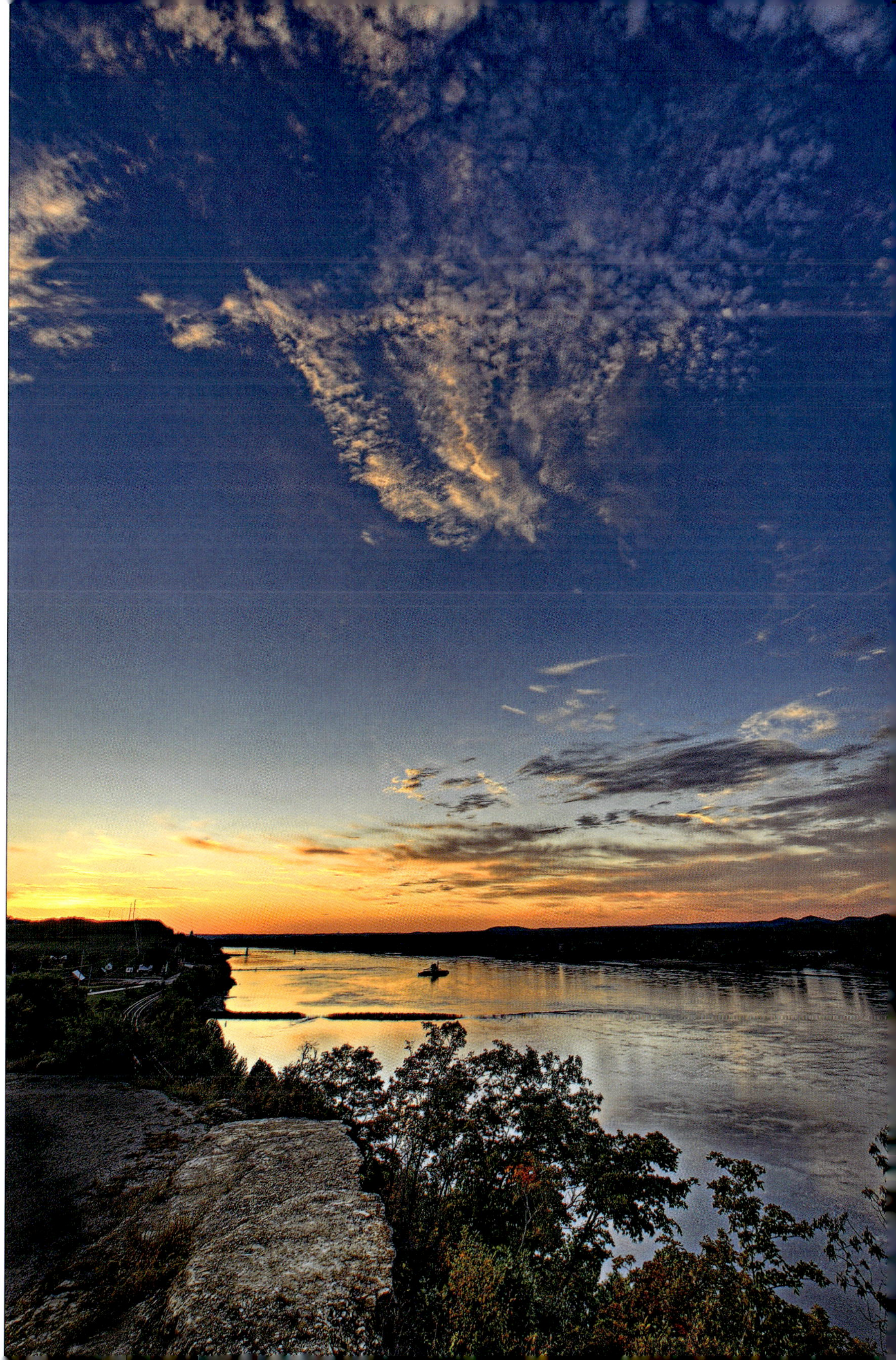

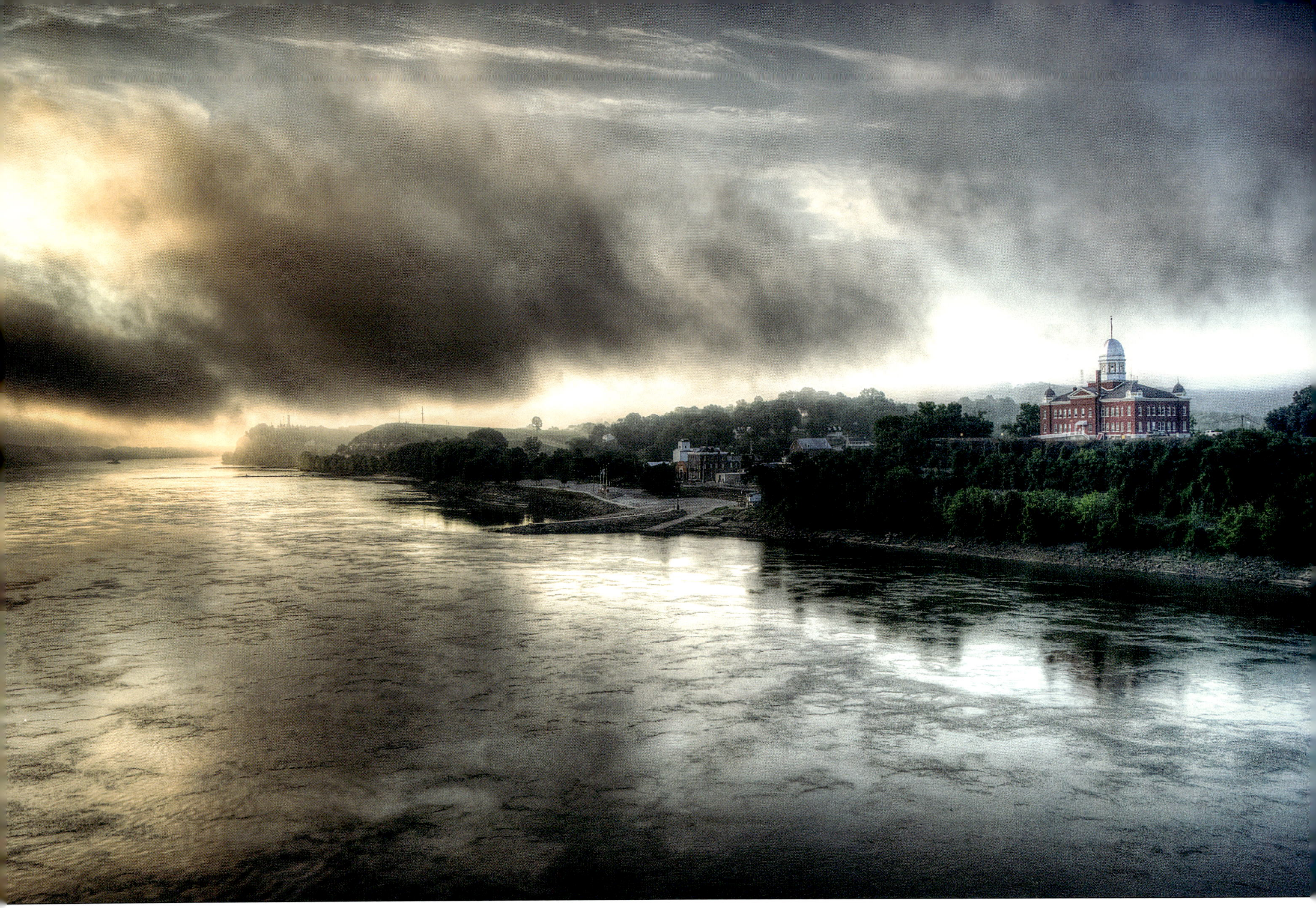

The Eitzen Gift

William Fields

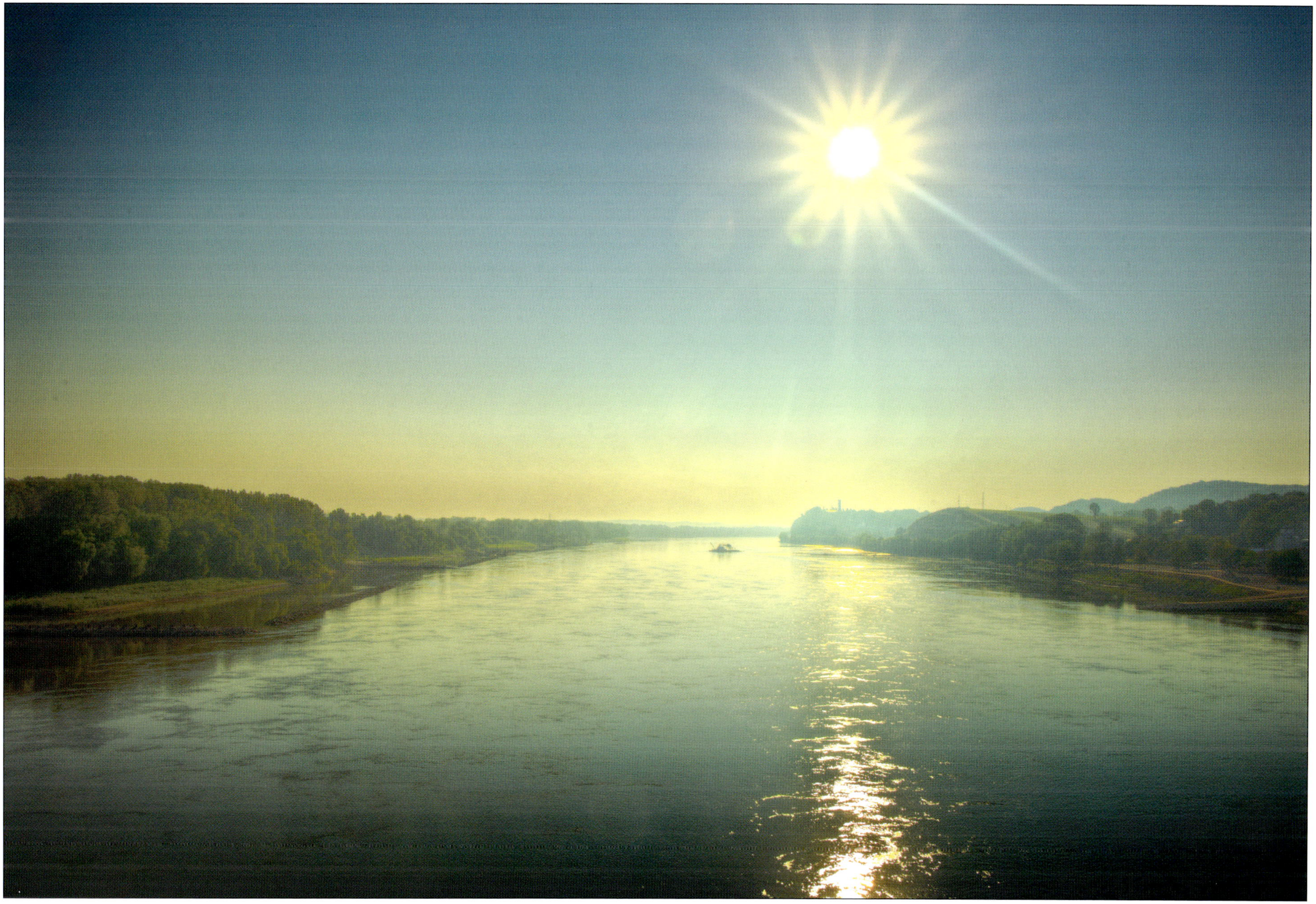

Ninety at Dawn
William Fields

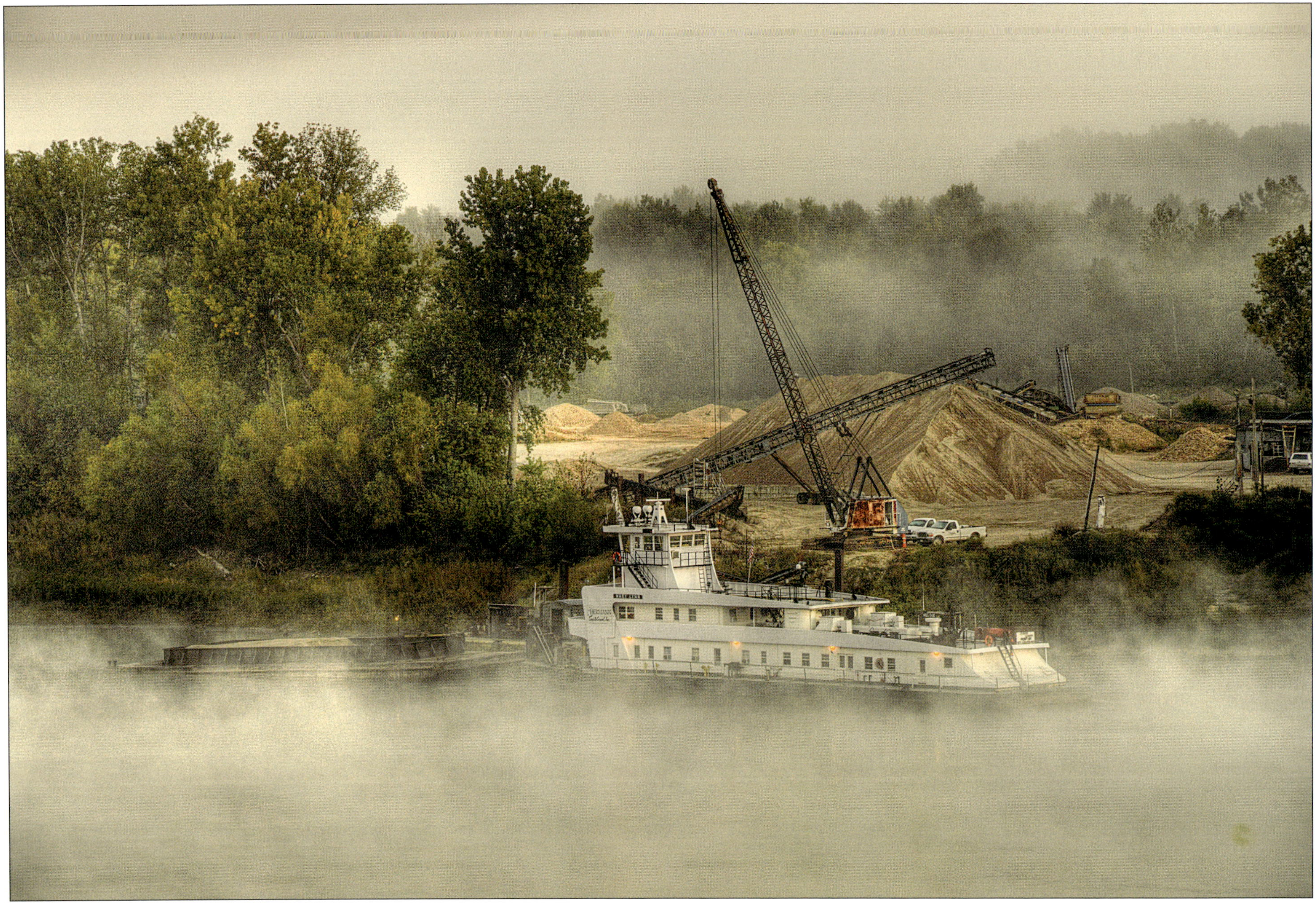

Give Us This Day
William Fields

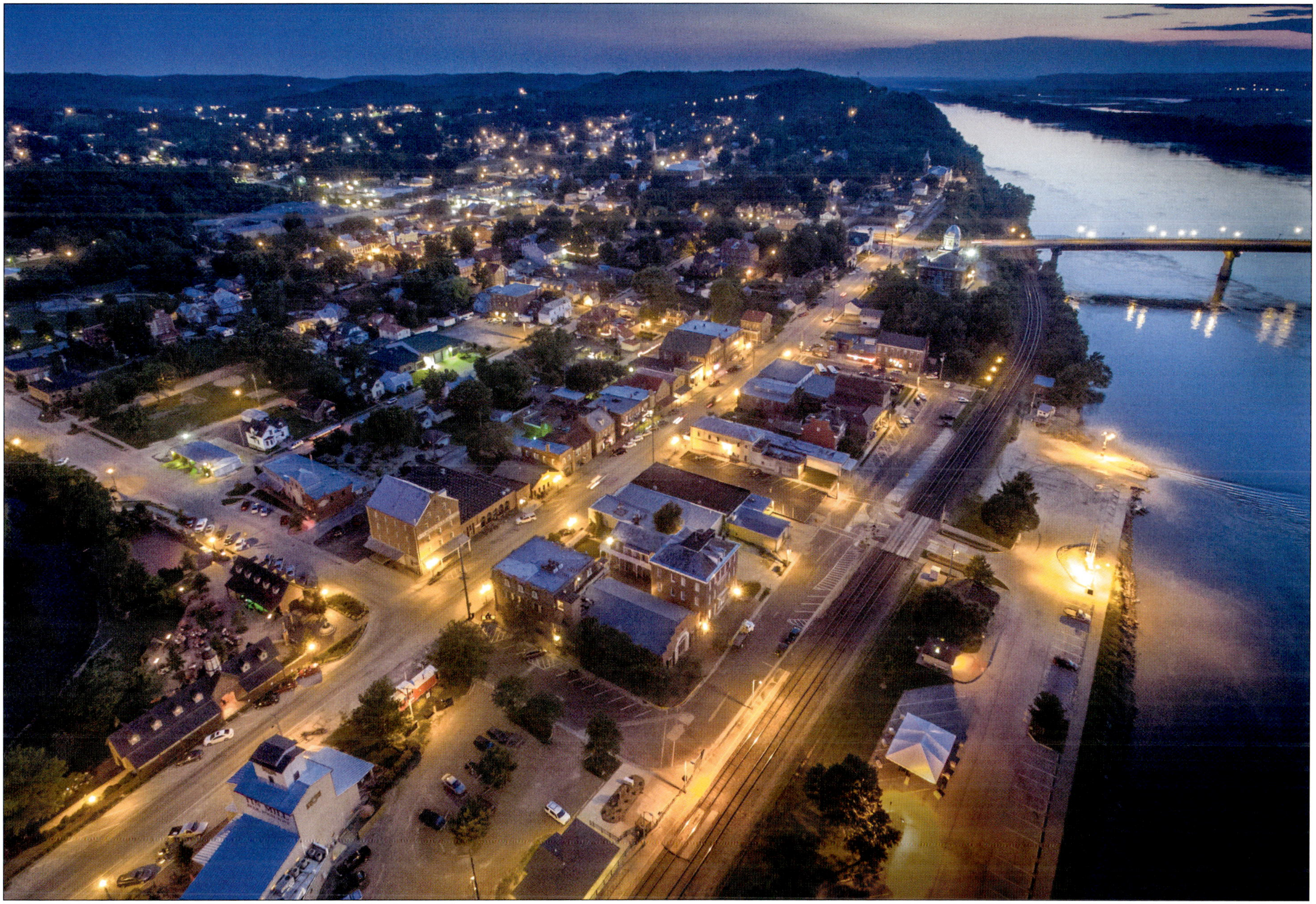

Hermann Aerial Nocturne
Tony Carosella

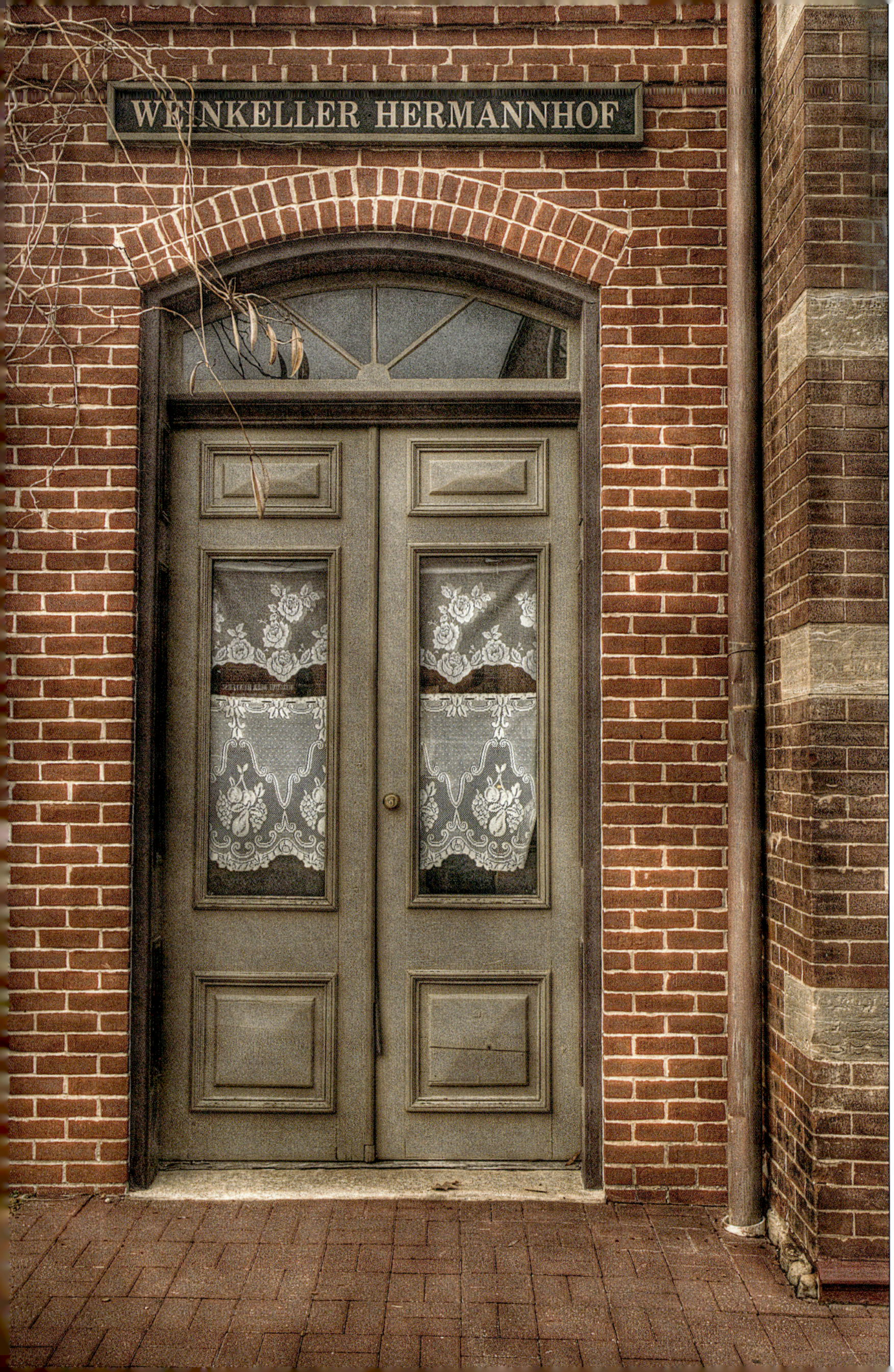

The Buildings

"Architecture is a visual art, and the buildings speak for themselves."
– Julia Morgan

The Weinkeller
William Fields

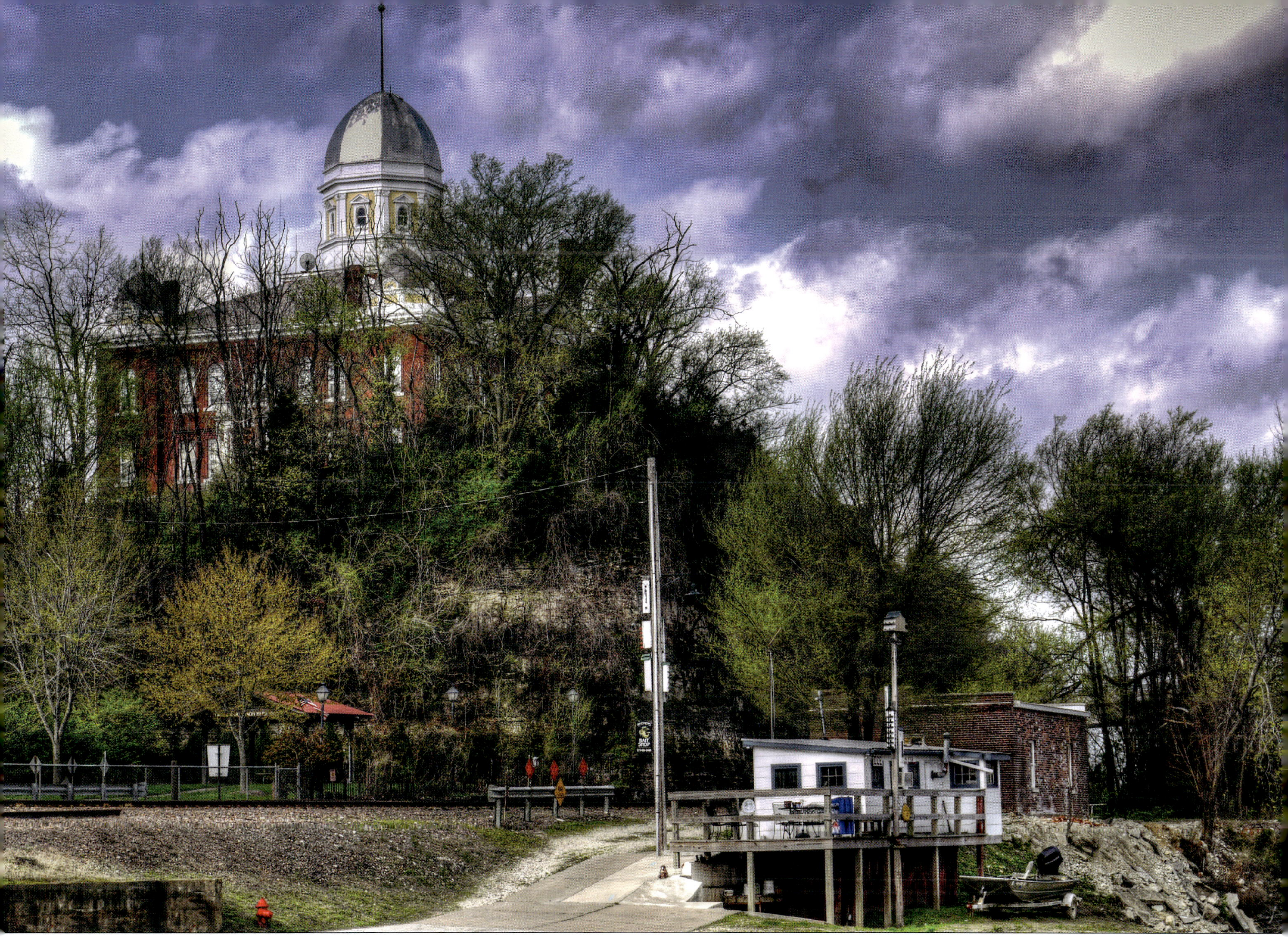

Fish Shack
William Fields

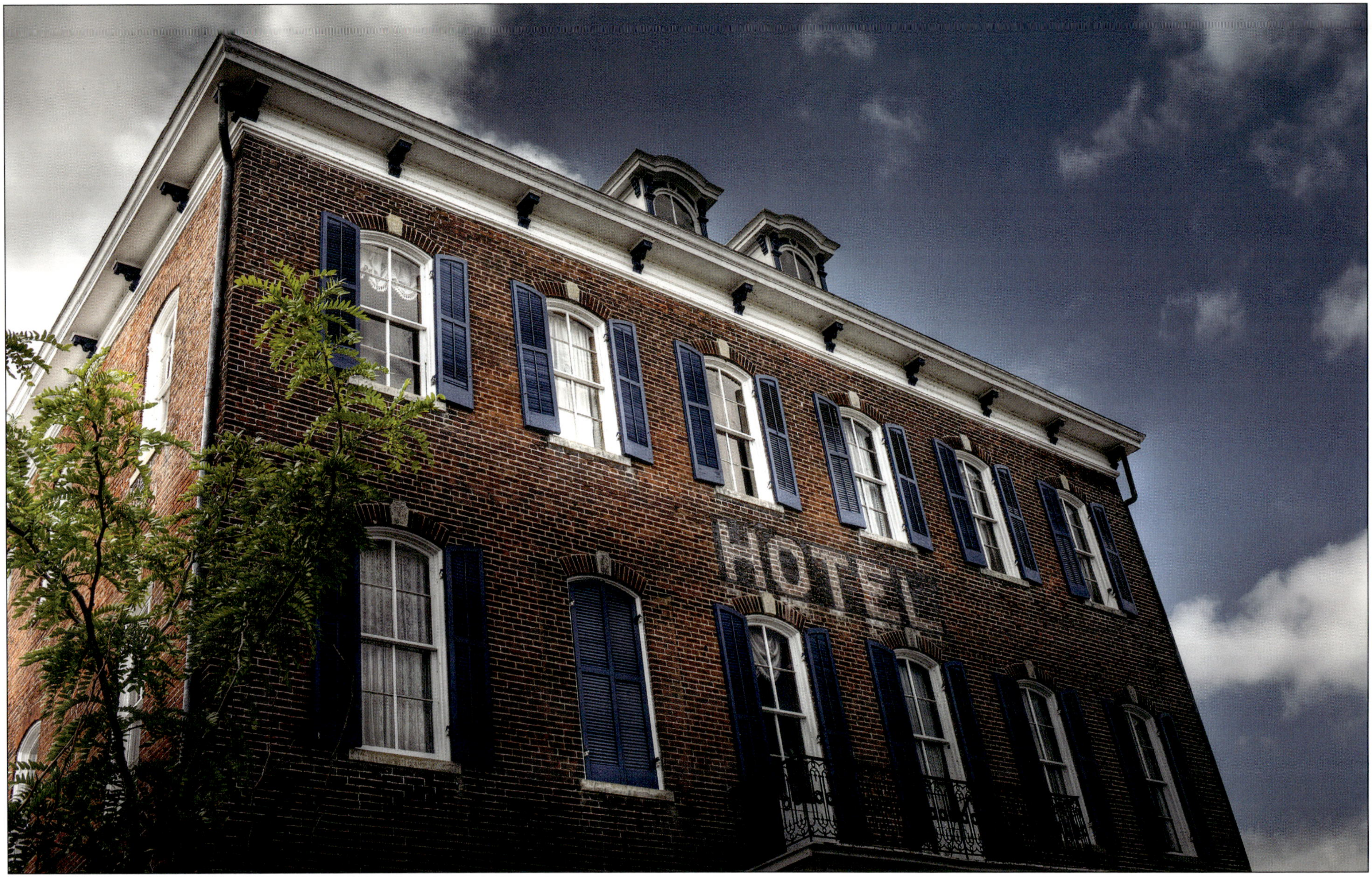

White House Hotel
William Fields

Zigzag Fencerow
William Fields

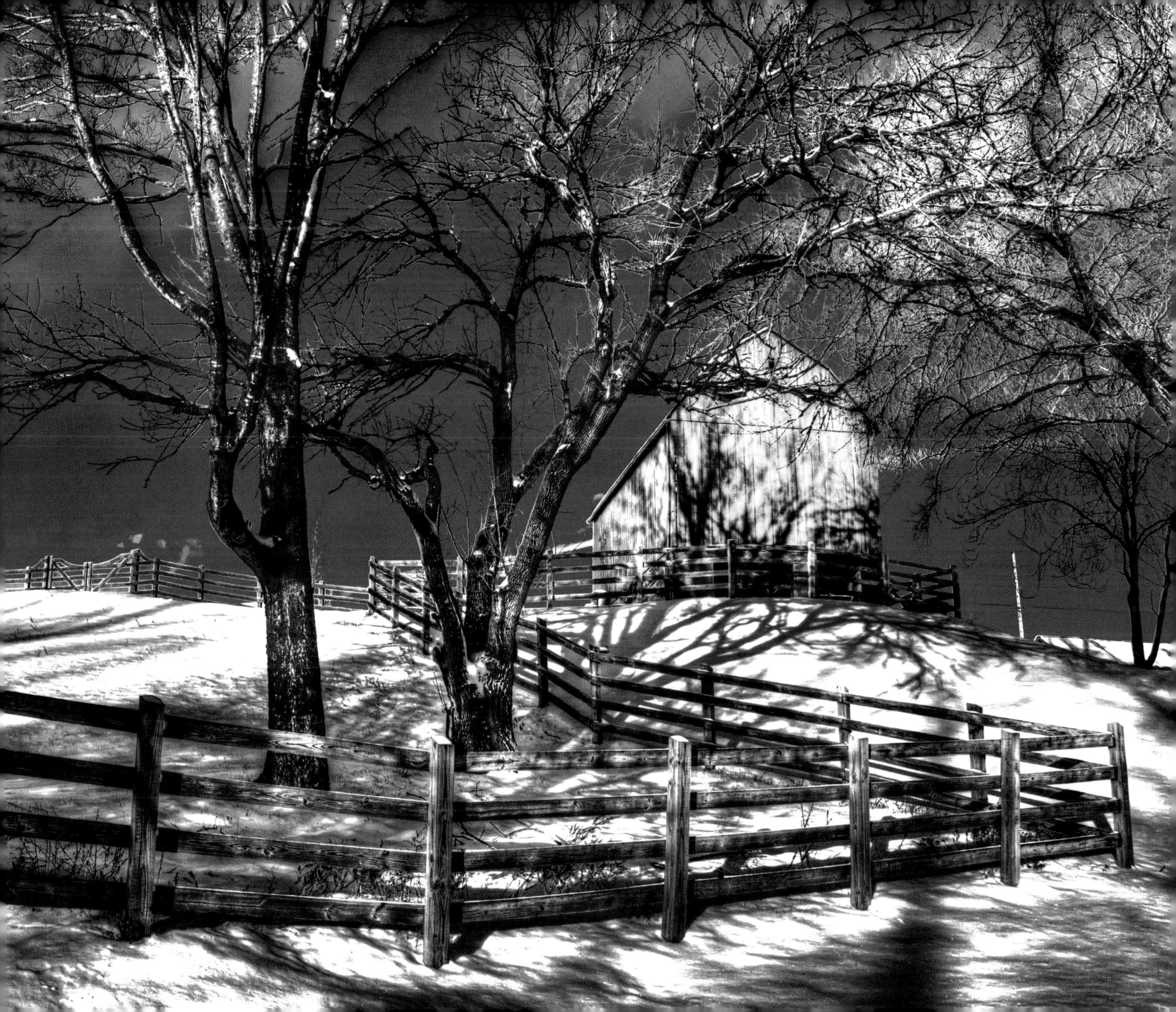

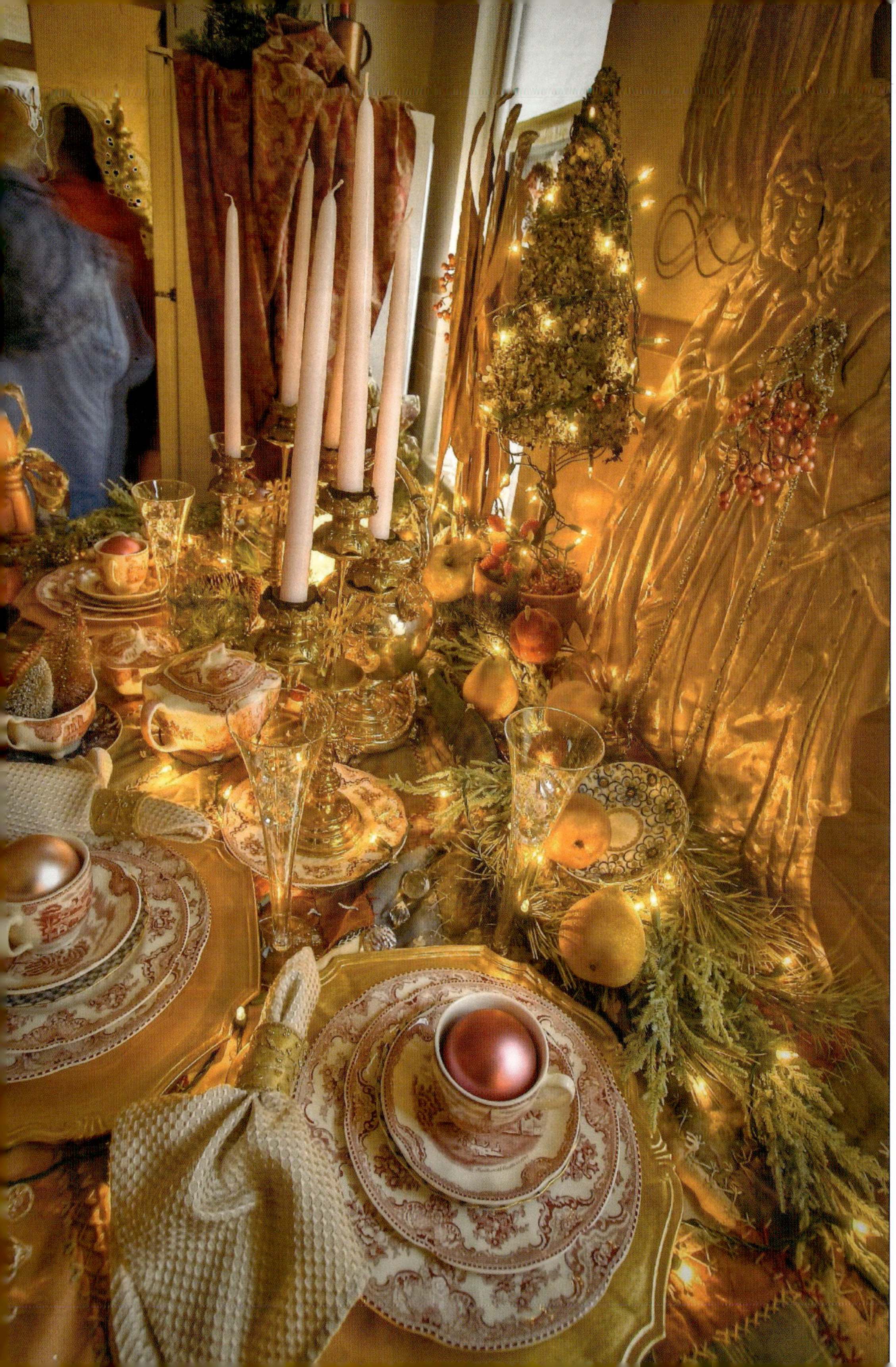

"The night has a thousand eyes
And the day but one;
Yet the light of the bright world dies
With the dying sun.
– Francis William Bordillon

Saint George Christmas Dinner

Tony Carosella

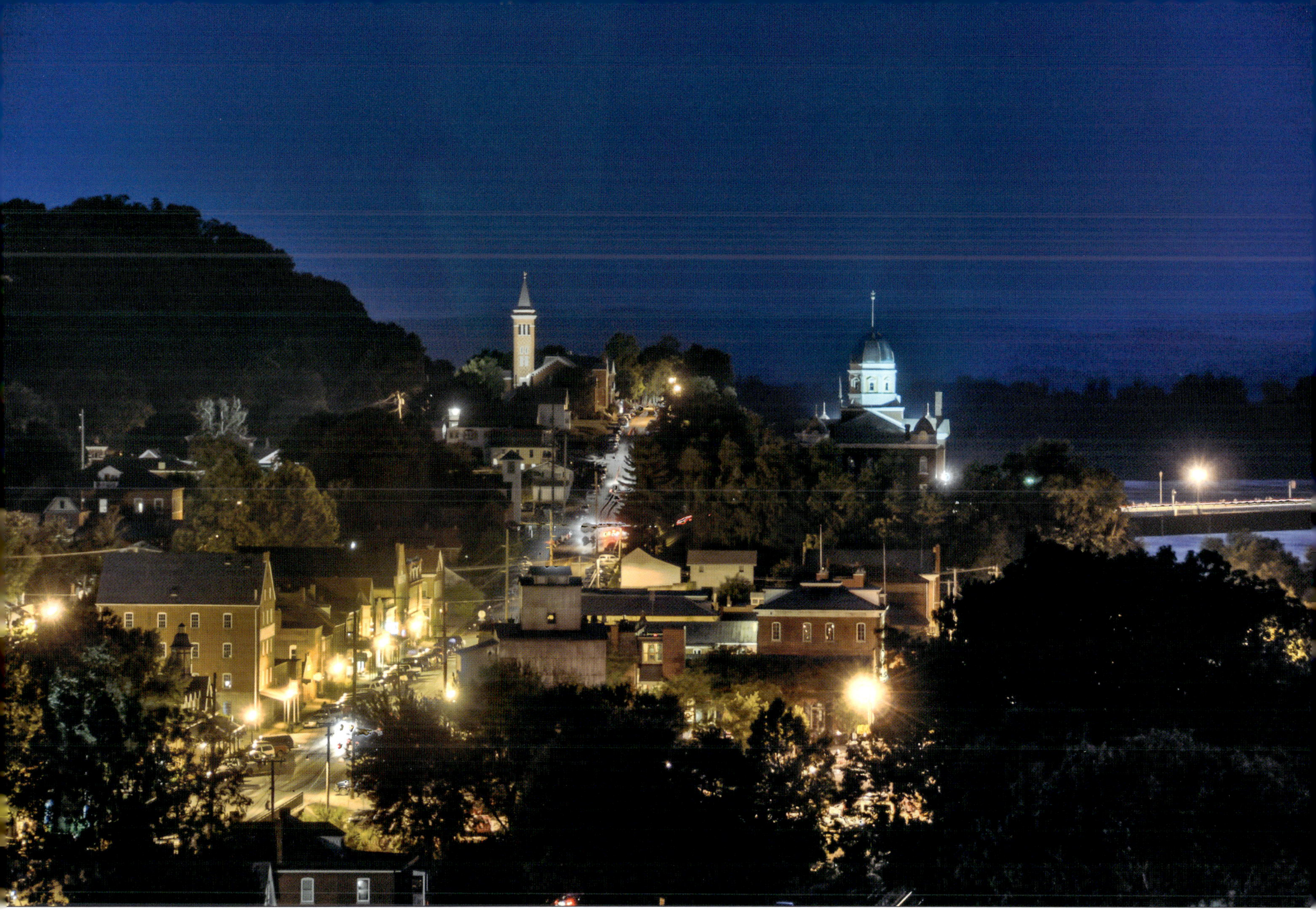

Hermann Nocturne
Tony Carosella

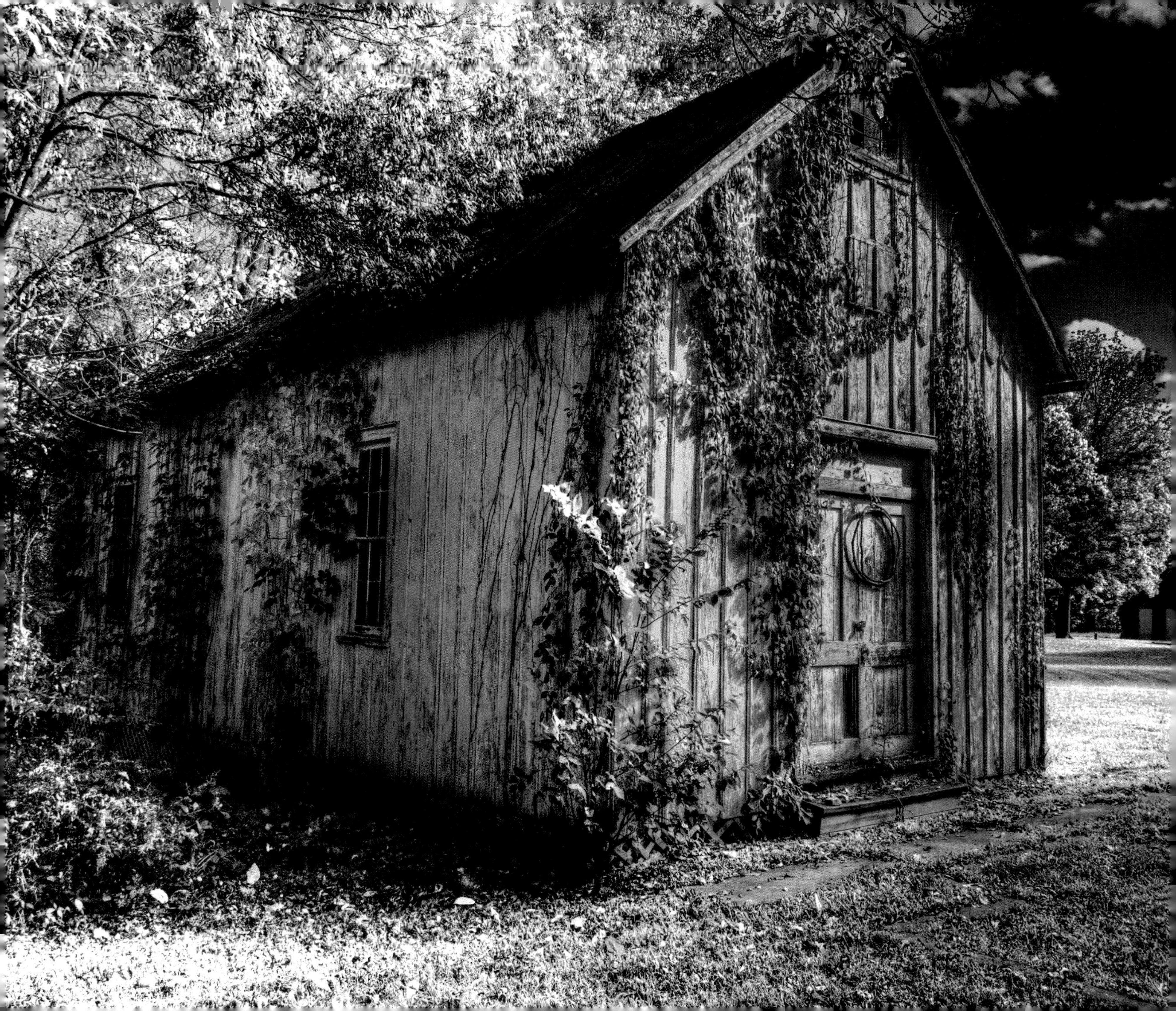

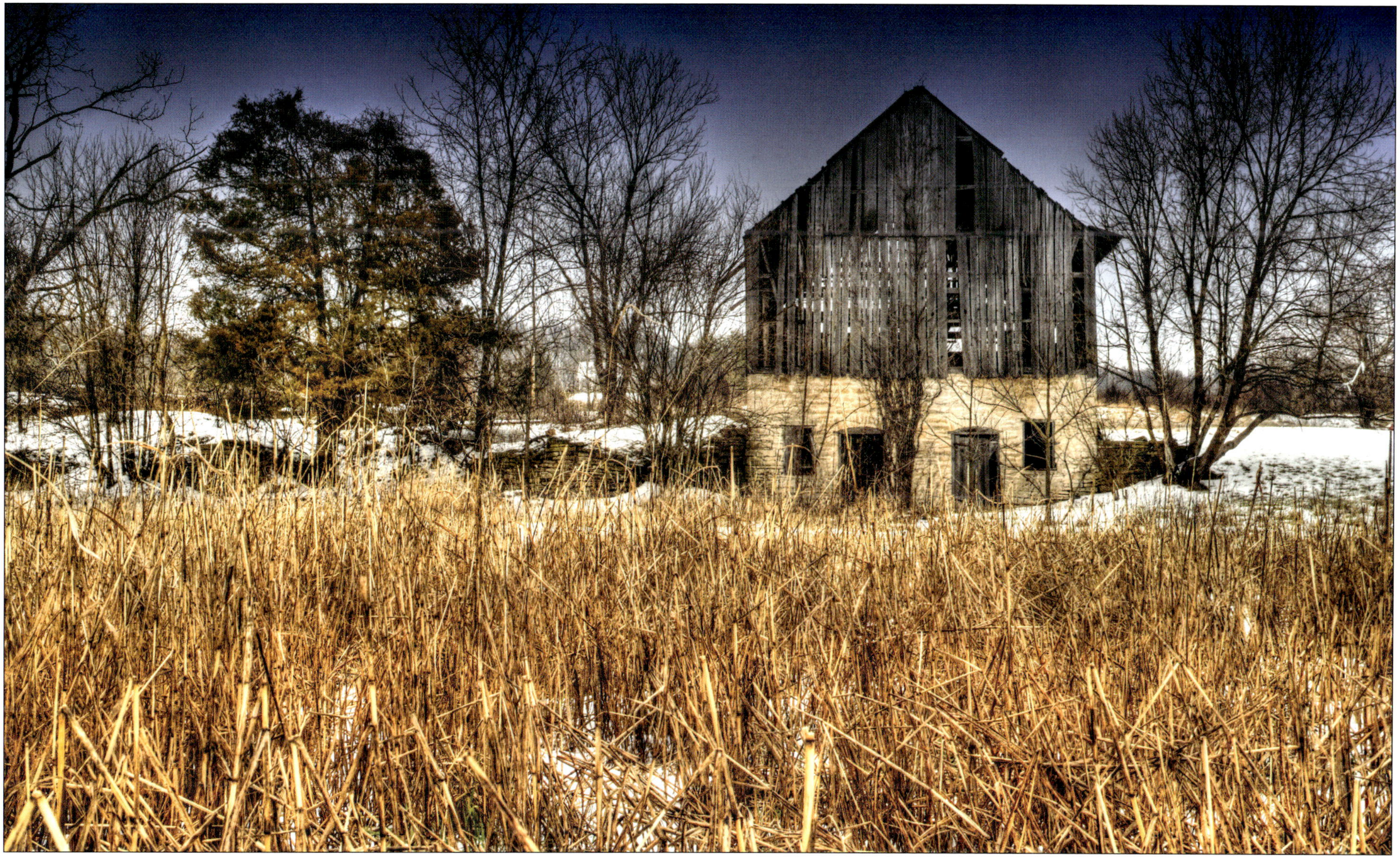

Stonewall II
William Fields

Gore Shed II
William Fields

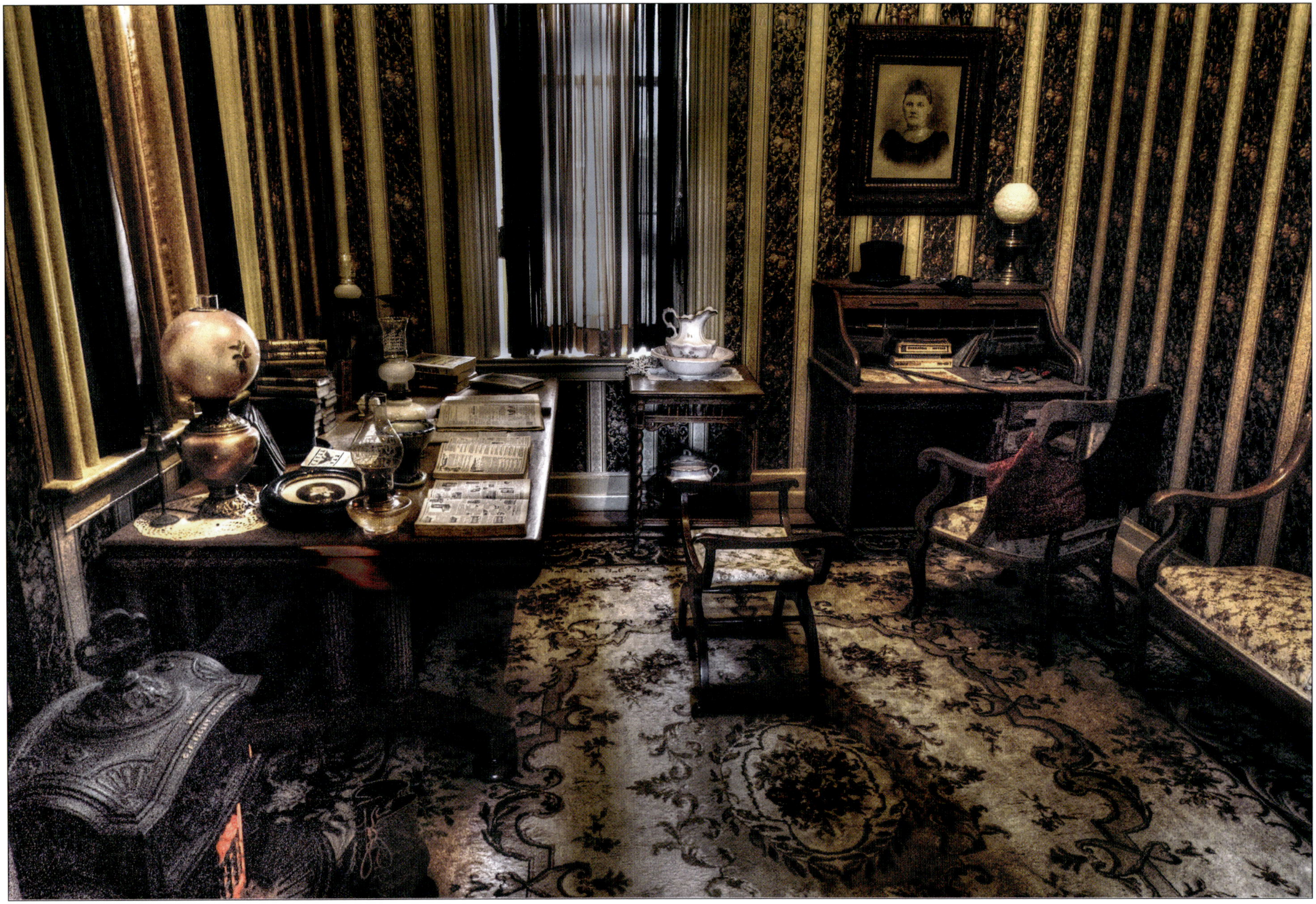

Grandfather's Office

William Fields

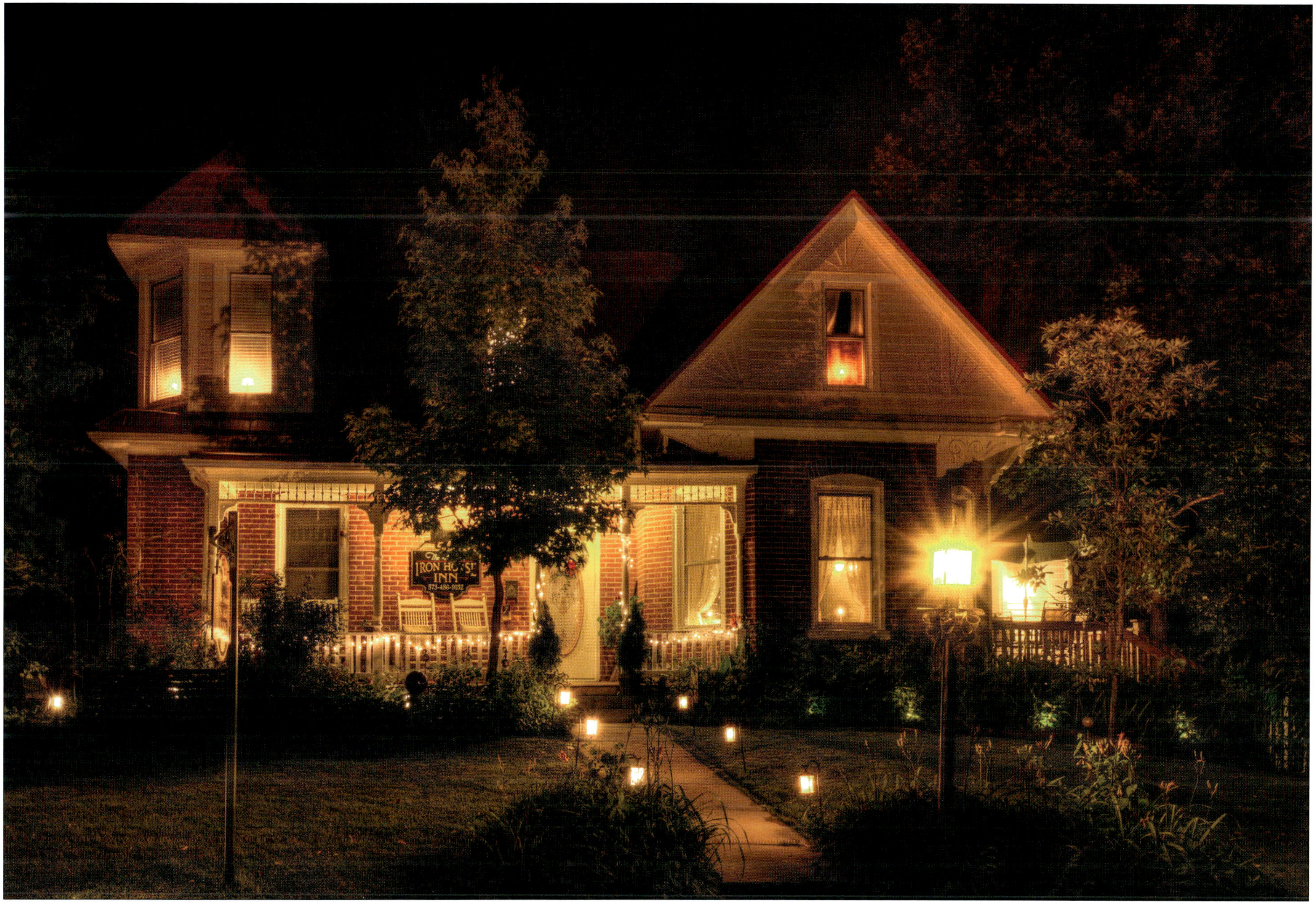

Iron Horse Nocturne

William Fields

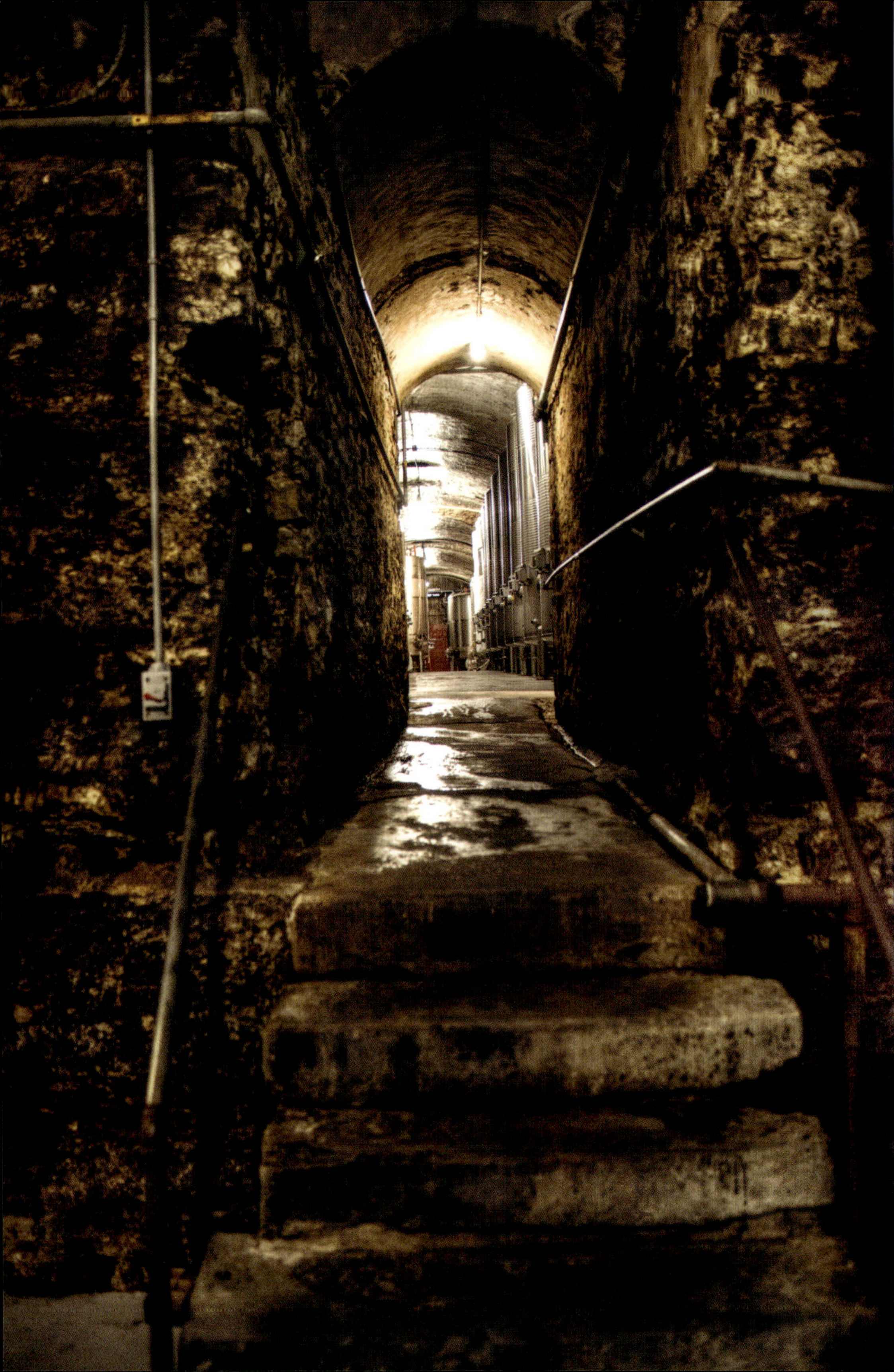

"Buildings, too, are children
of Earth and Sun."
– Frank Lloyd Wright

Wine making and vineyard cultivation are one of the most important industries in Hermann. The cellars are where the alchemy happens.
– William Fields

In the Cellar

William Fields

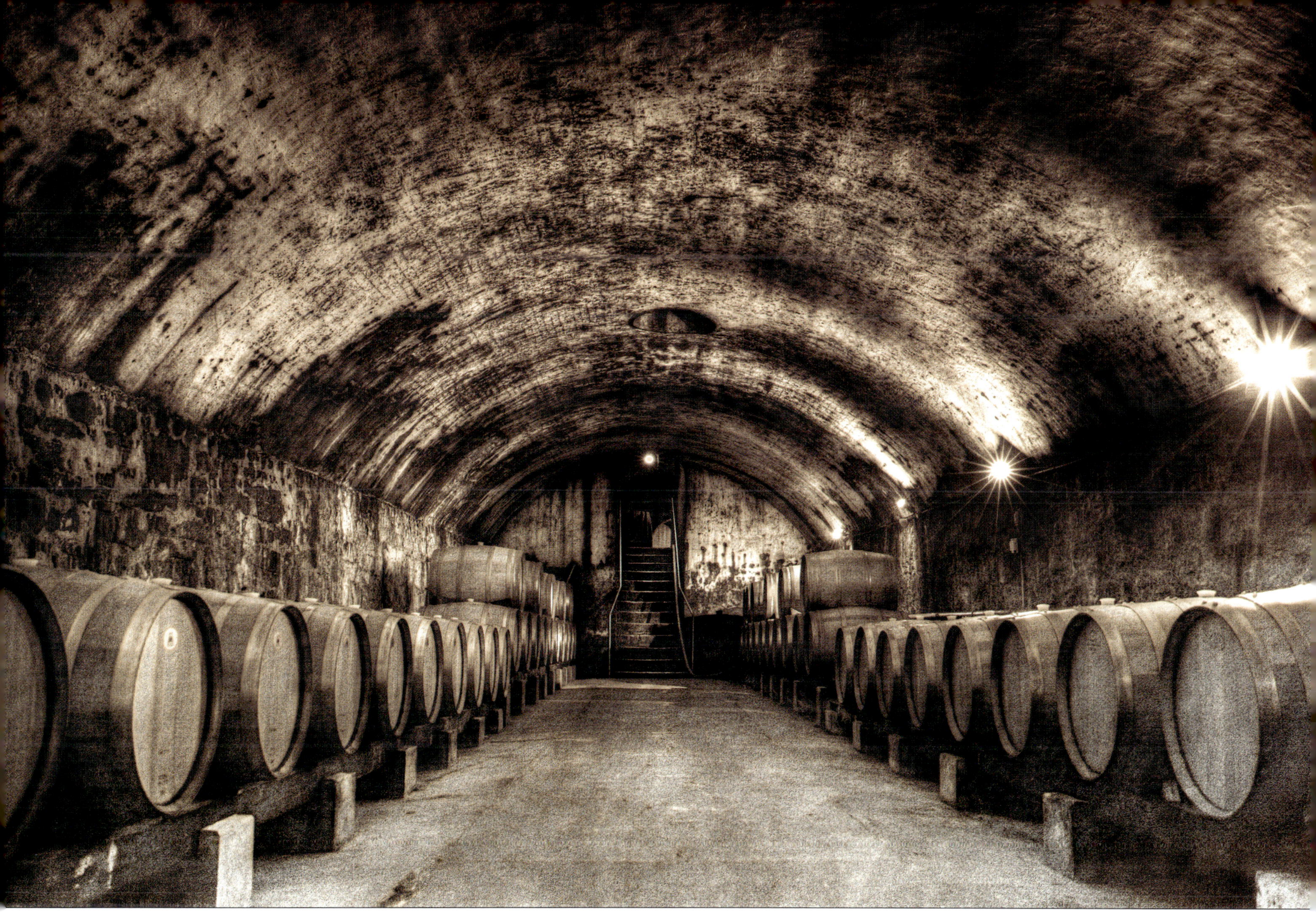

Row by Row
William Fields

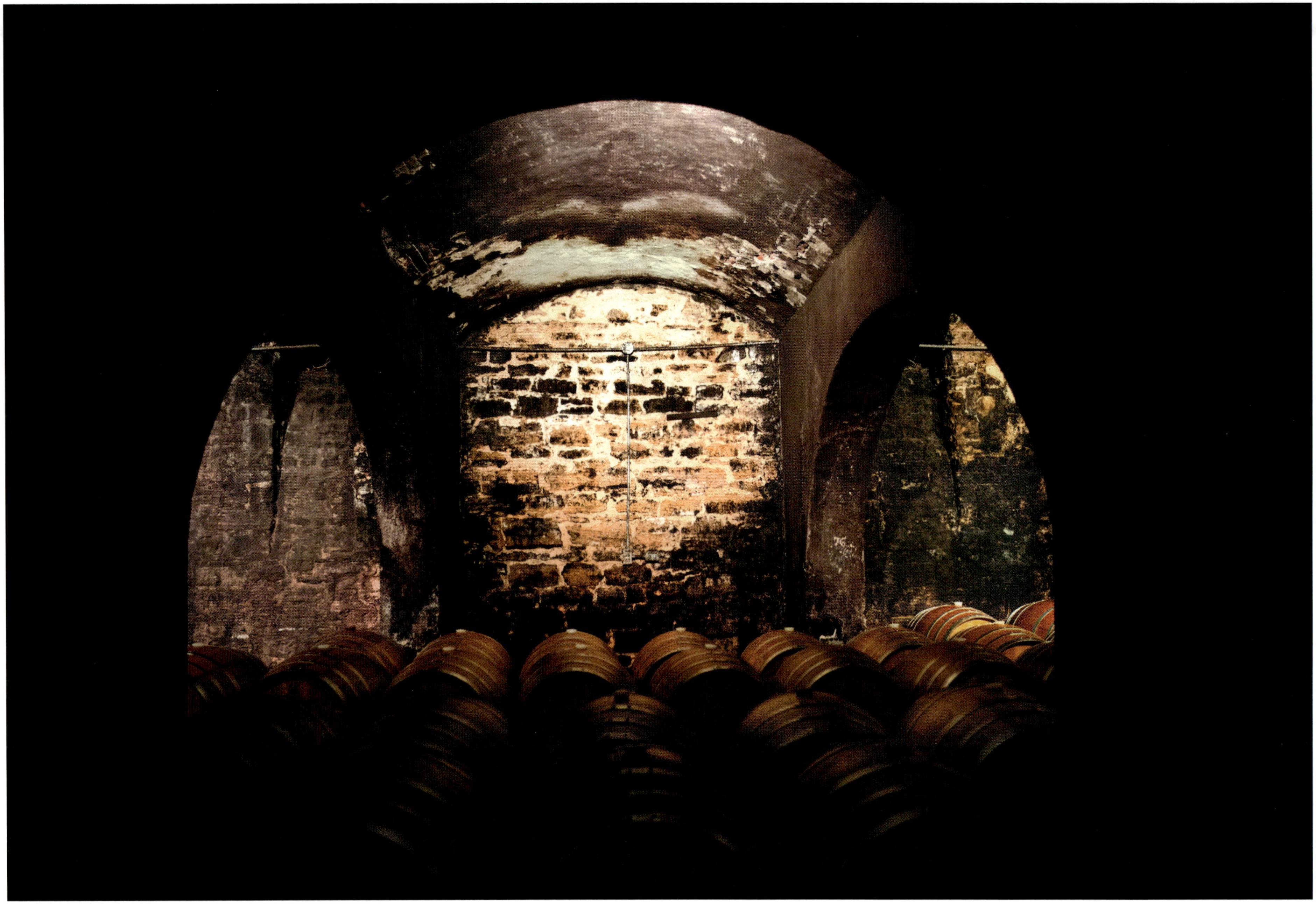

An Overarching Concern
William Fields

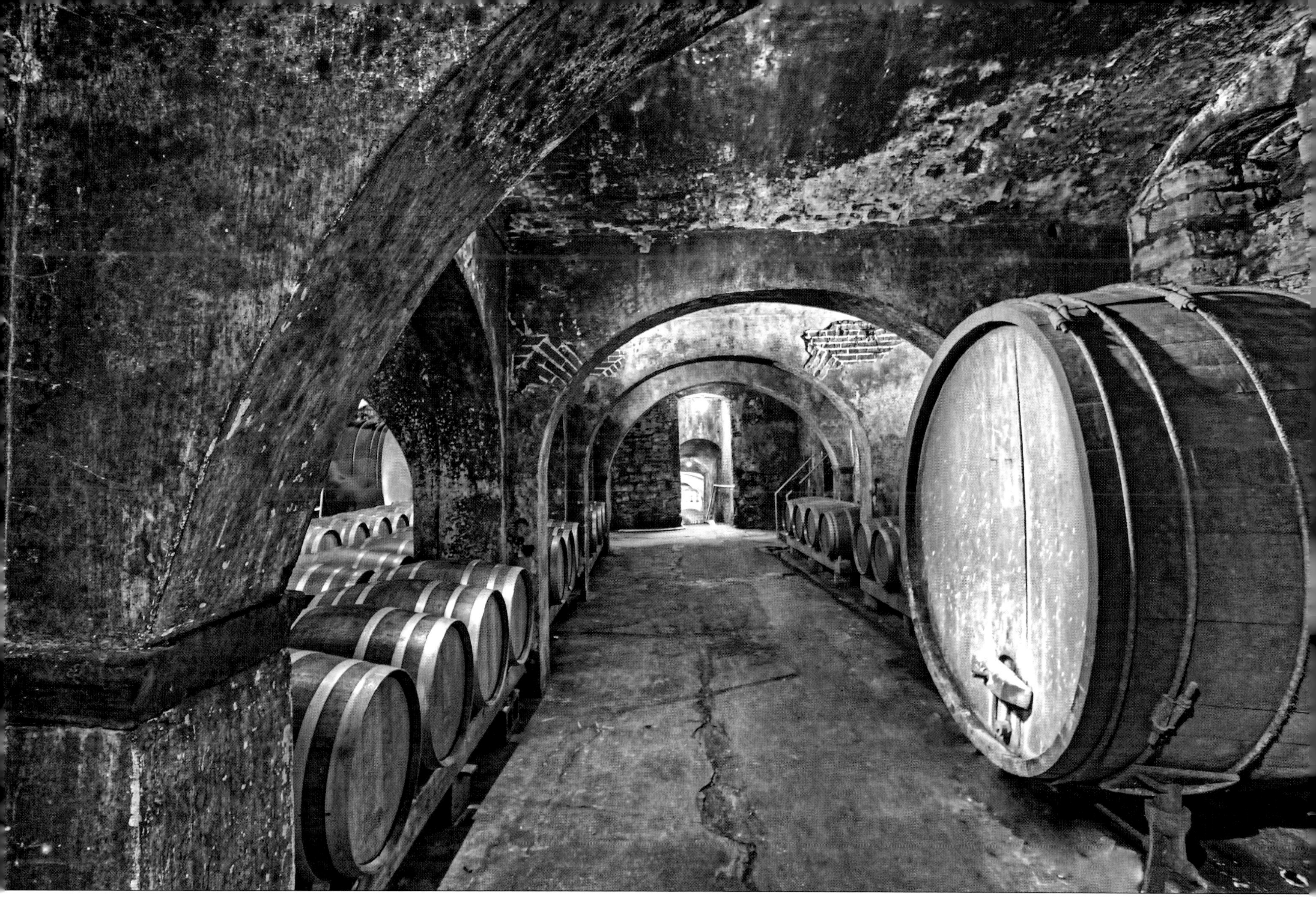

Hermannhof Cellar
Tony Carosella

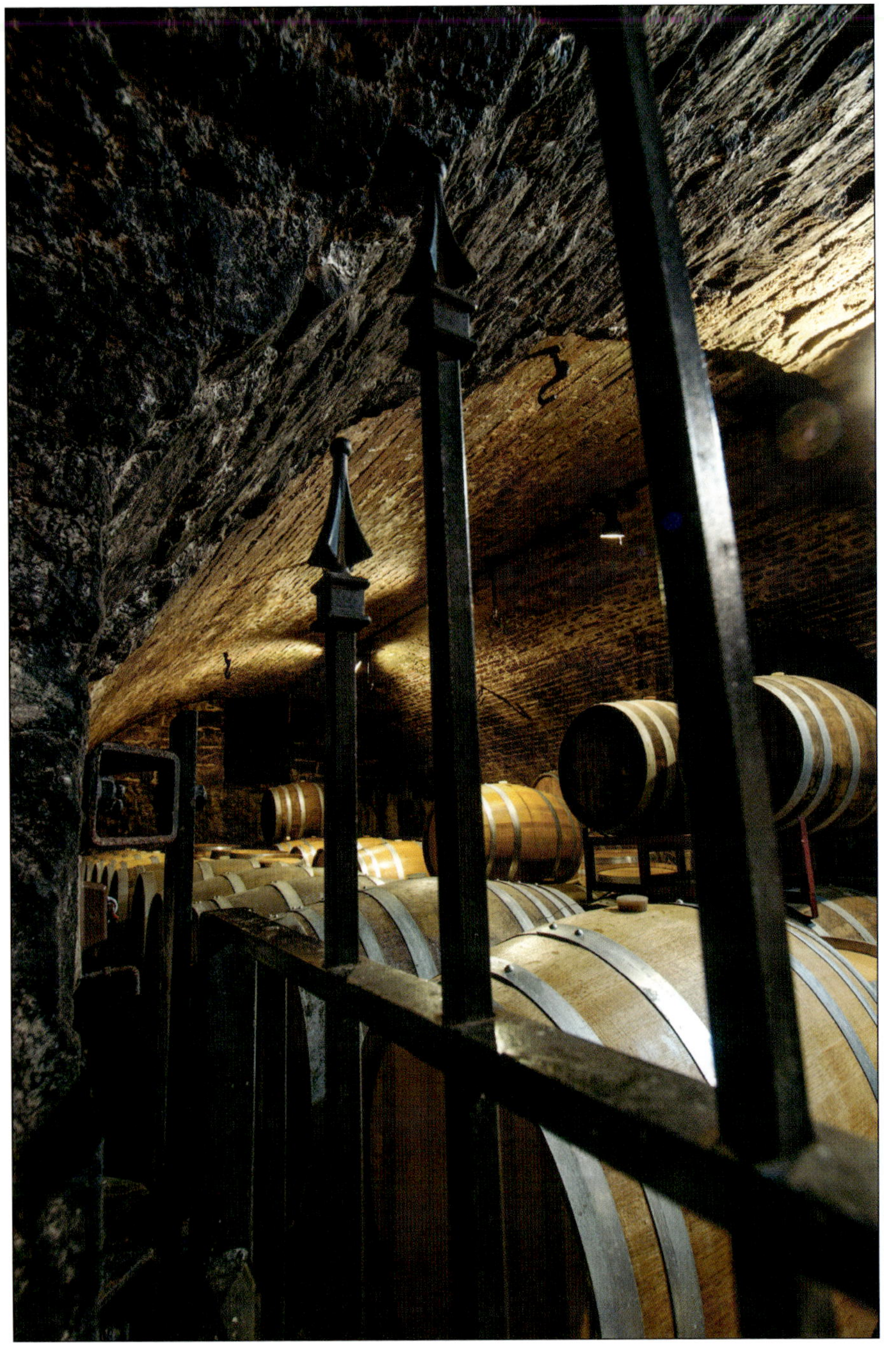

Behind the Bars
Tony Carosella

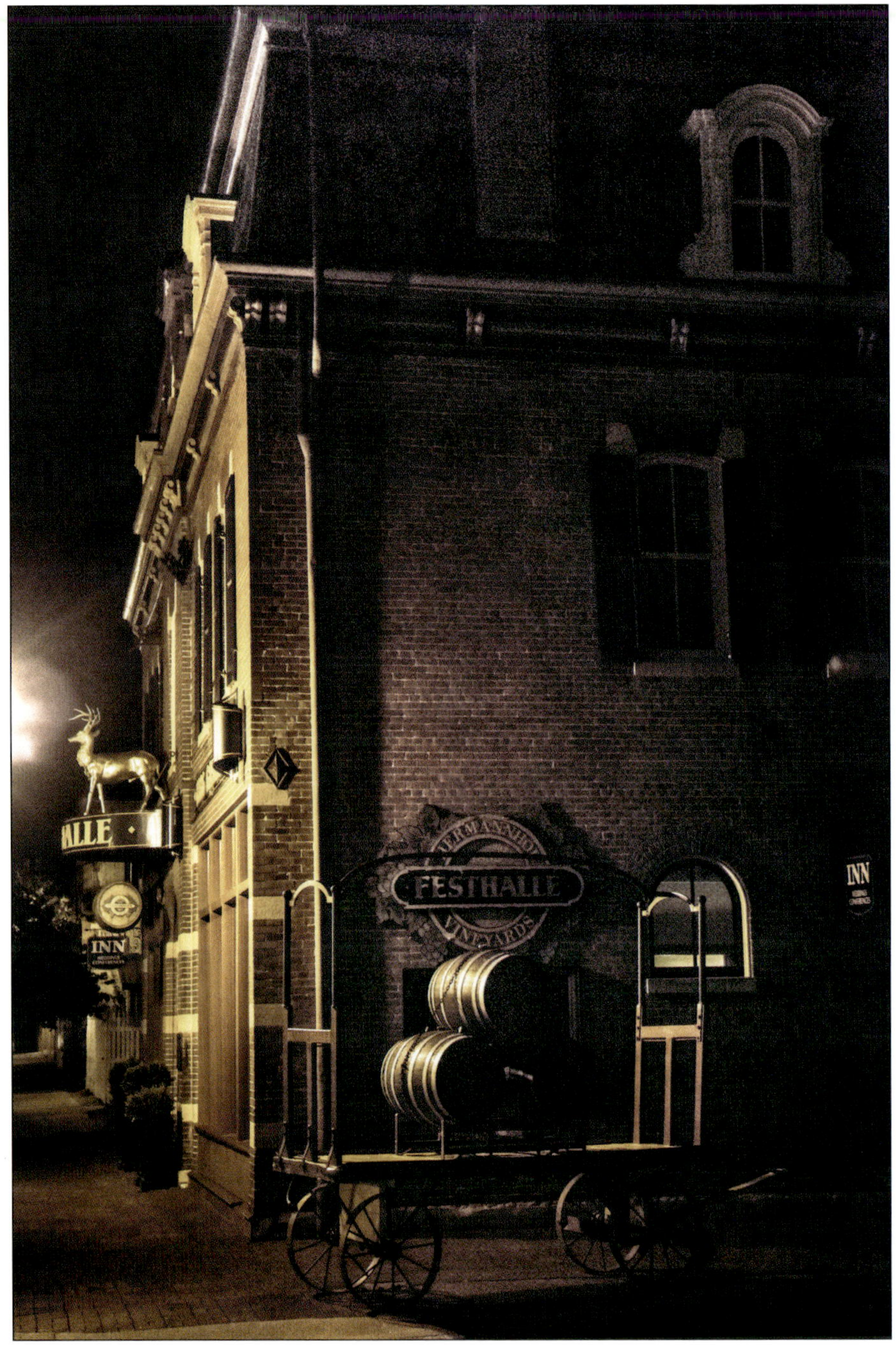

Festhalle Nocturne
William Fields

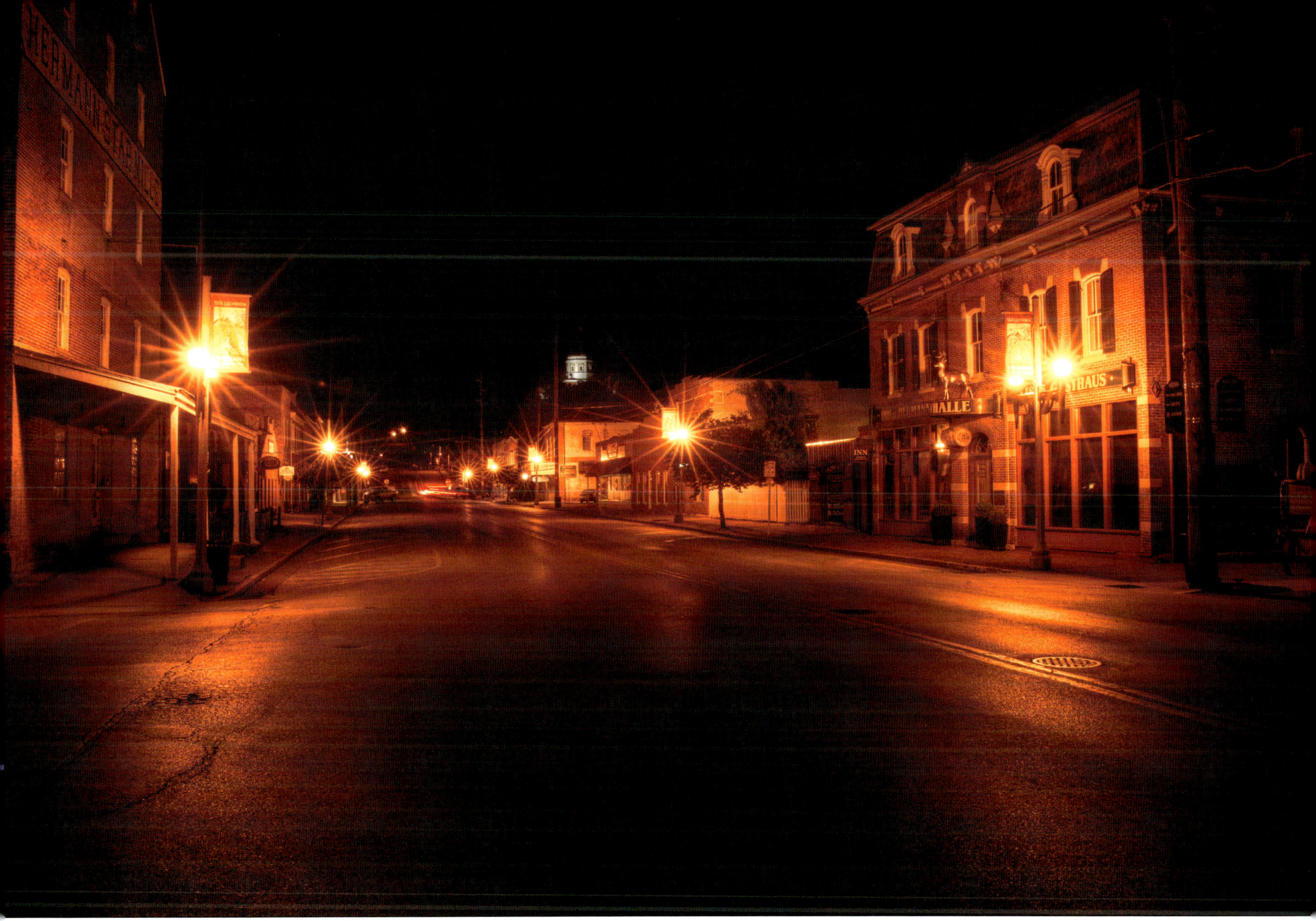

First Street Nocturne
William Fields

George Bayer Statue

Tony Carosella

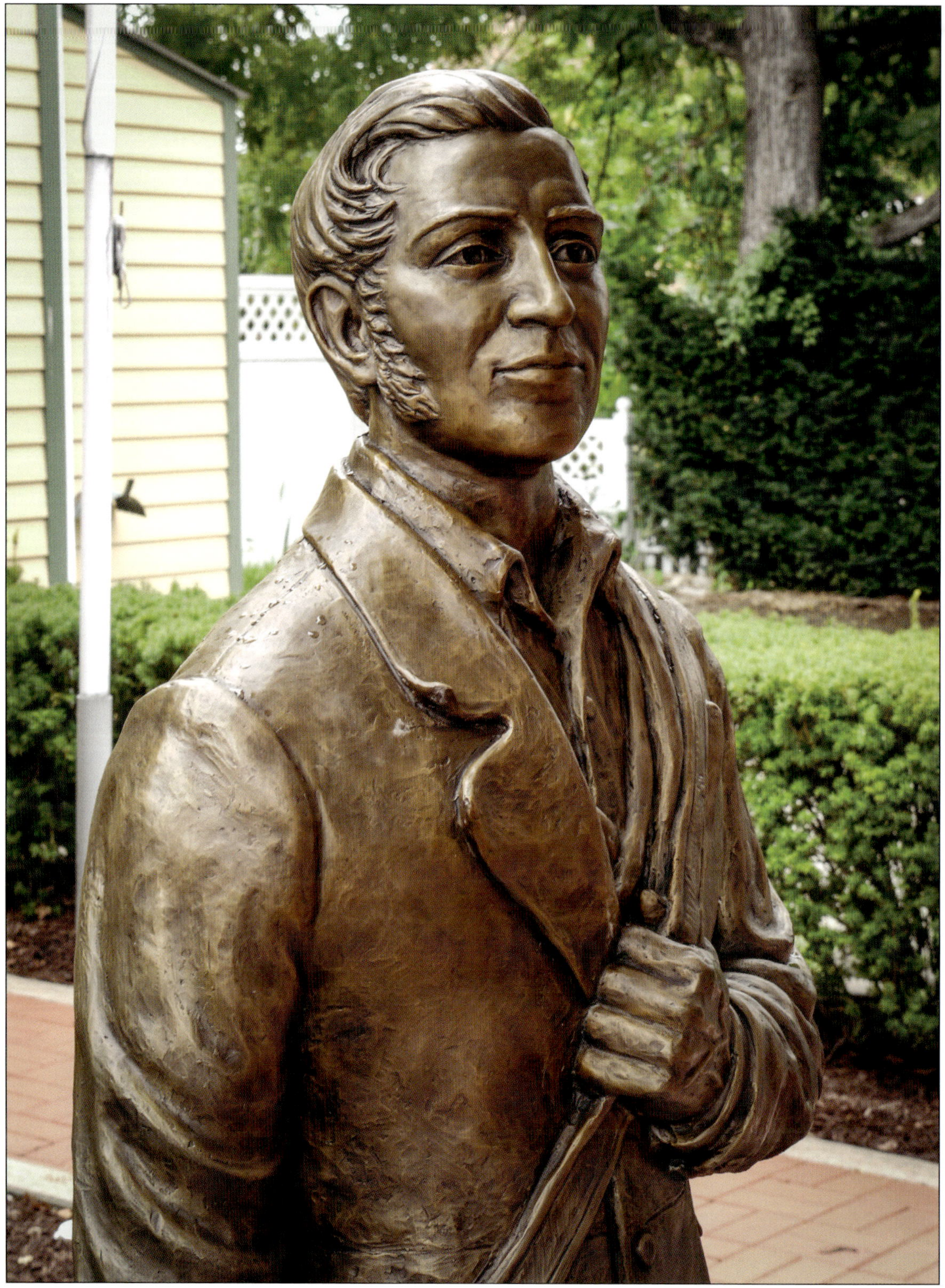

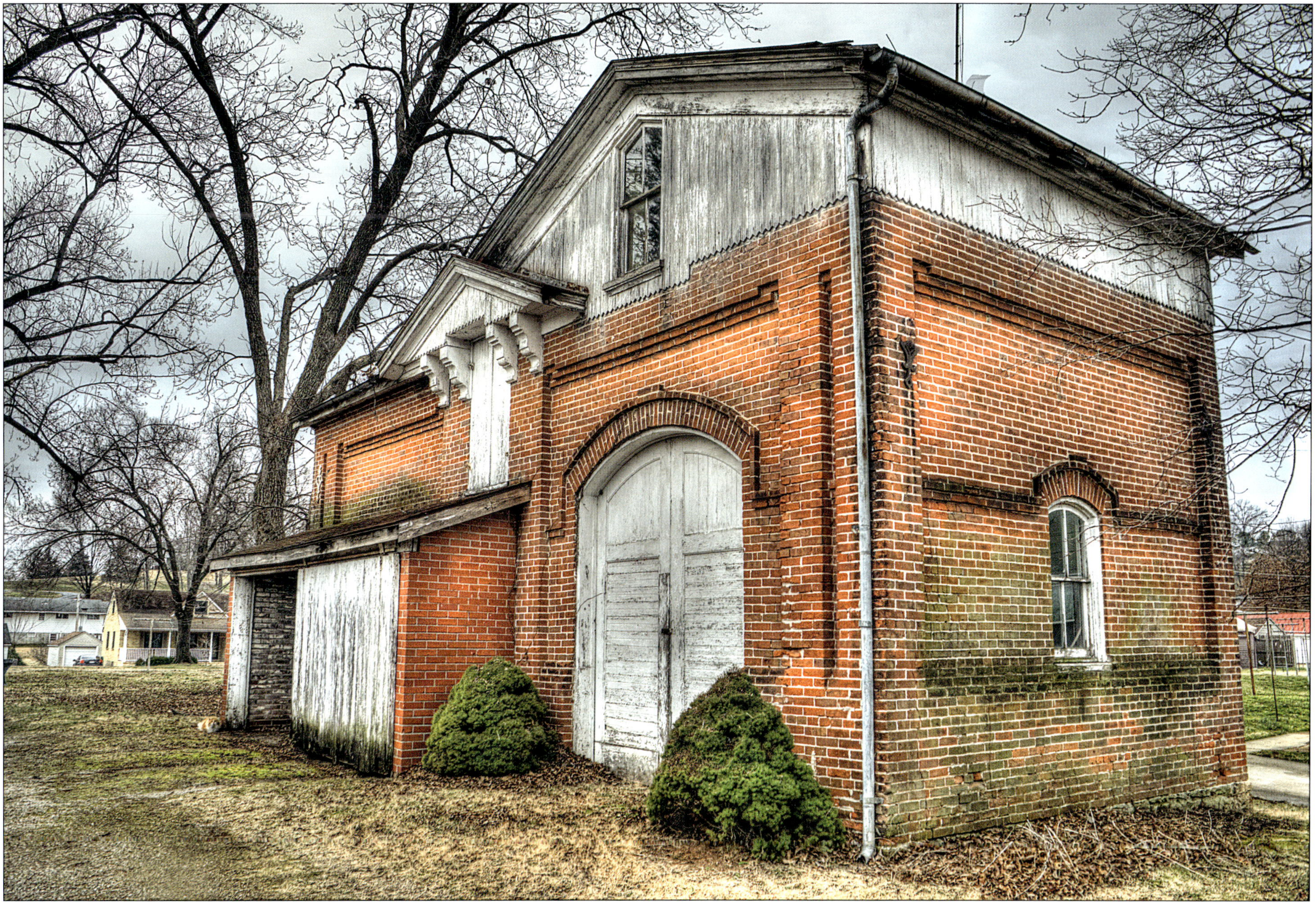

Beneath the Flowing Tide of Time
William Fields

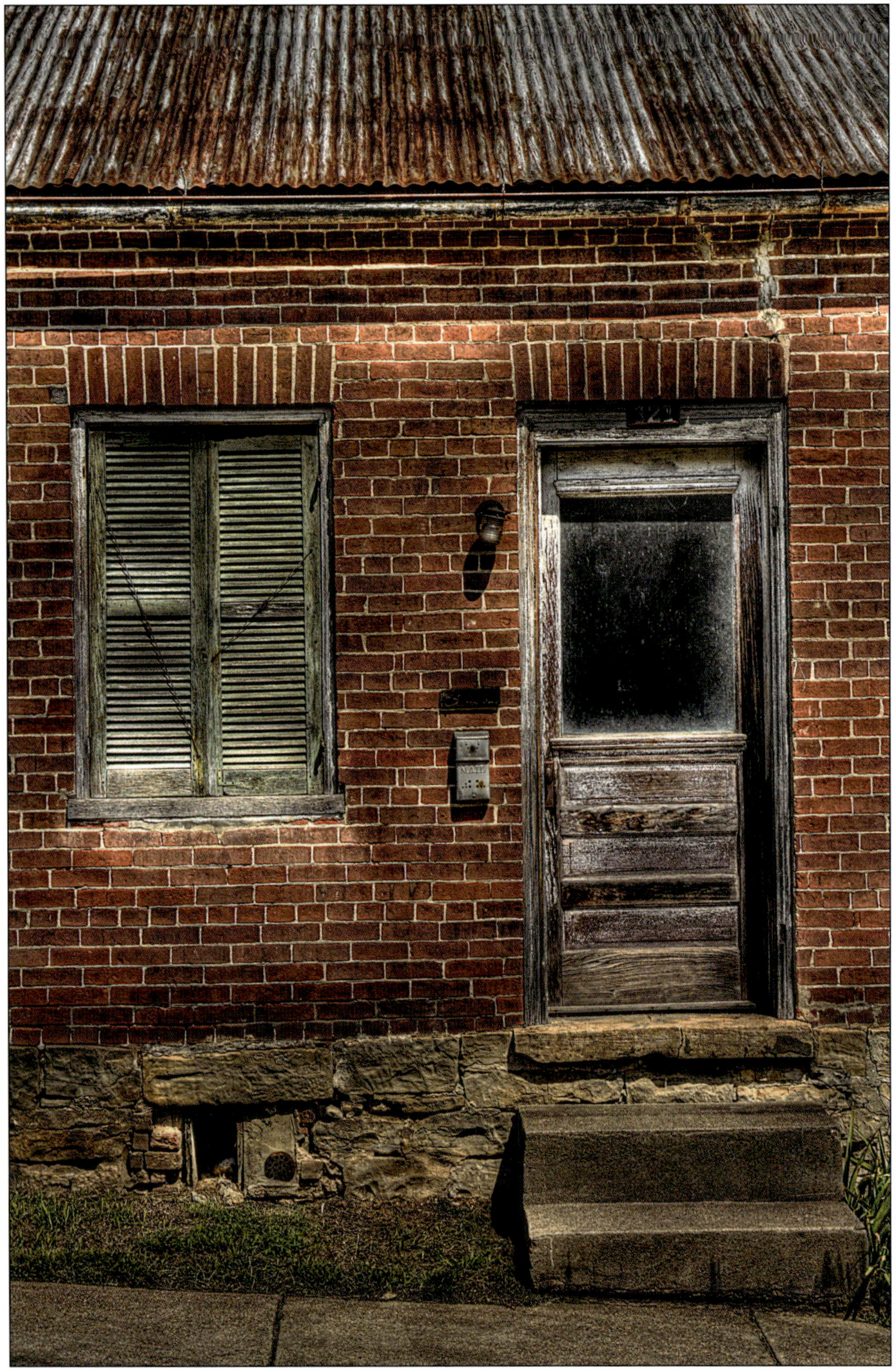

Green Shutters

William Fields

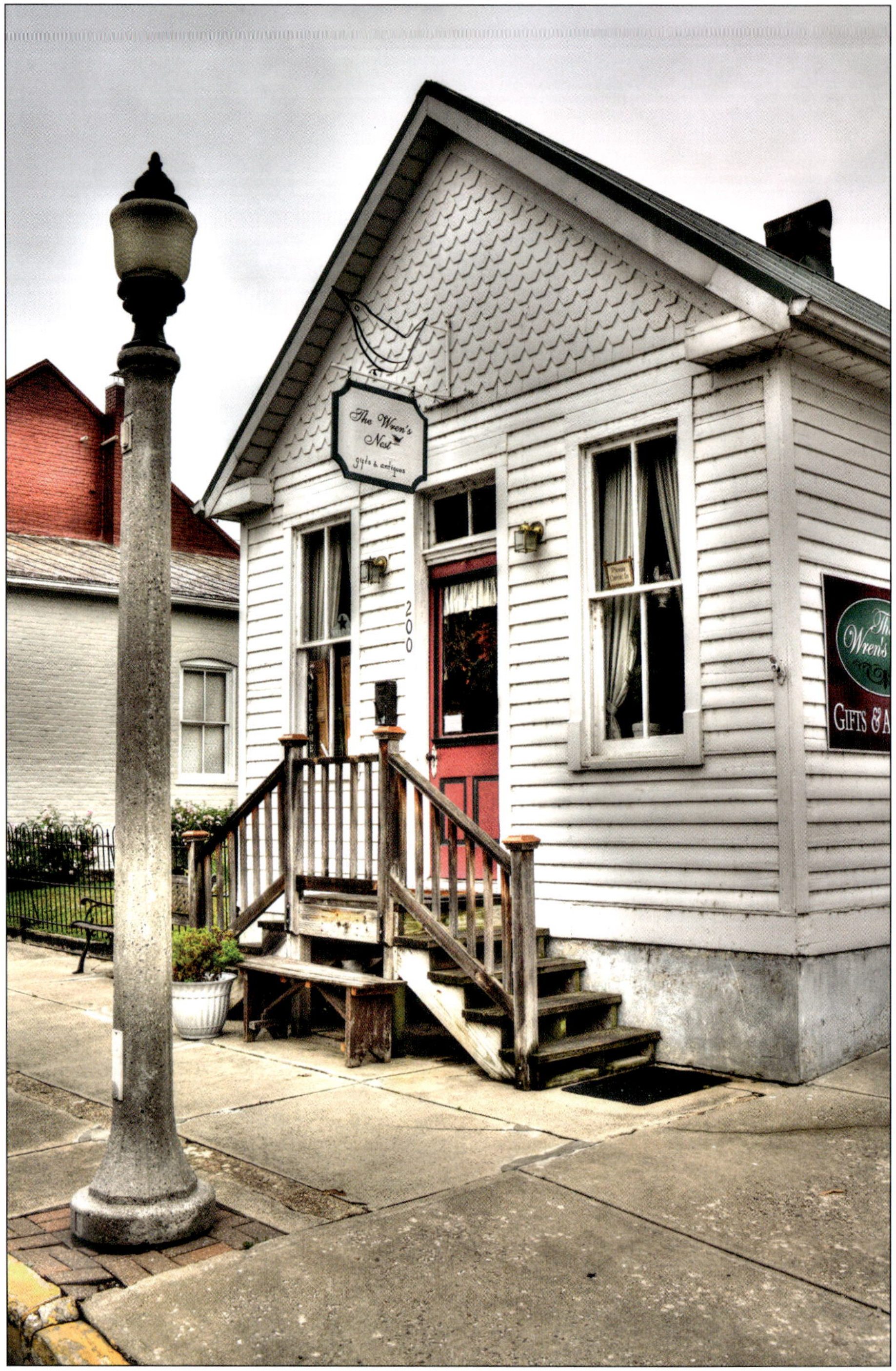

Wren's Nest Redux

William Fields

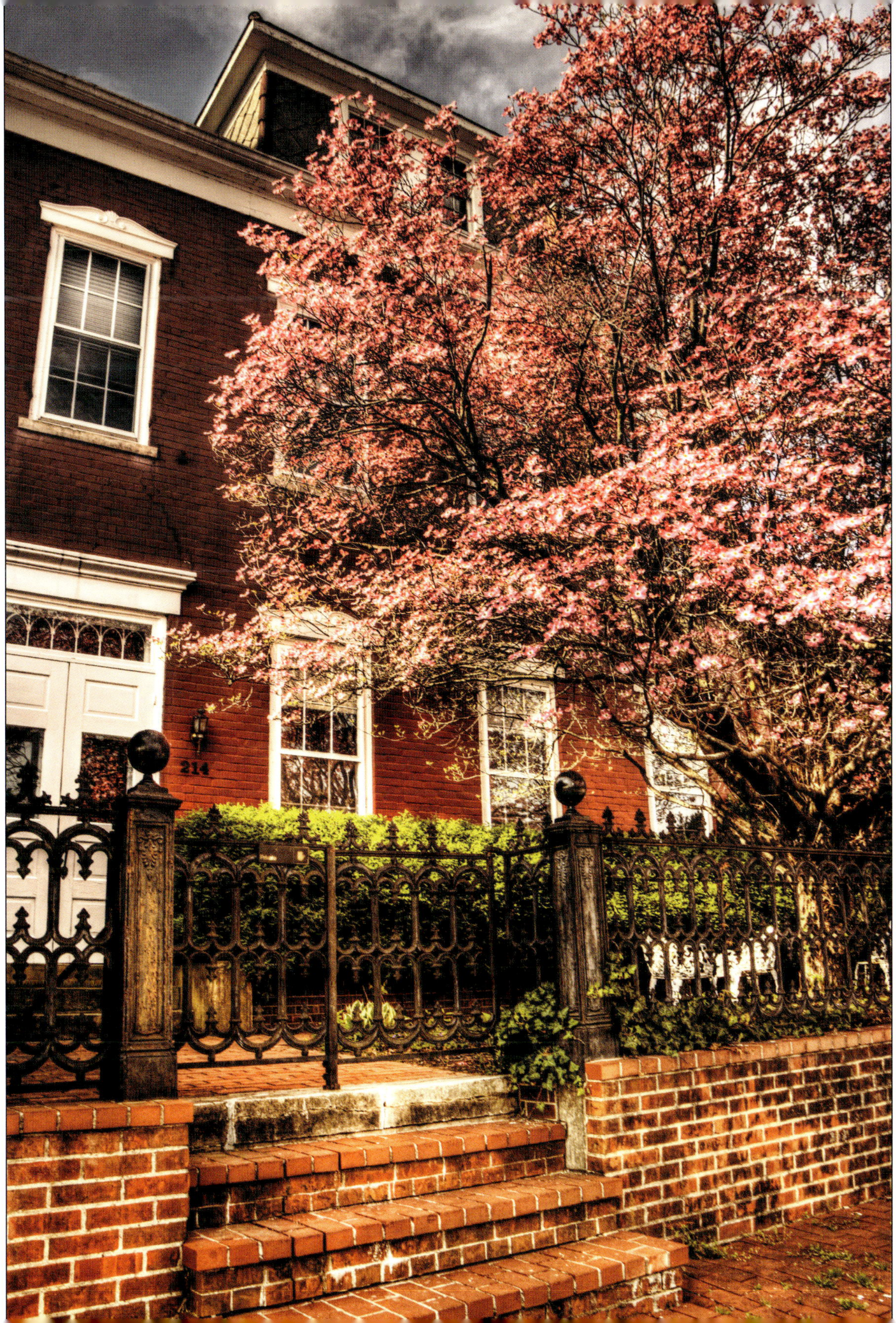

Kolbe Haus, April

William Fields

Hermann Aerial

Tony Carosella

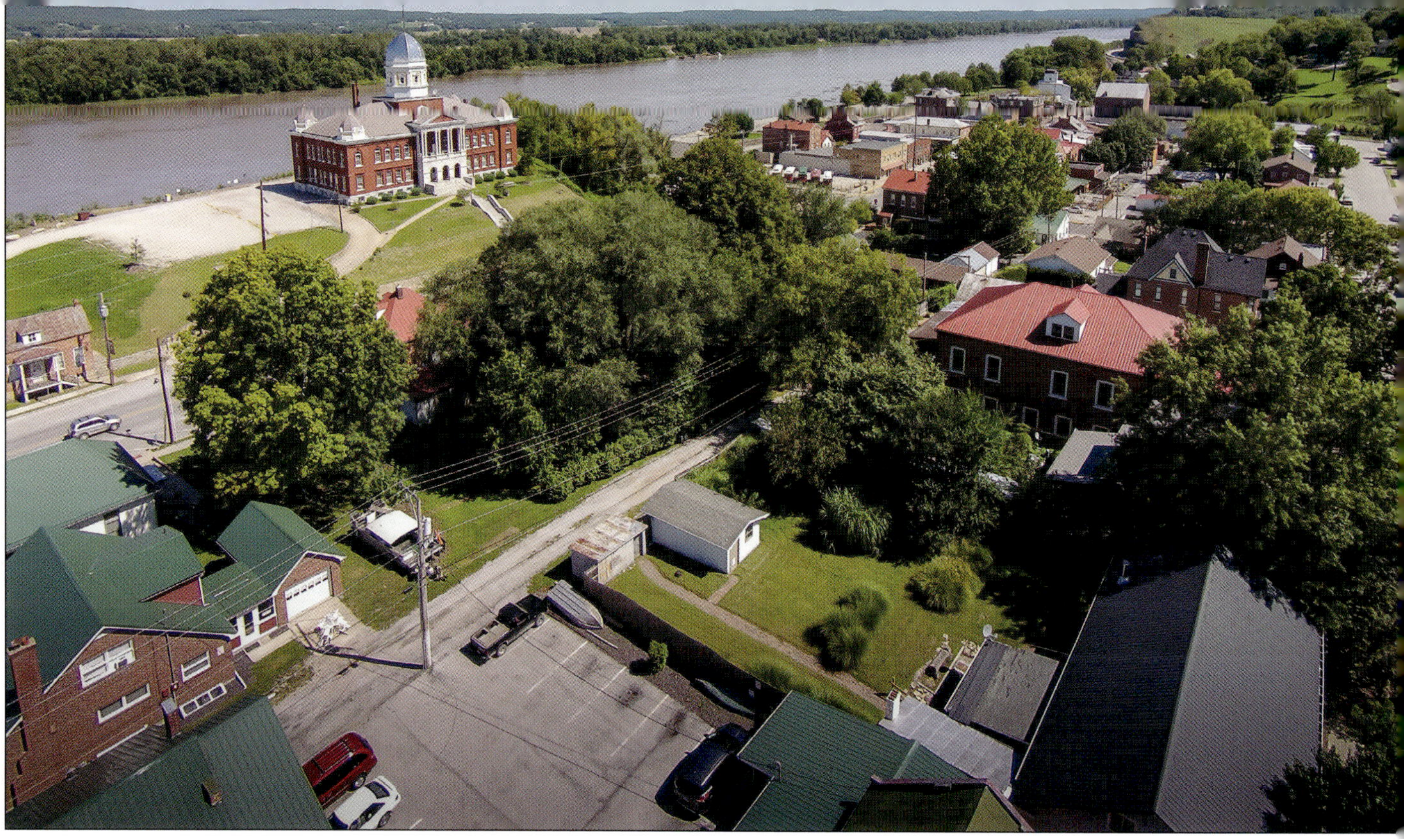

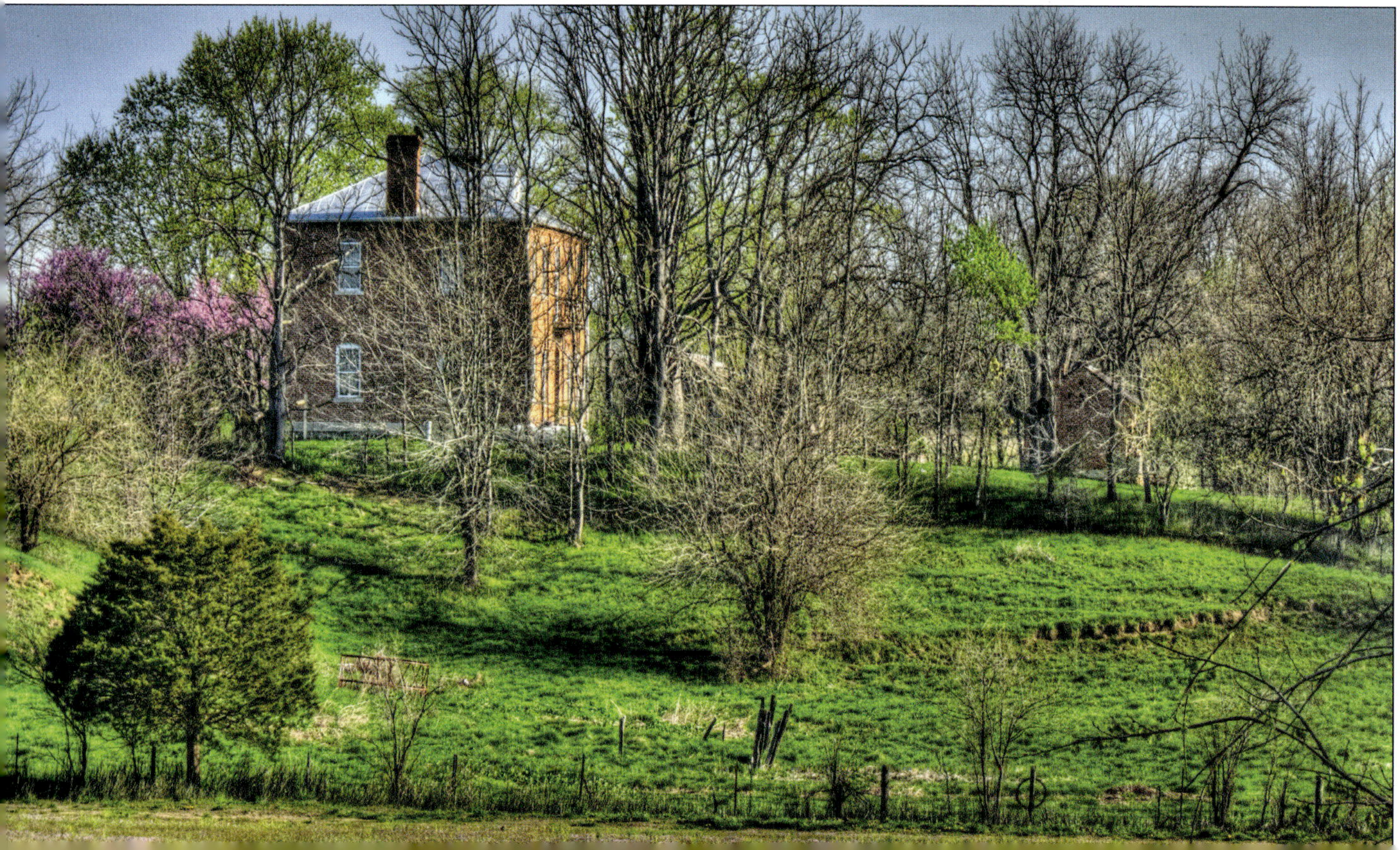

Brick Farmhouse, Peace Valley

William Fields

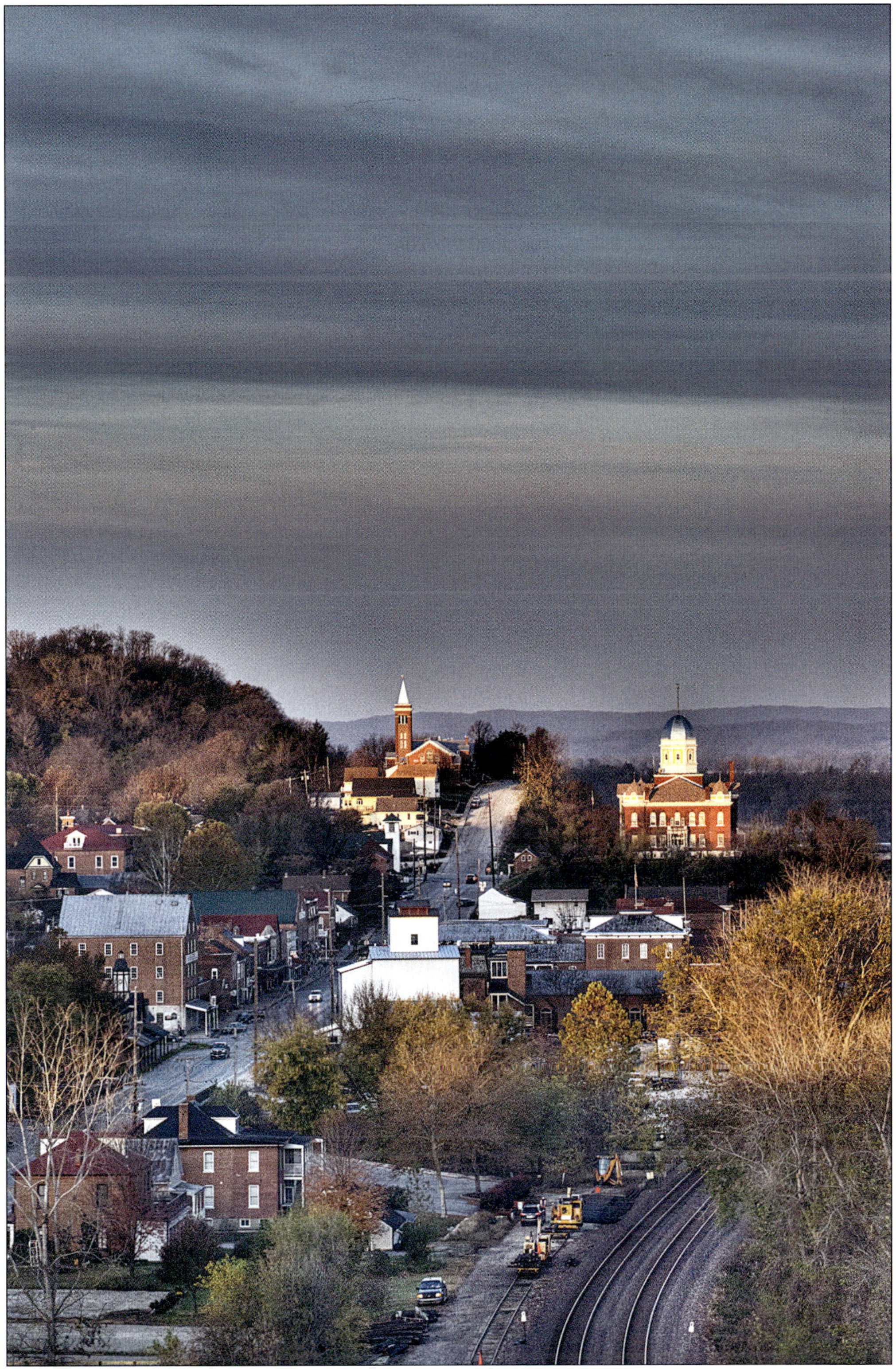

Hermann Dawn from Bluff

William Fields

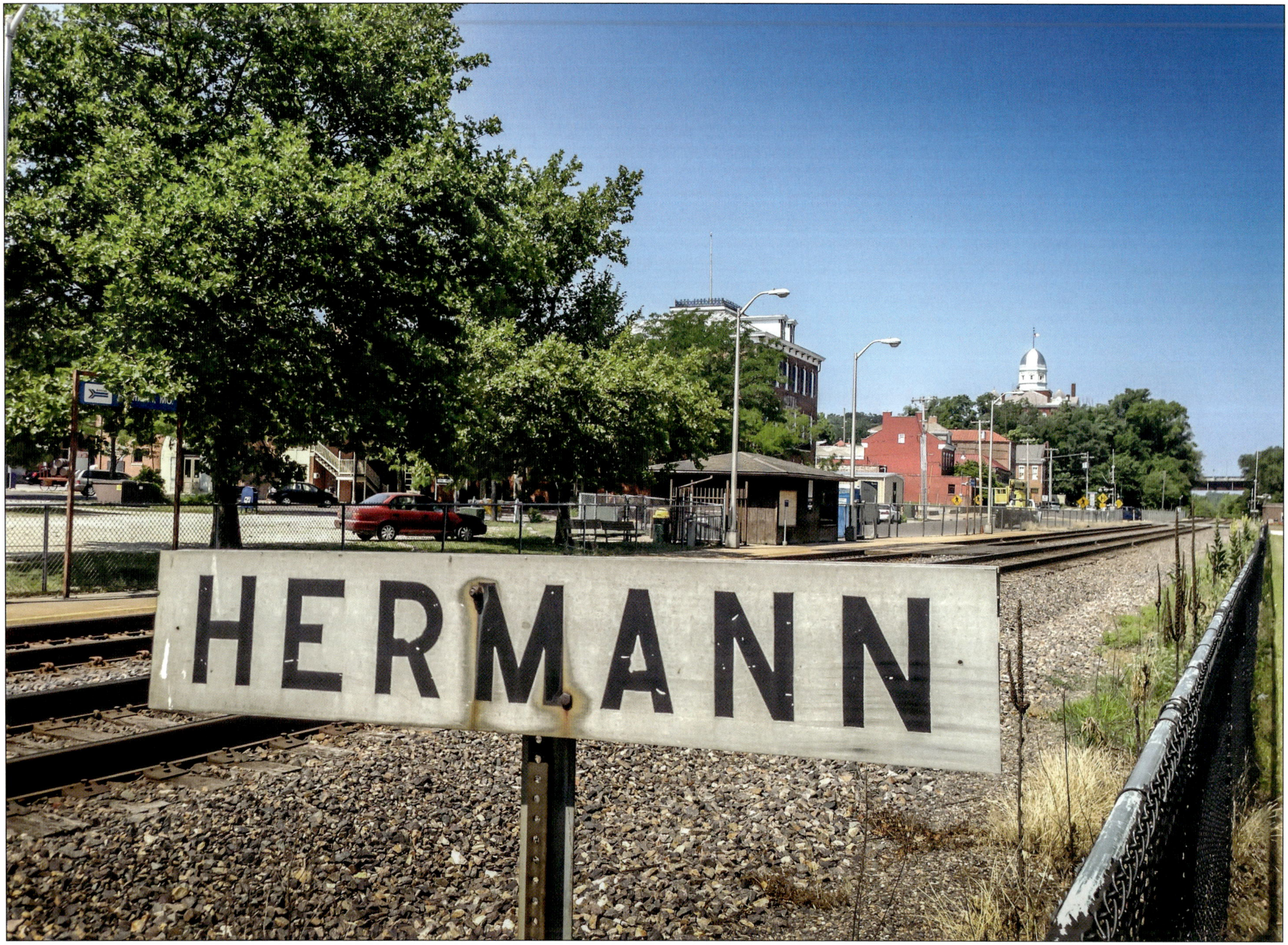

At the Depot
Tony Carosella

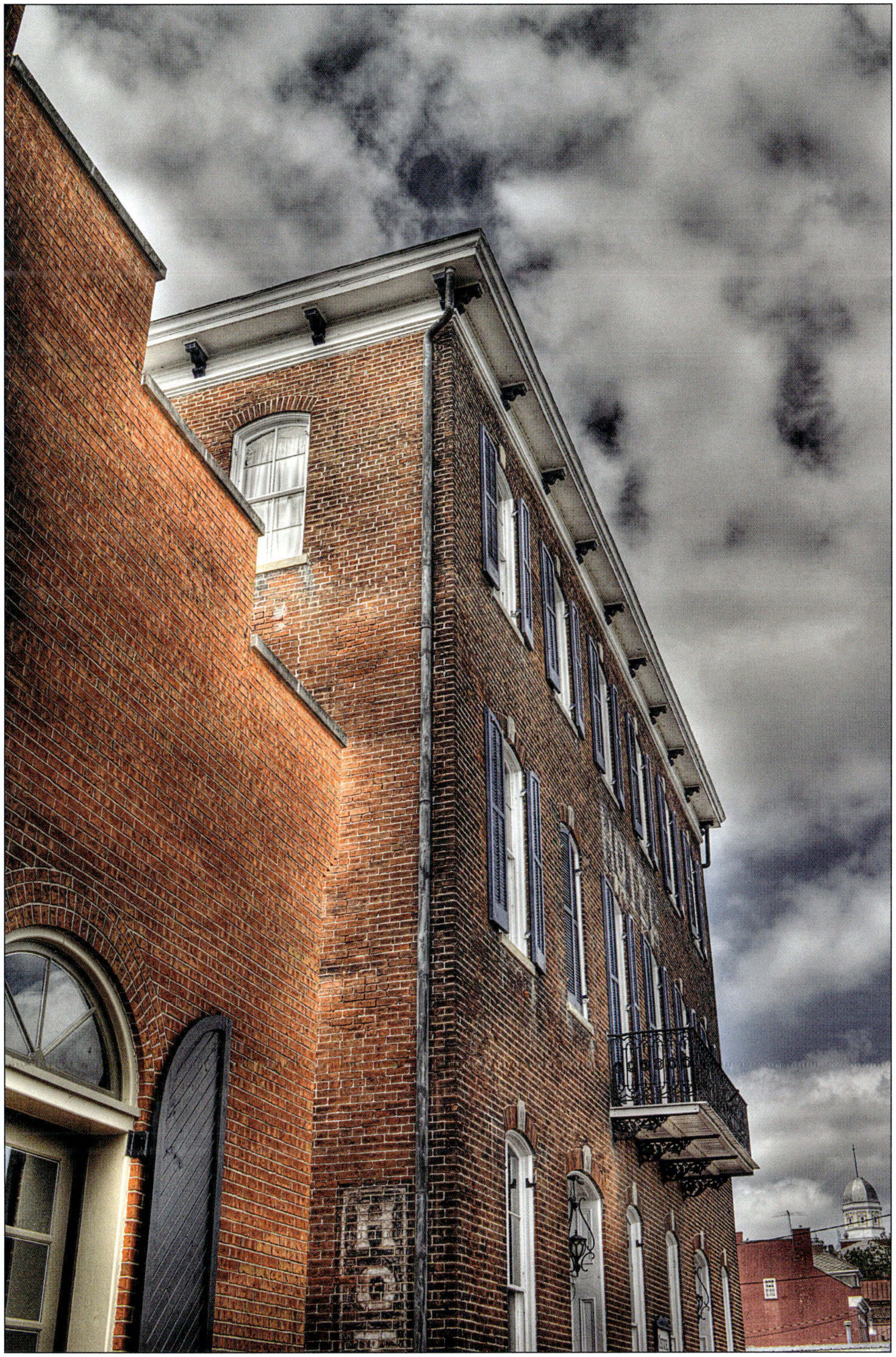

White House with Courthouse

William Fields

Sharp Corner

Tony Carosella

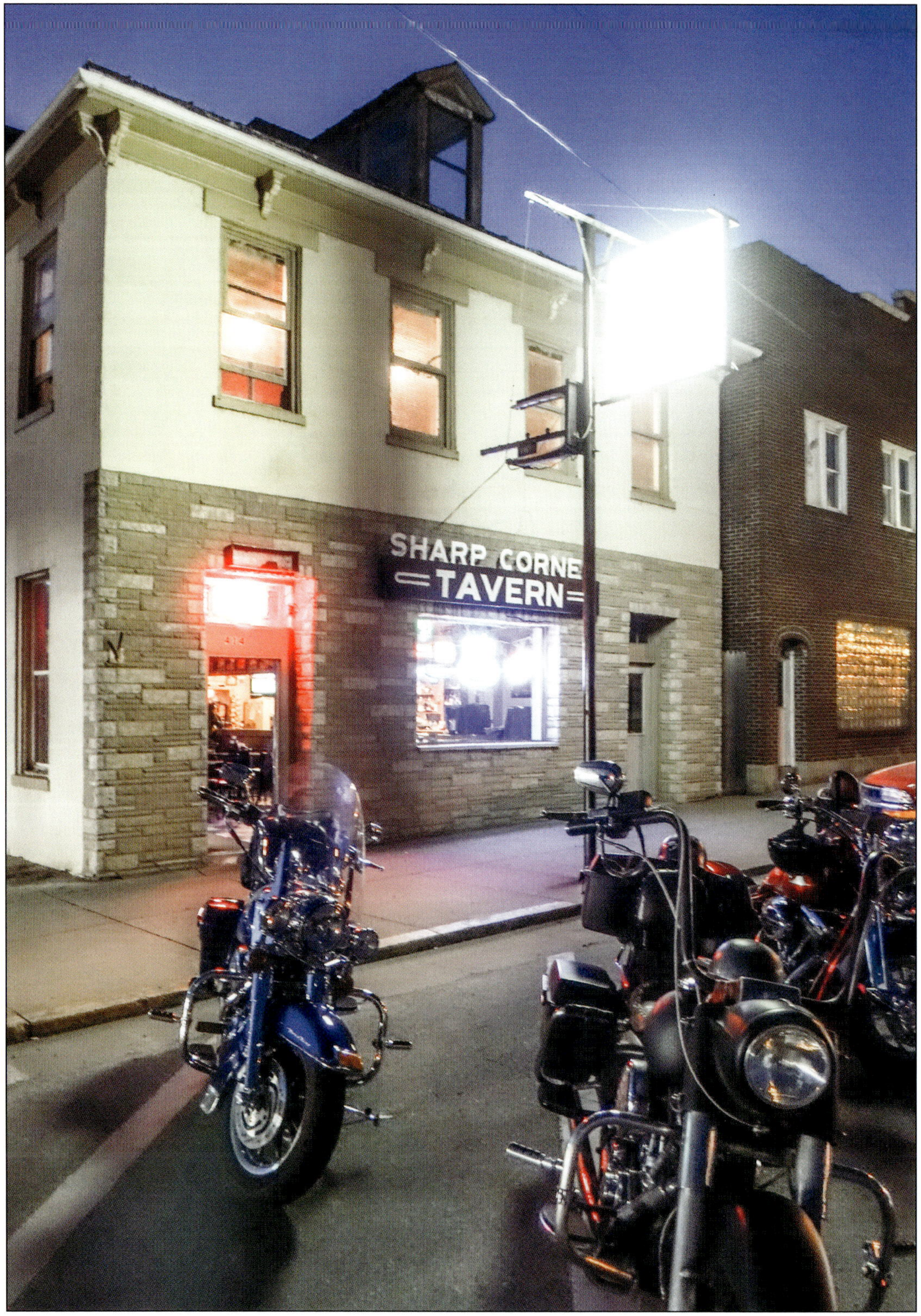

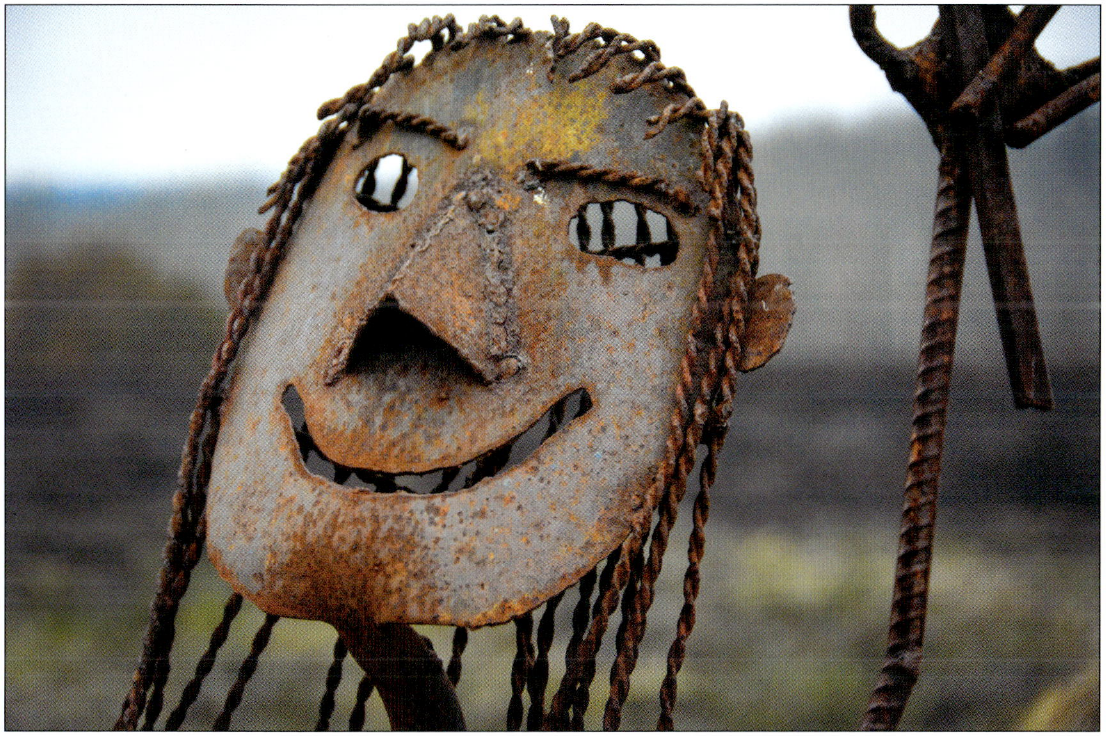

Joey's Sculpture

Tony Carosella

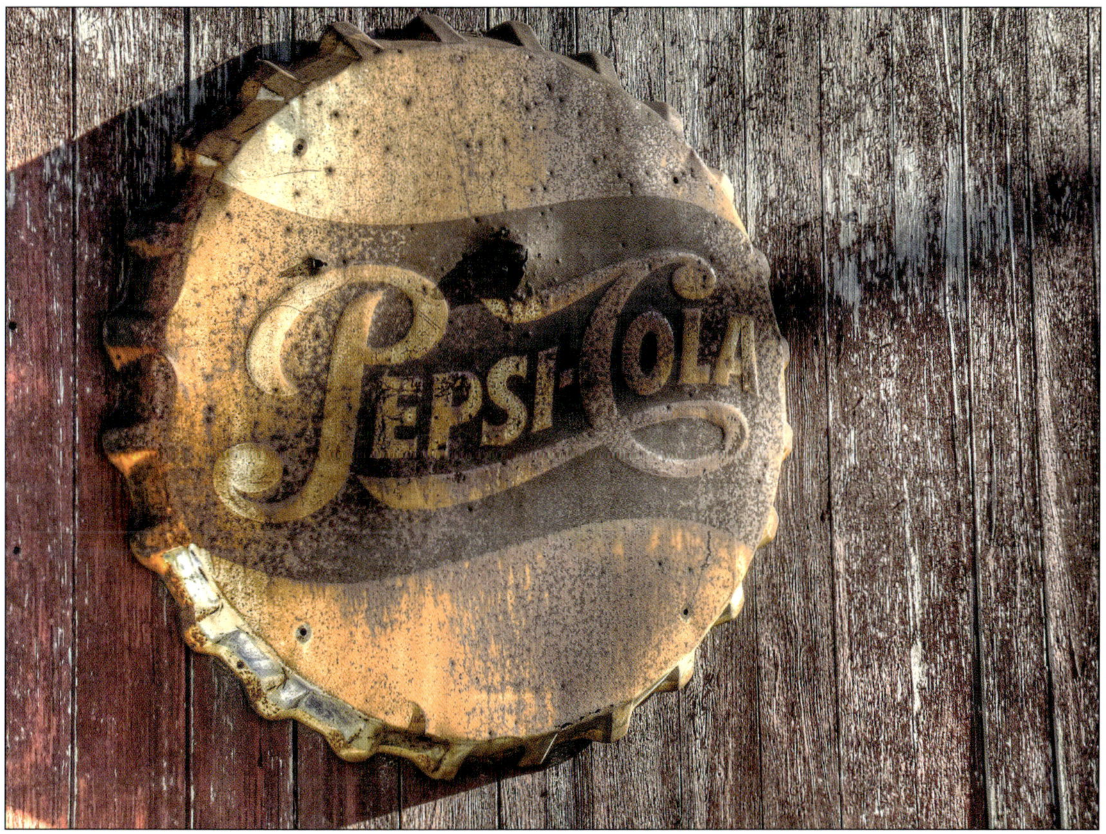

Pepsi II

William Fields

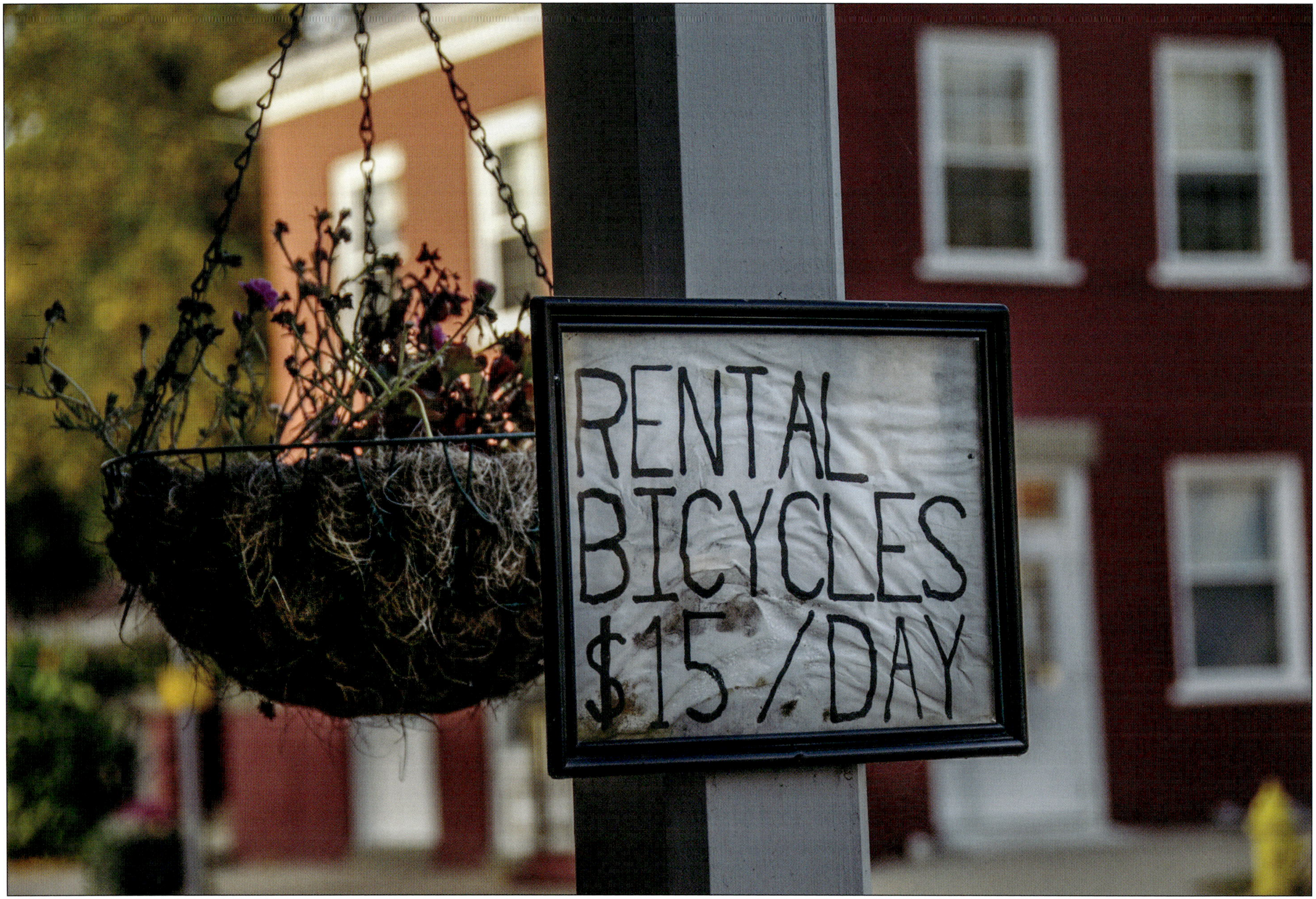

Rental Bicycles
Tony Carosella

"Through the valleys, softly creeping
'Mid the tree-tops, tempest-tossed,
See the cloud-forms seeking, peeping
For the loved ones that are lost.
Not for storm or sunshine resting,
Will they slacken or desist,
Or grow weary in their questing
For the children of the mist."
– Frank Dalby Davison
from *Children of the Mist*

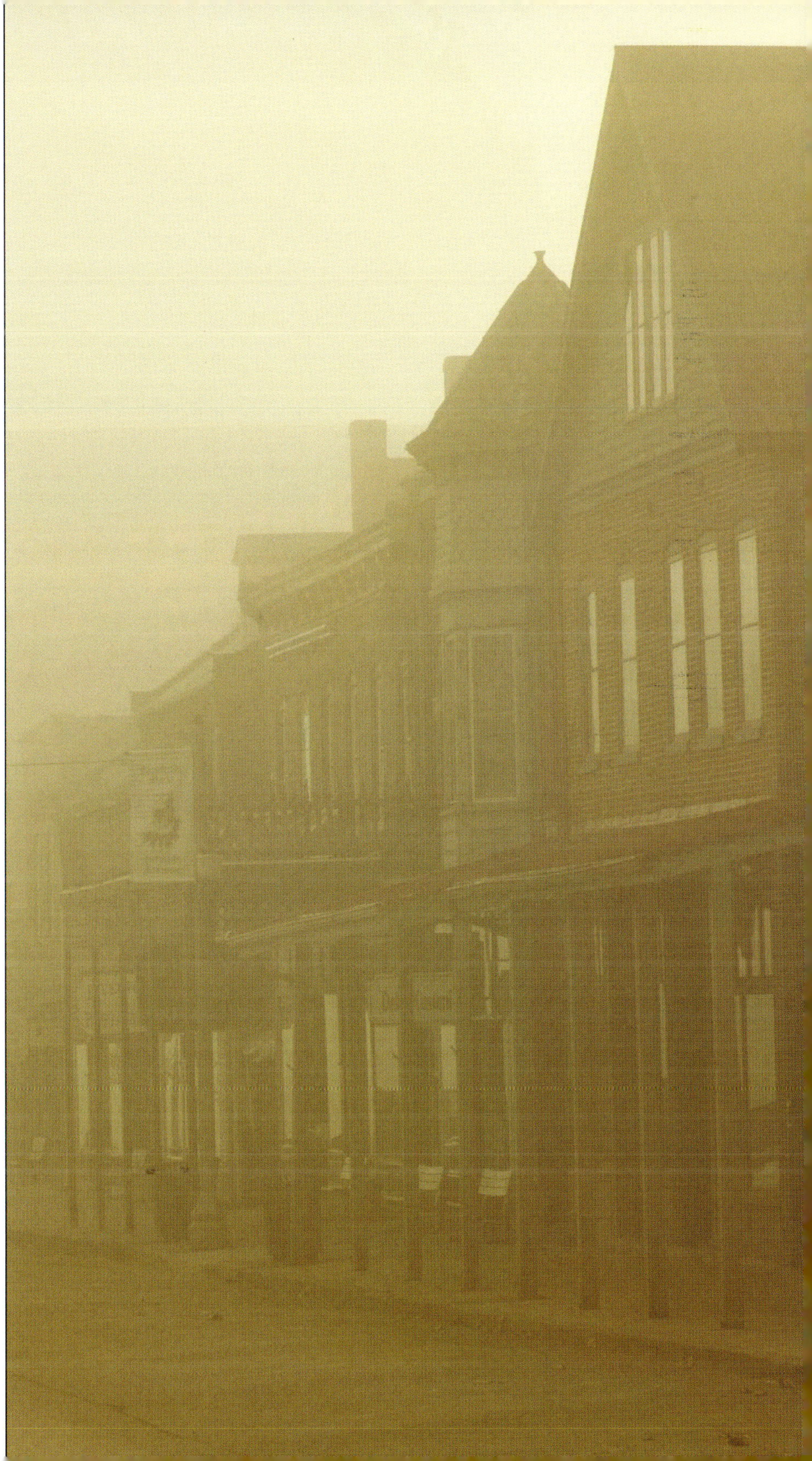

First Street Fog
Tony Carosella

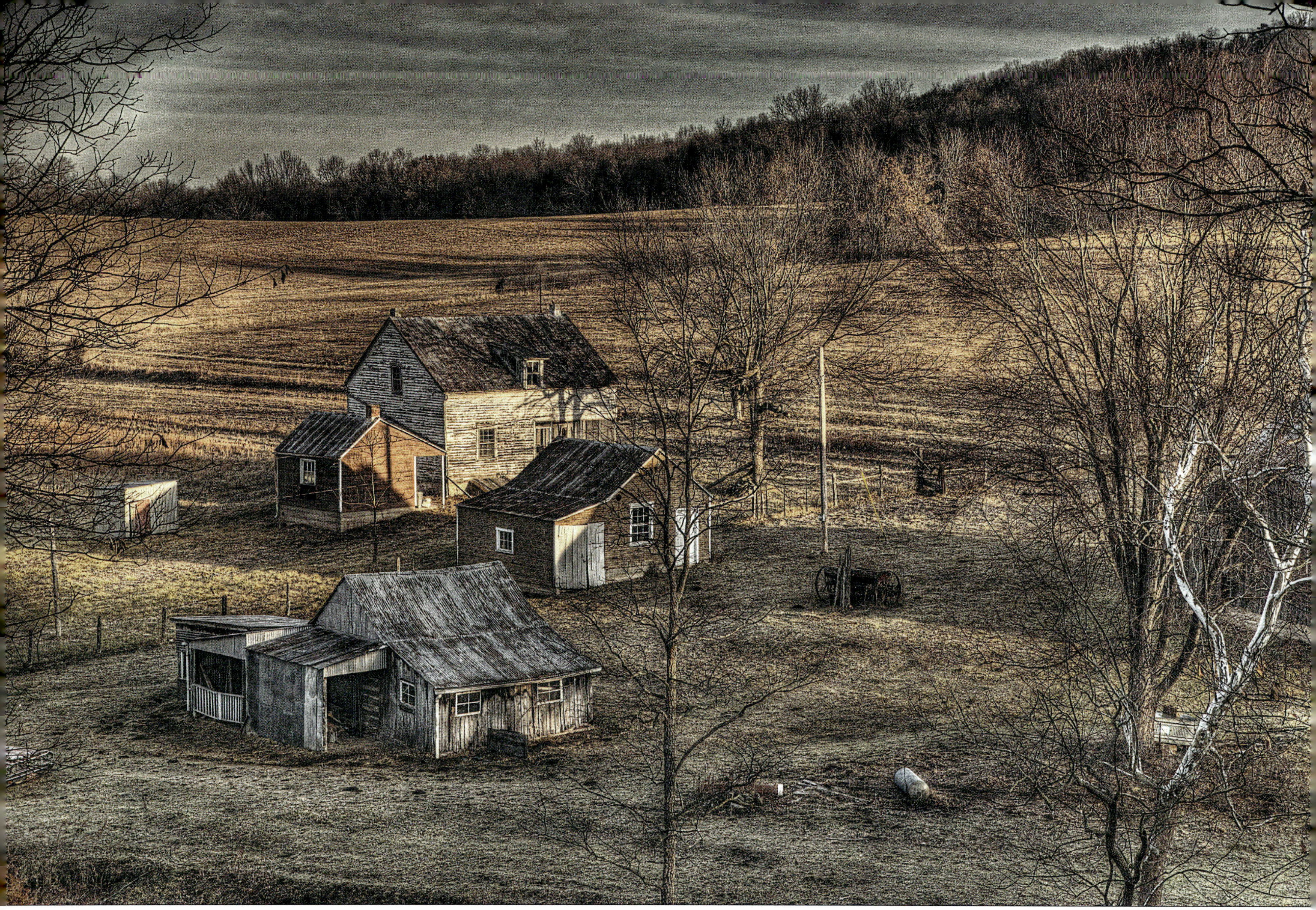

Farmer in the Dell
William Fields

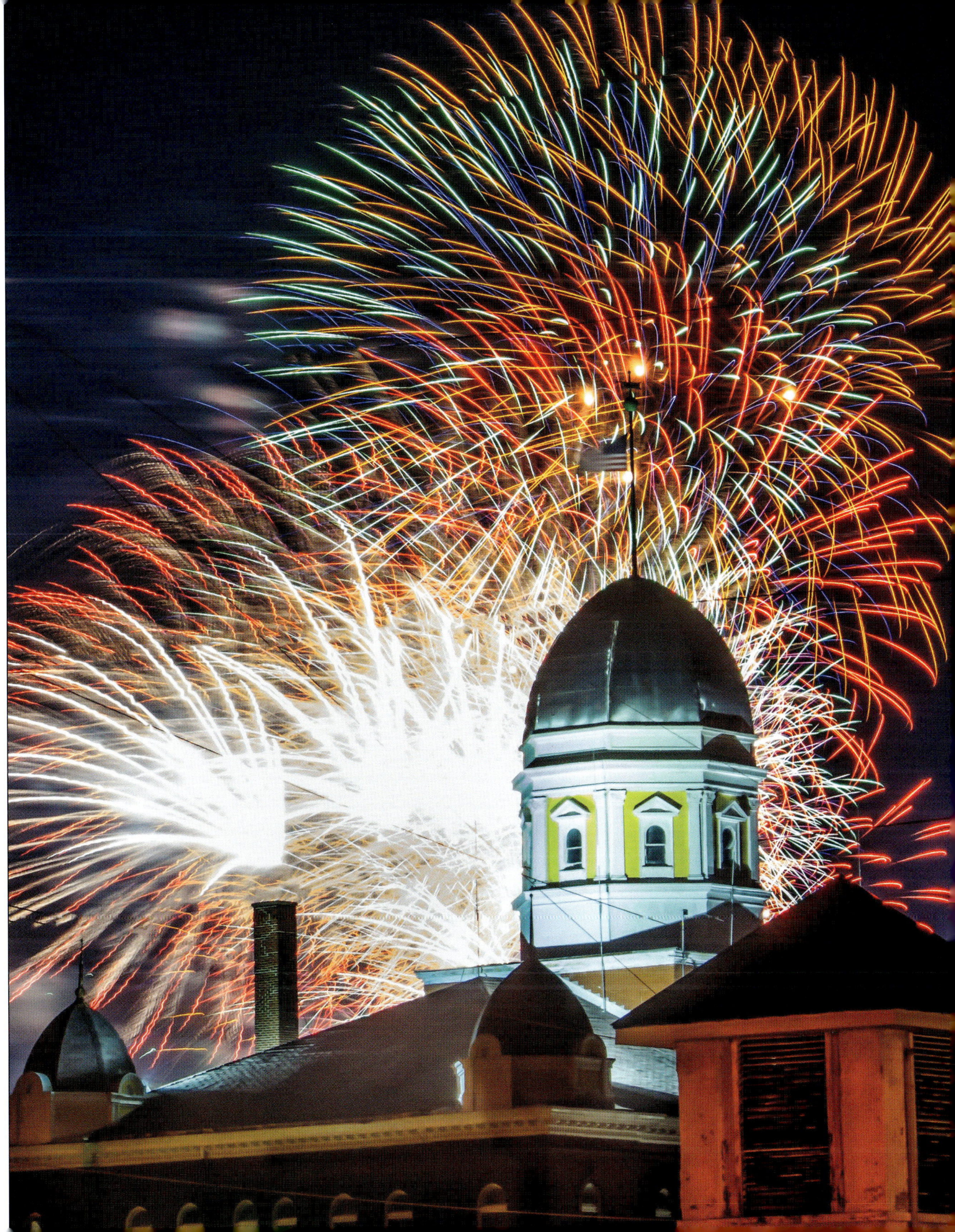

Courthouse 4th
Tony Carosella

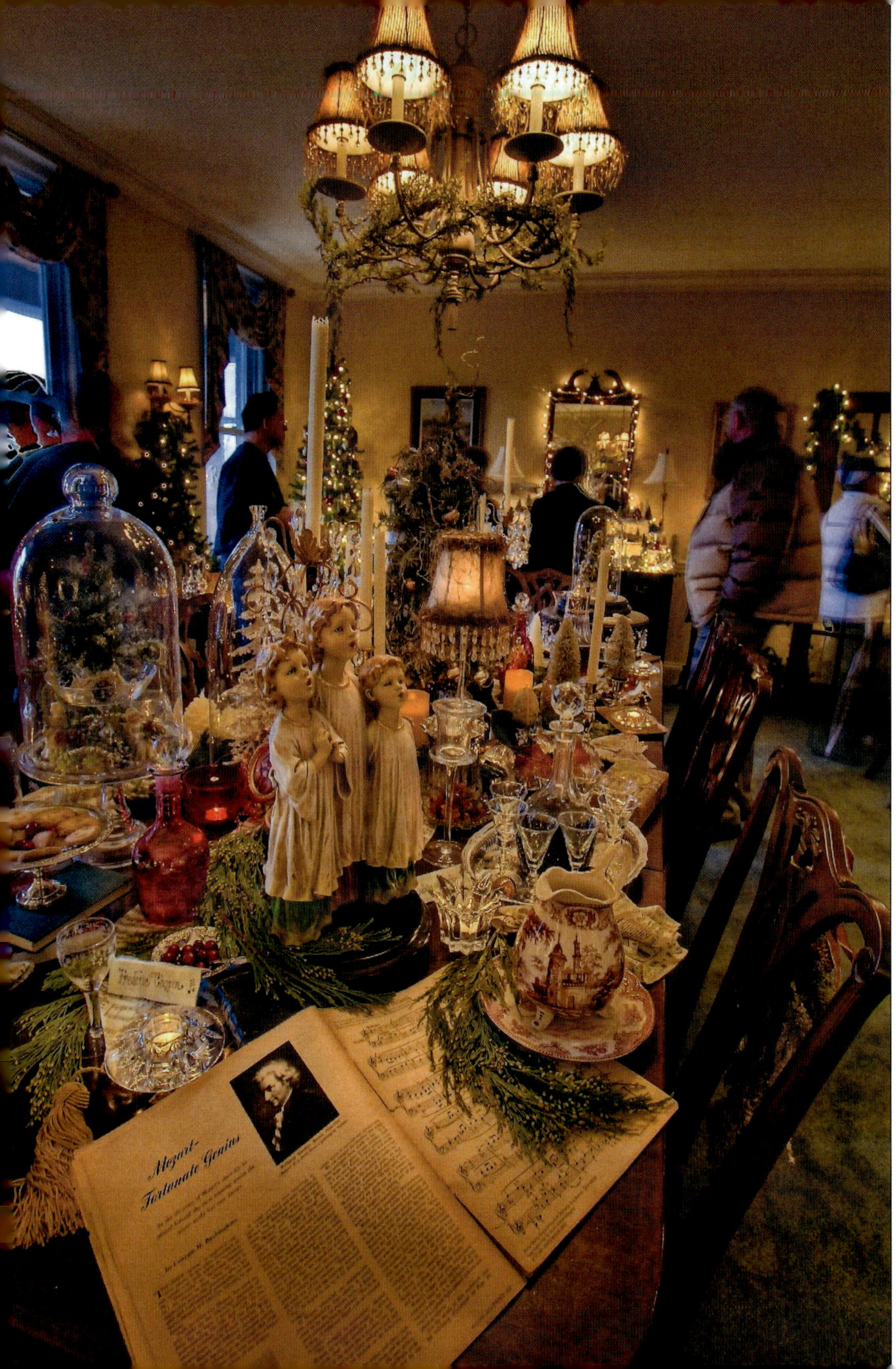

Each year at Christmas time, Father Bill Debo, pastor of Saint George Church, demonstrated his training as a designer by decorating the rectory from top to bottom. People came from miles around in cars, in buses and by train to see the astonishing world that Father Bill assembled. There was no charge to view the rectory. Free will donations were collected for the benefit of the Ministerial Alliance, which supports the Food Pantry and does other charitable work in Hermann. Father Bill has moved on and the Rectory Christmas decorations are no more.

– William Fields and Tony Carosella

The Rectory Dining Room in St. George at Christmas

Tony Carosella

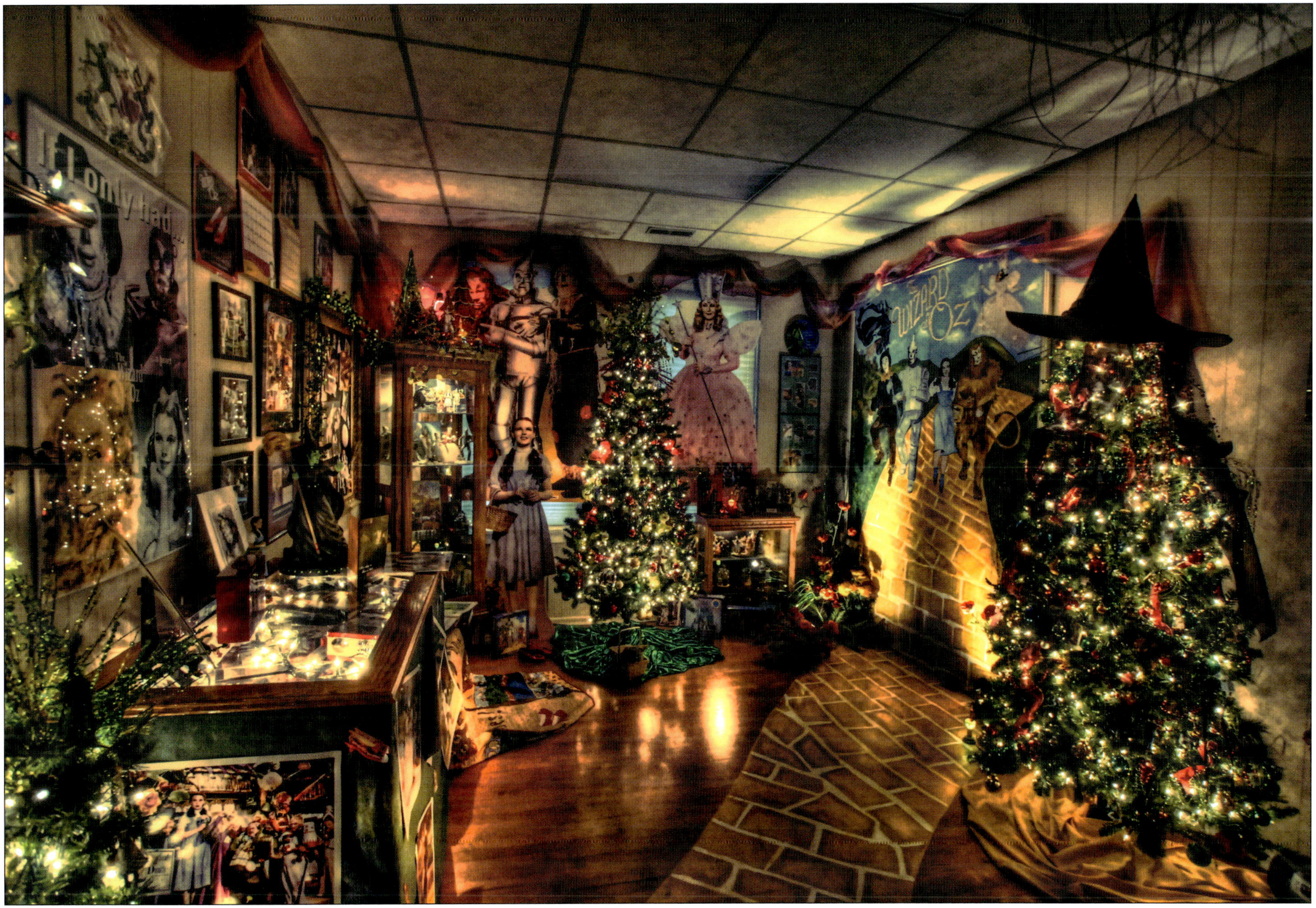

Yellow Brick Road
Tony Carosella

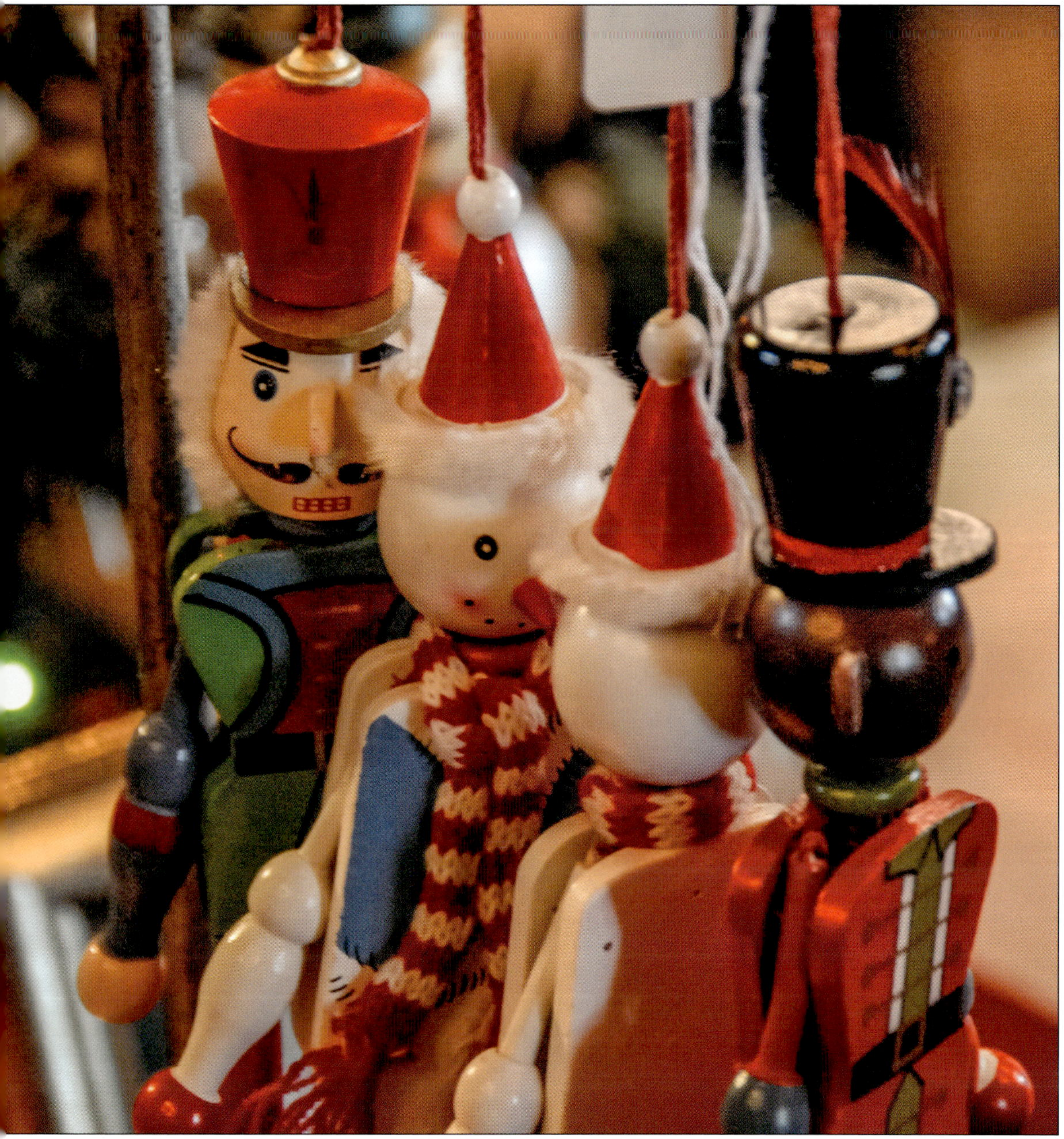

Kristkindl Markt
Tony Carosella

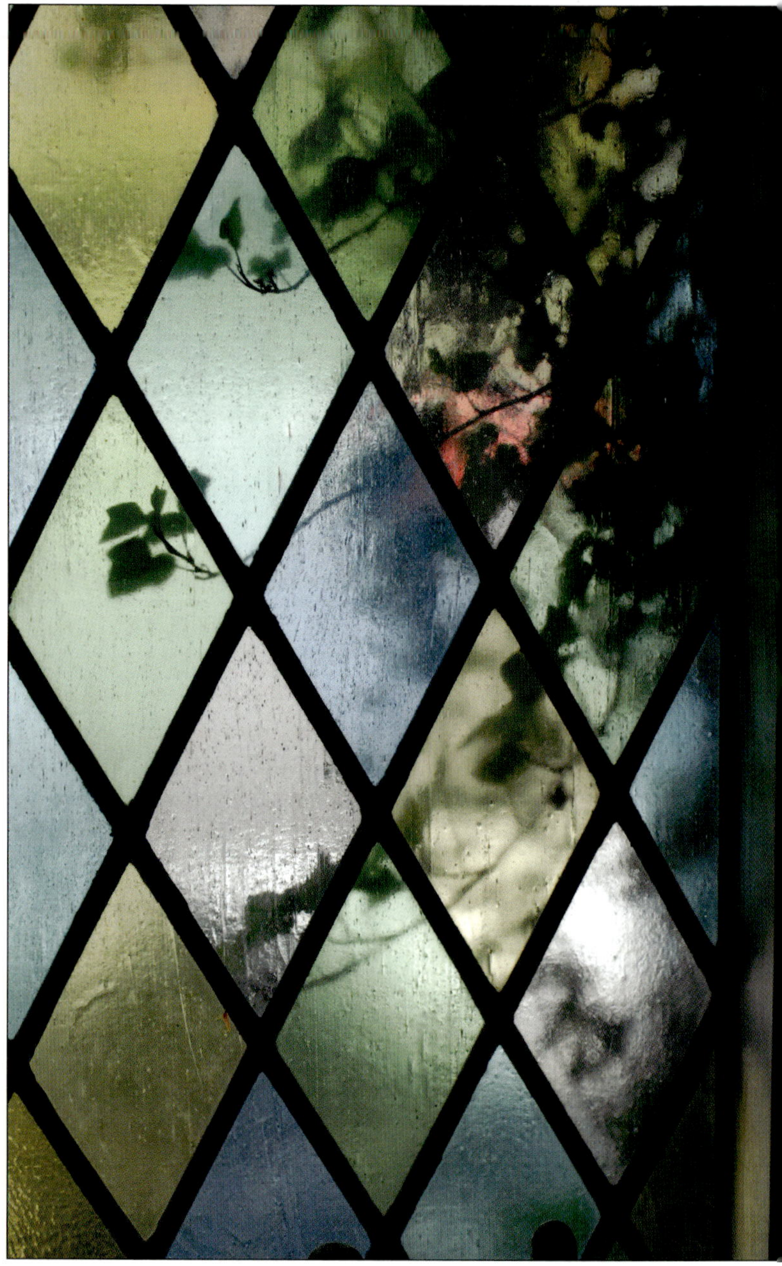

Stained Glass
Tony Carosella

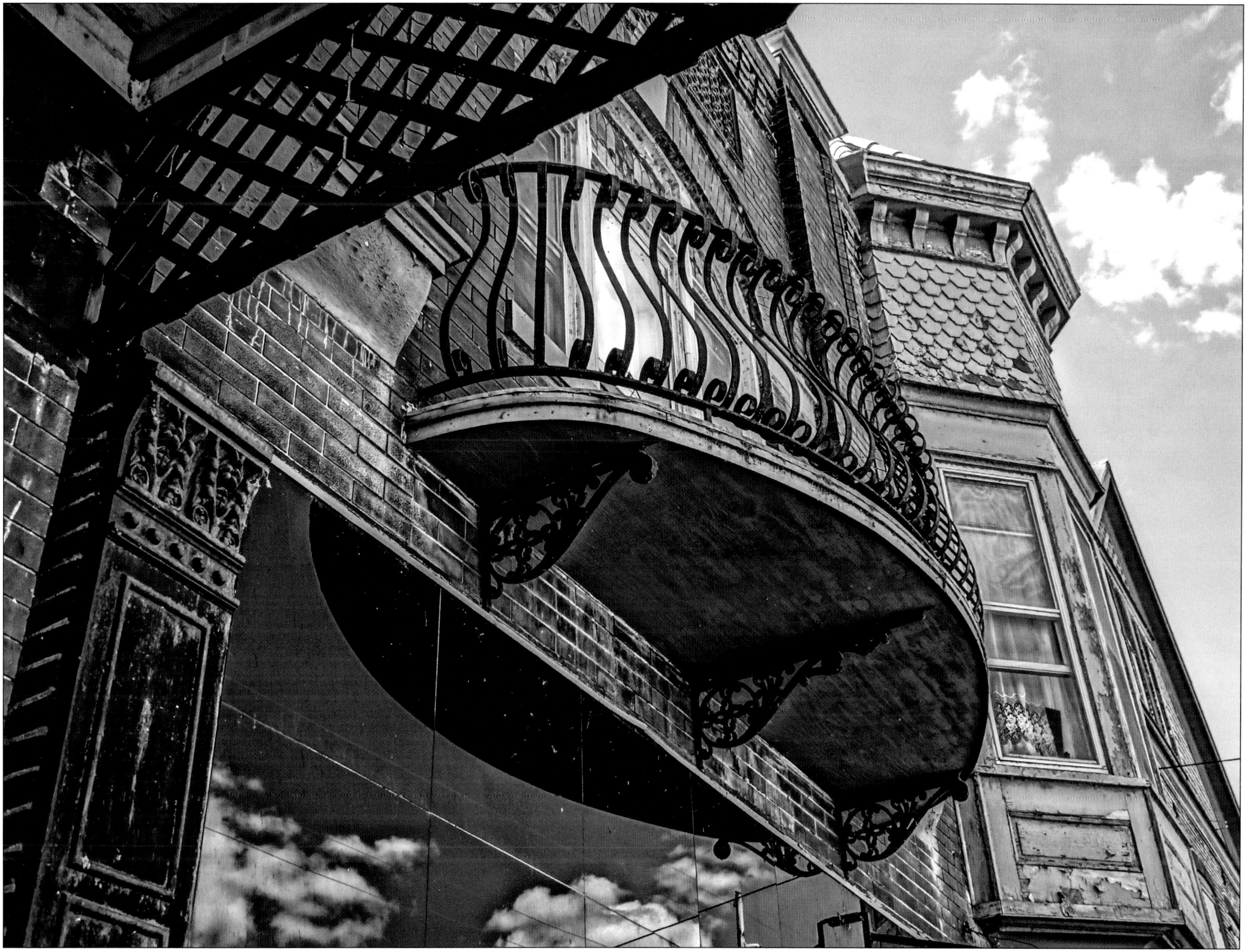

Balcony Bottom
Tony Carosella

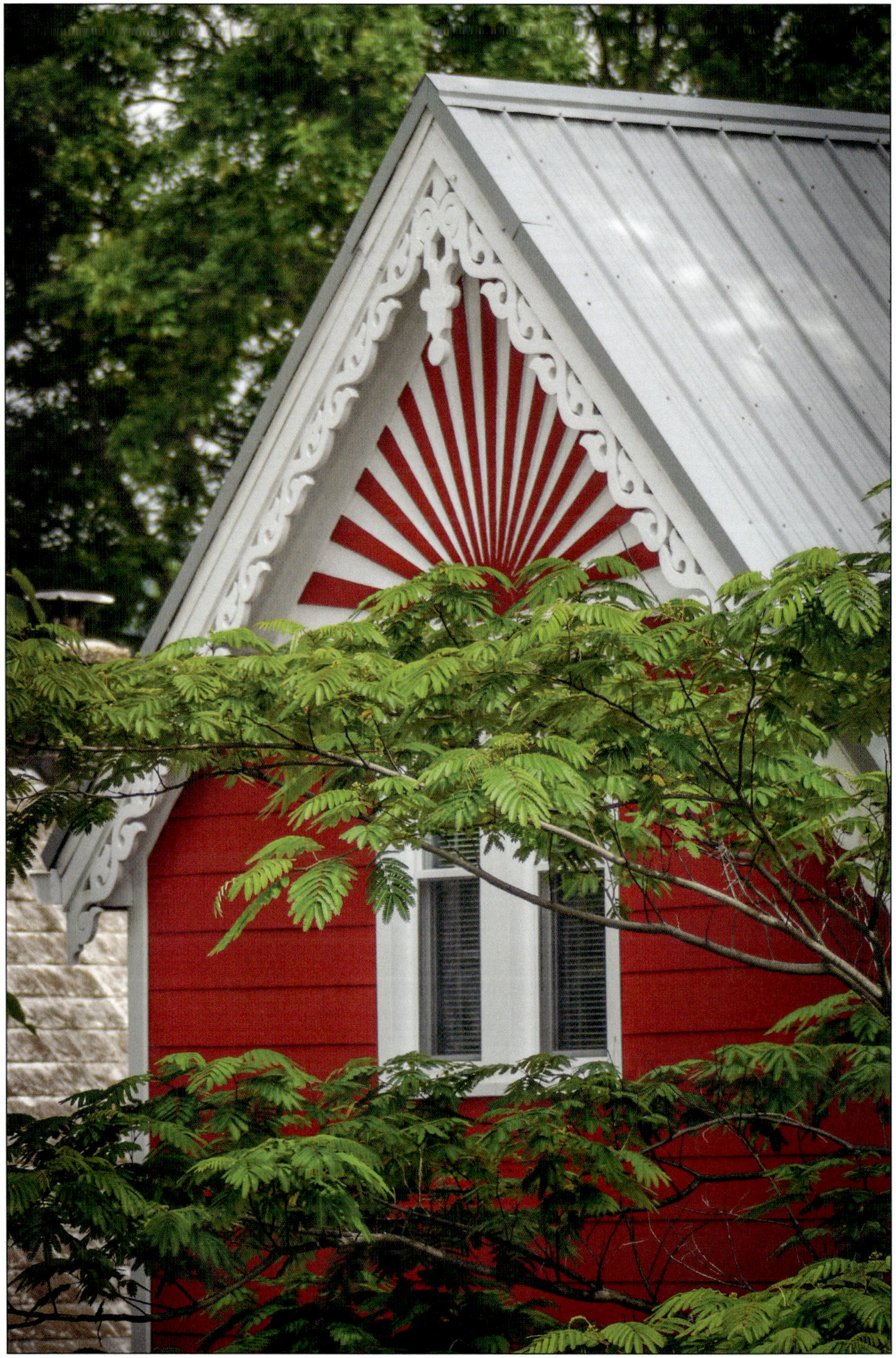

Gingerbread Inn
Tony Carosella

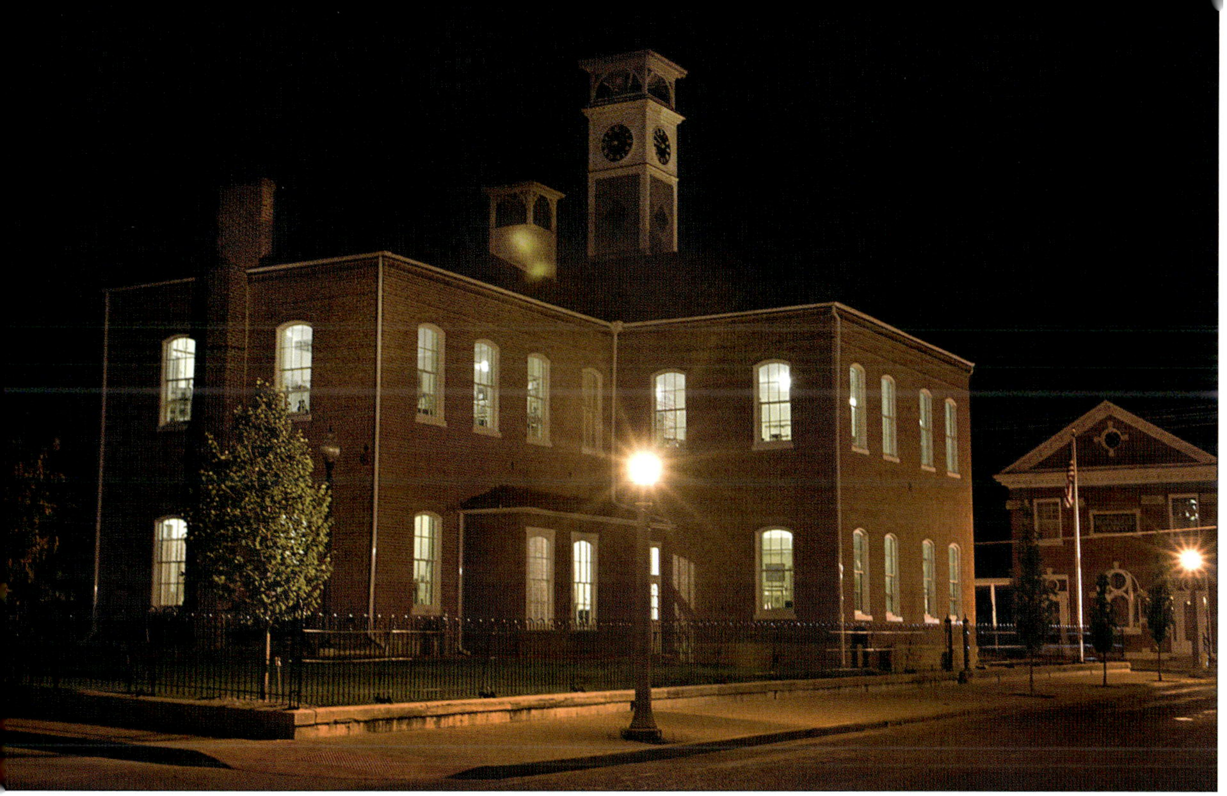

Schoolhouse West
William Fields

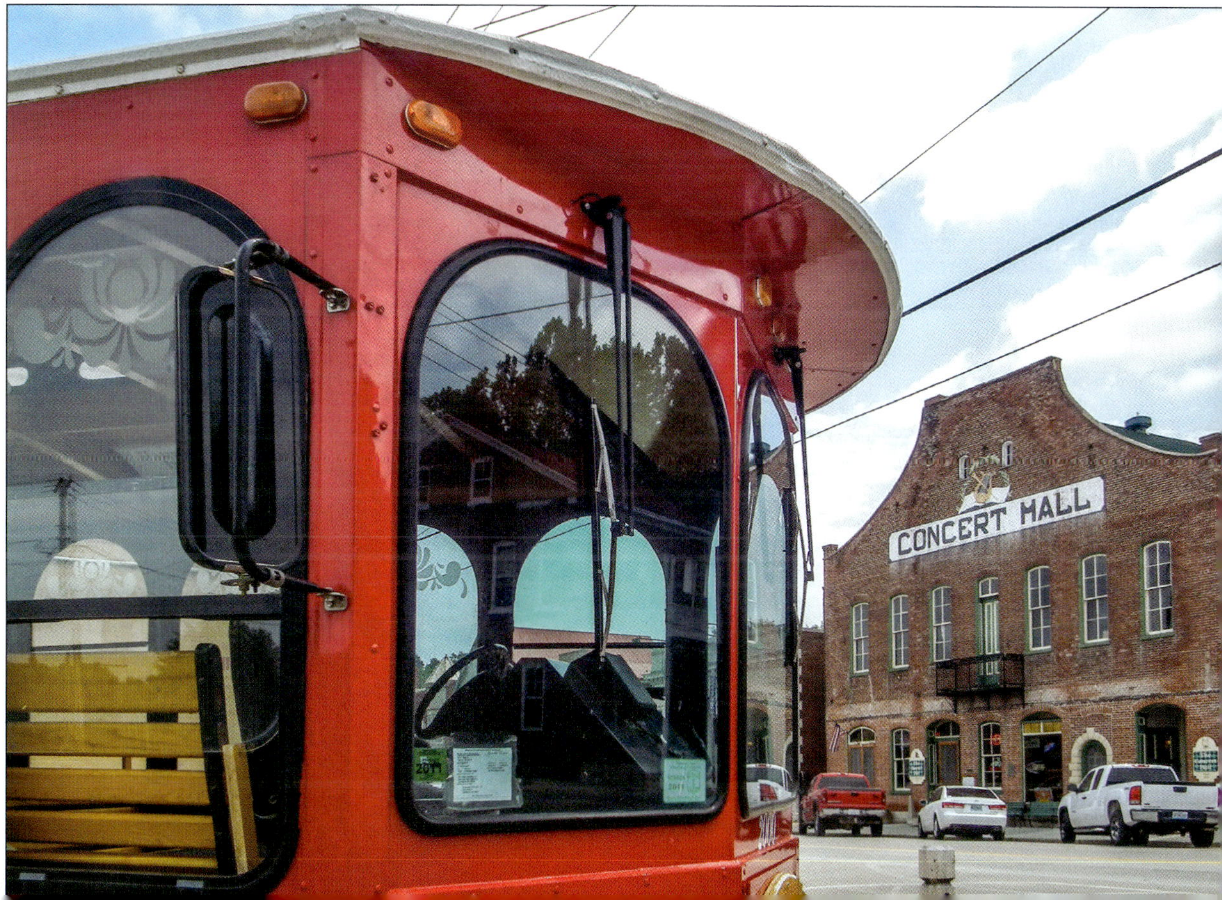

Trolley and Barrel
Tony Carosella

Captain Manwaring
William Fields

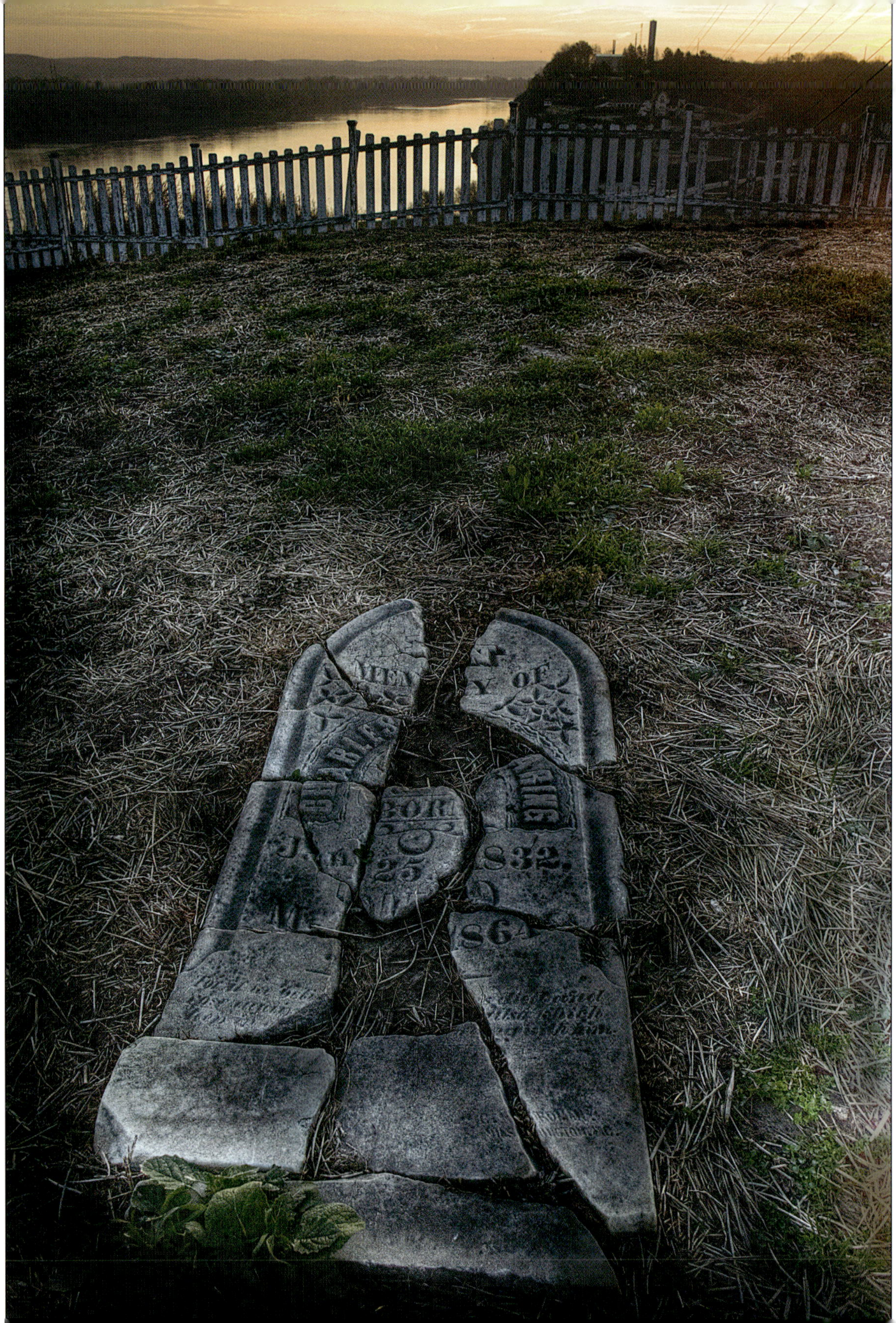

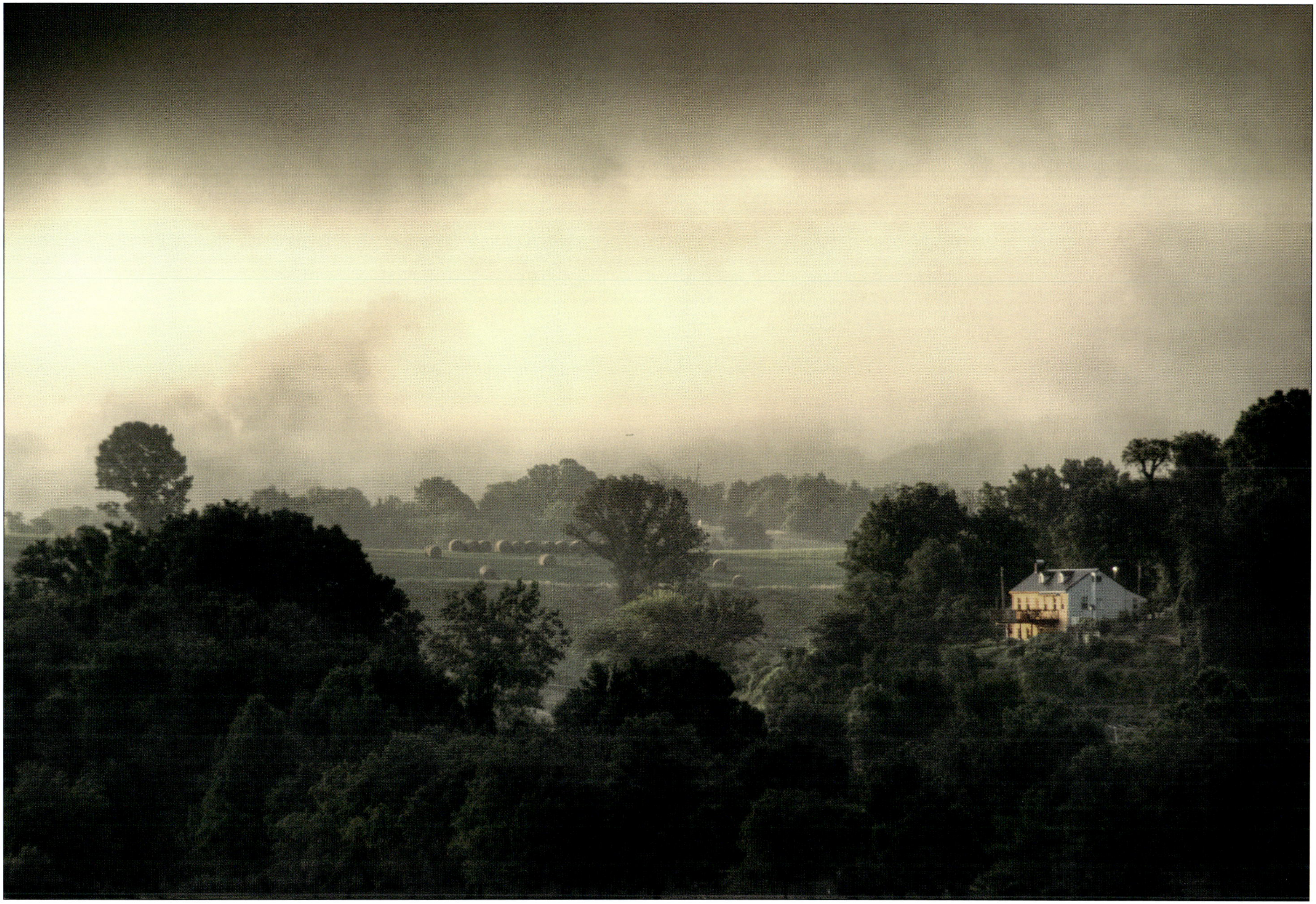

Johann Setzer House

William Fields

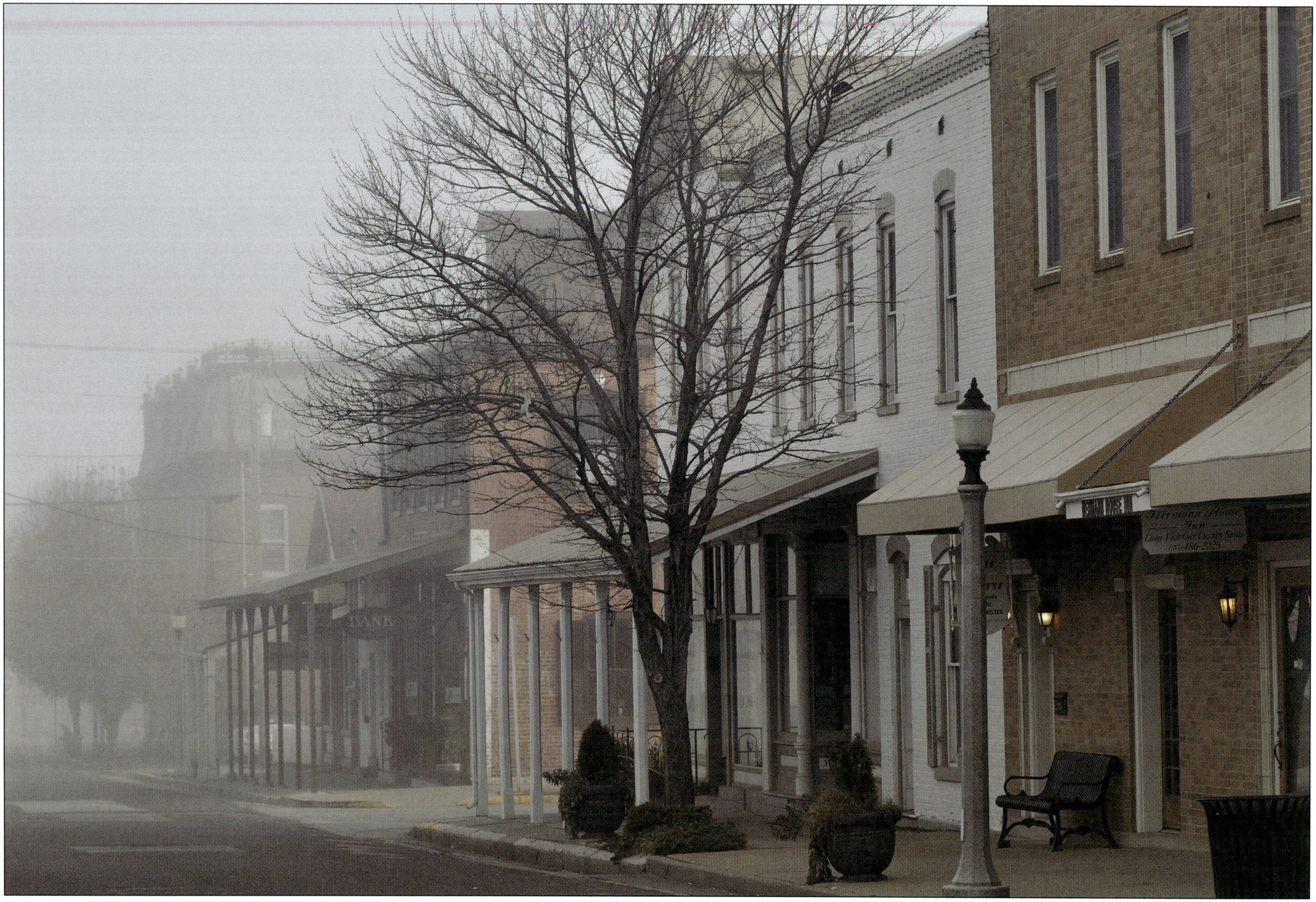

Alone in the Early Morning Mist

Tony Carosella

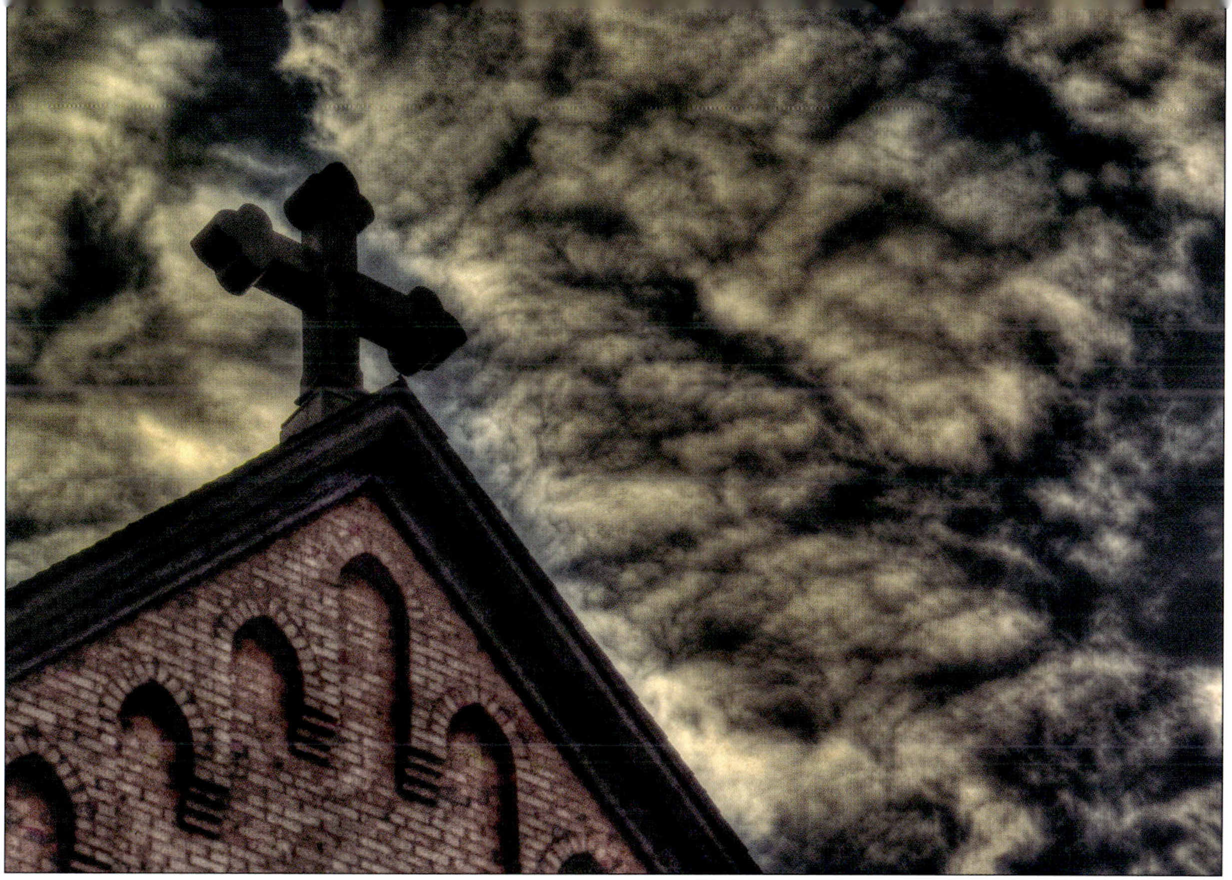

Saint George Against the Dragon
William Fields

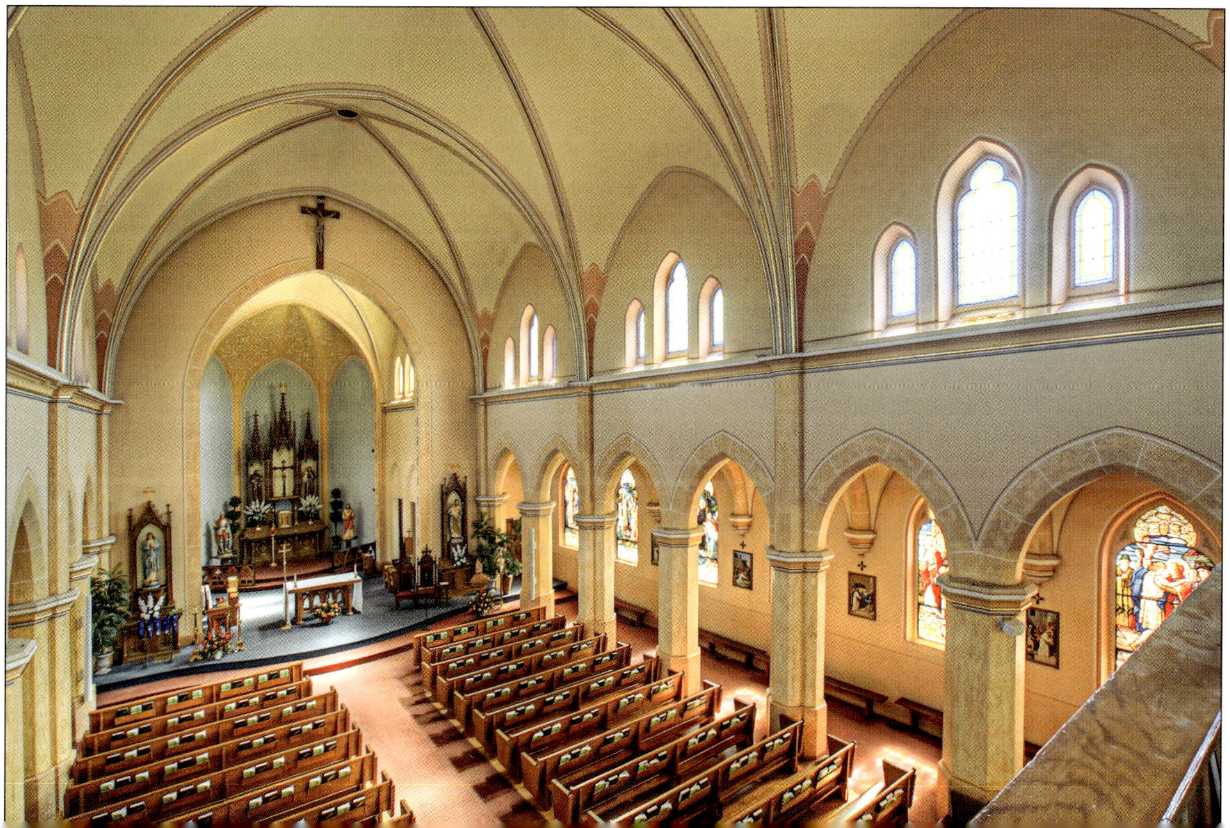

Saint George from the Choir Loft
Tony Carosella

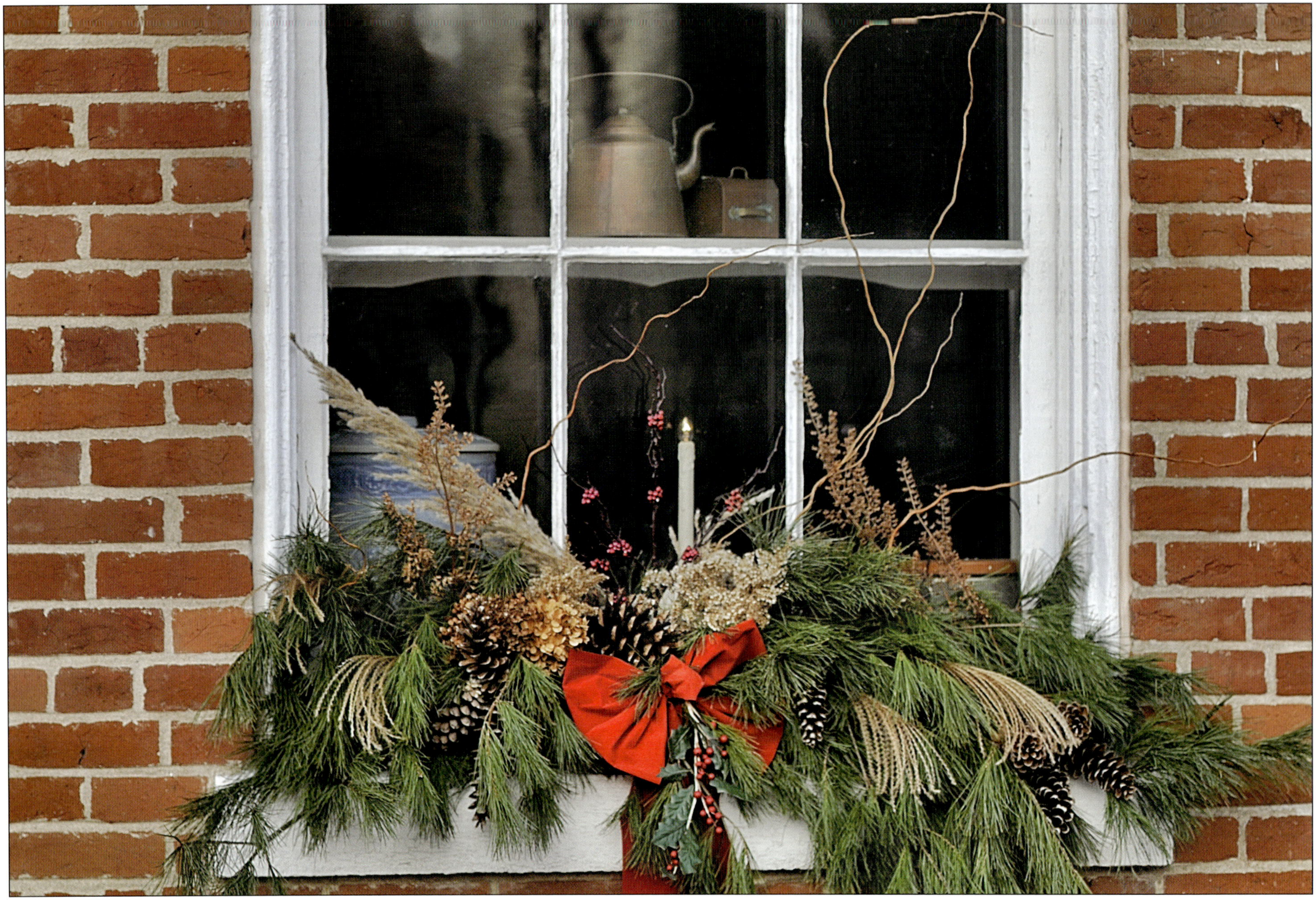

Window Dressing
Tony Carosella

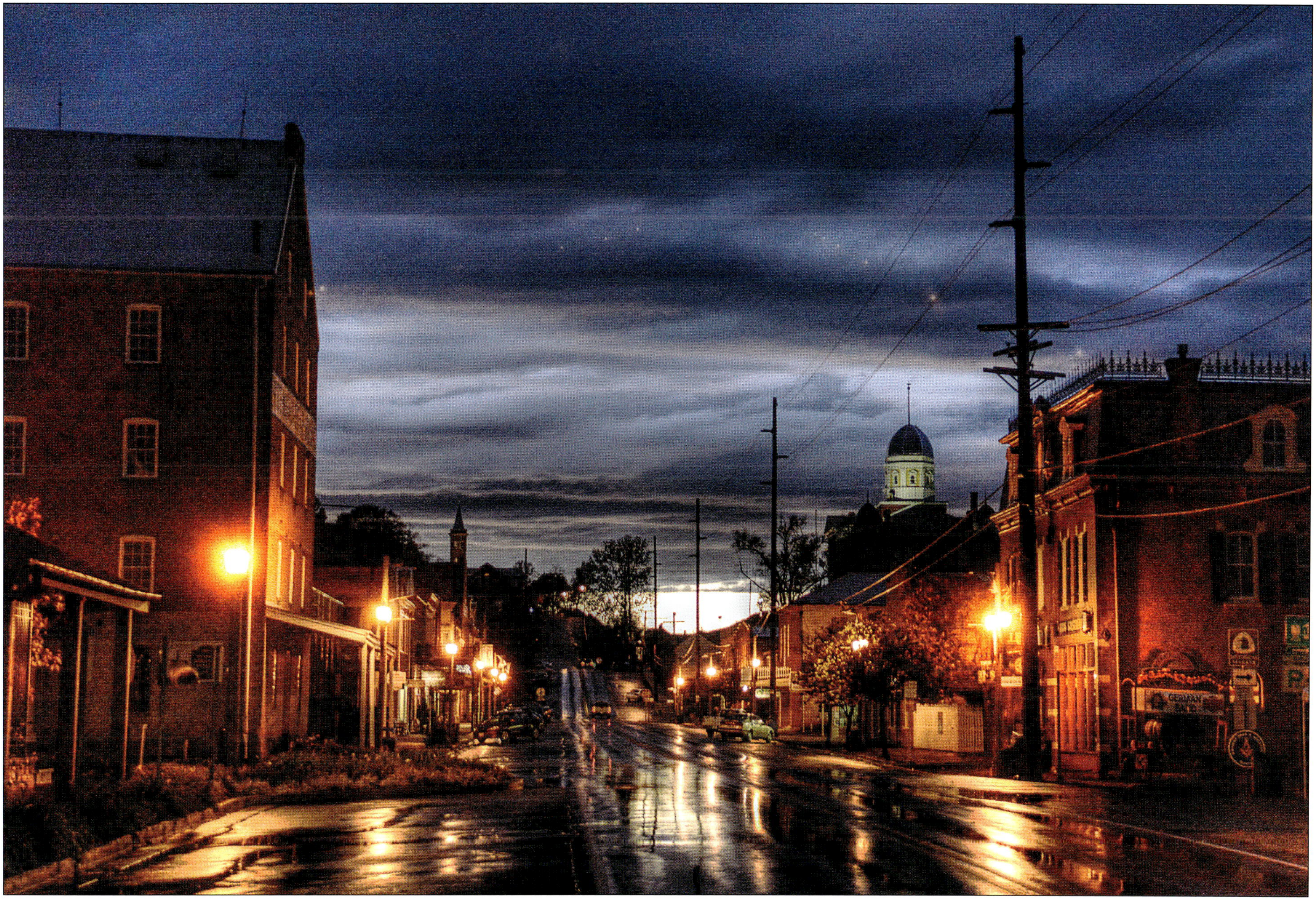

First Street Dusk
William Fields

Yellow Brick Cottage

Tony Carosella

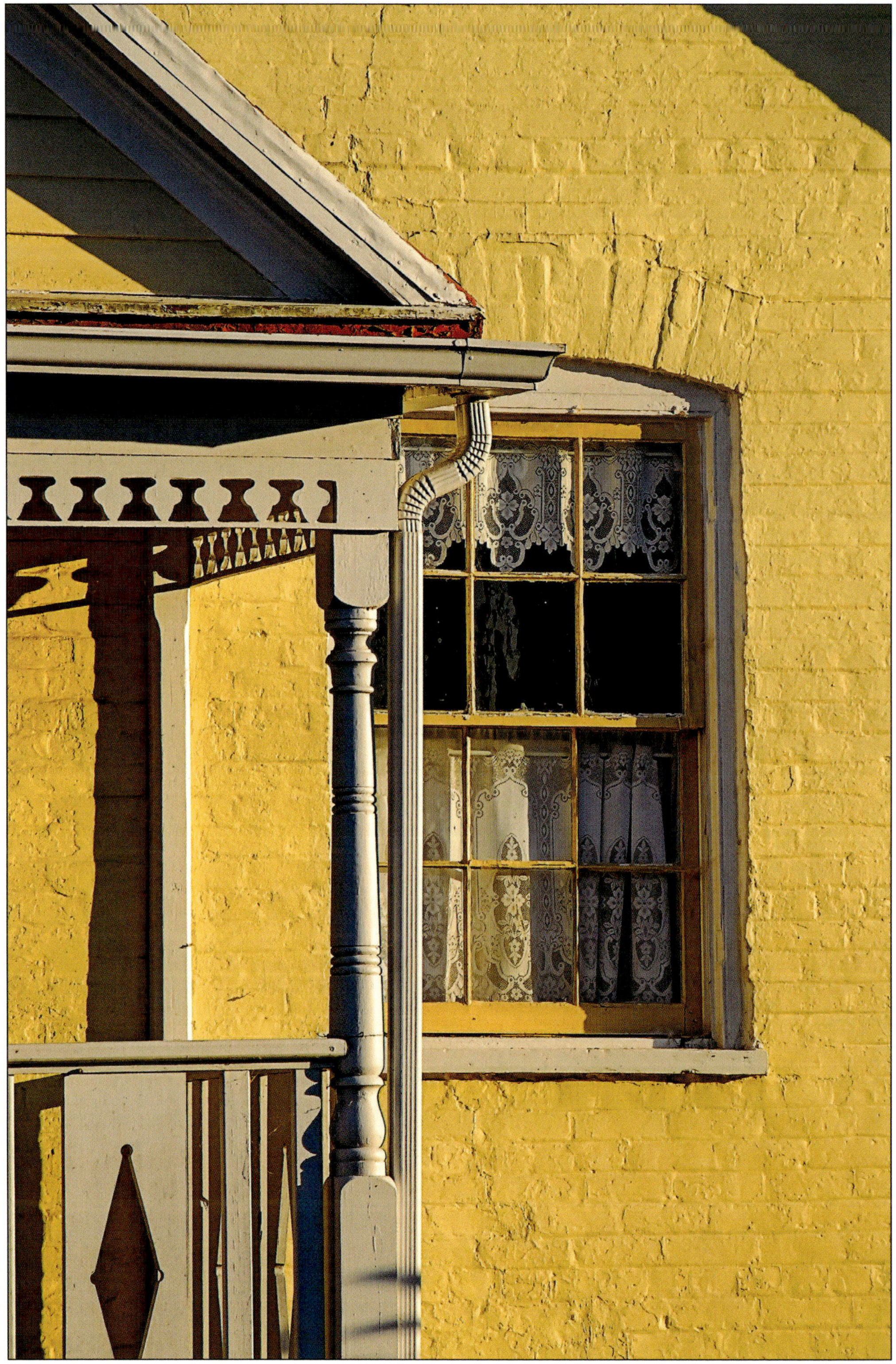

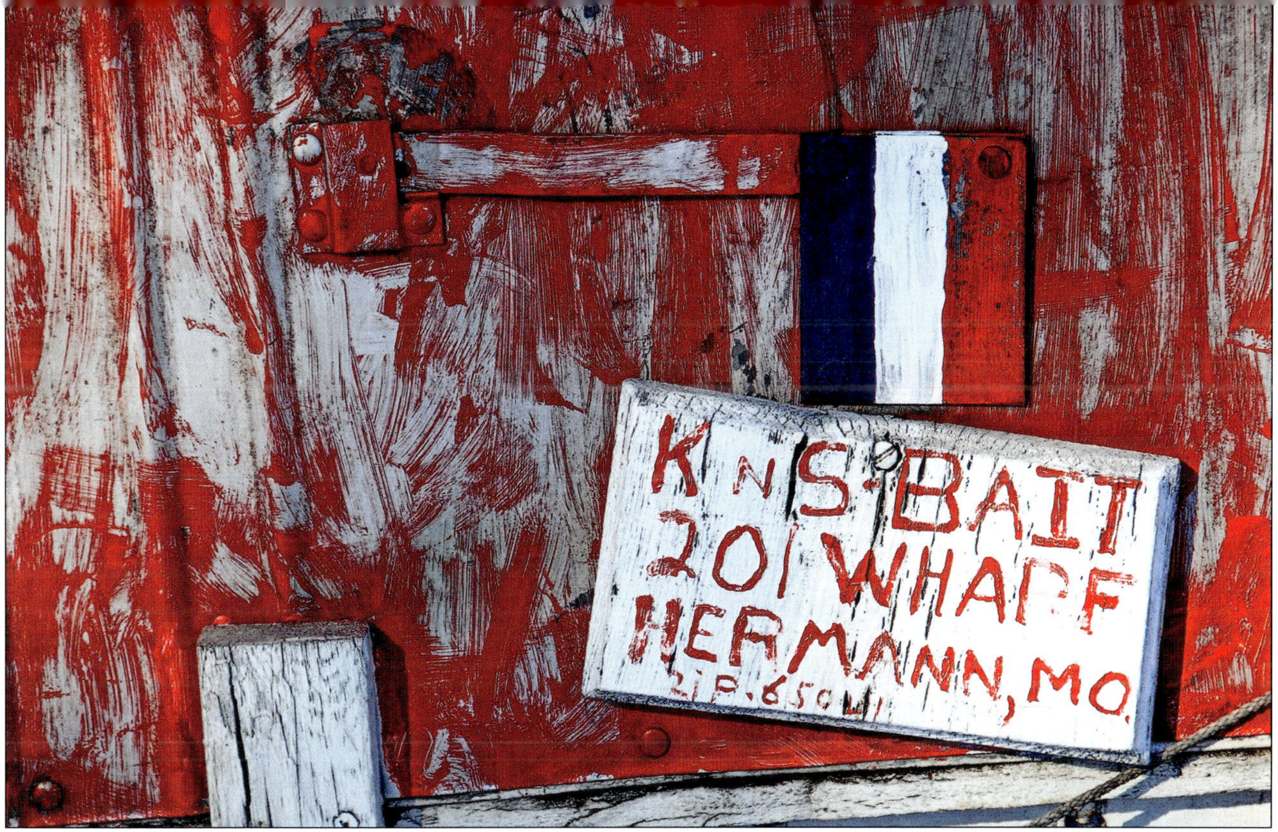

Baitshop Mailbox
Tony Carosella

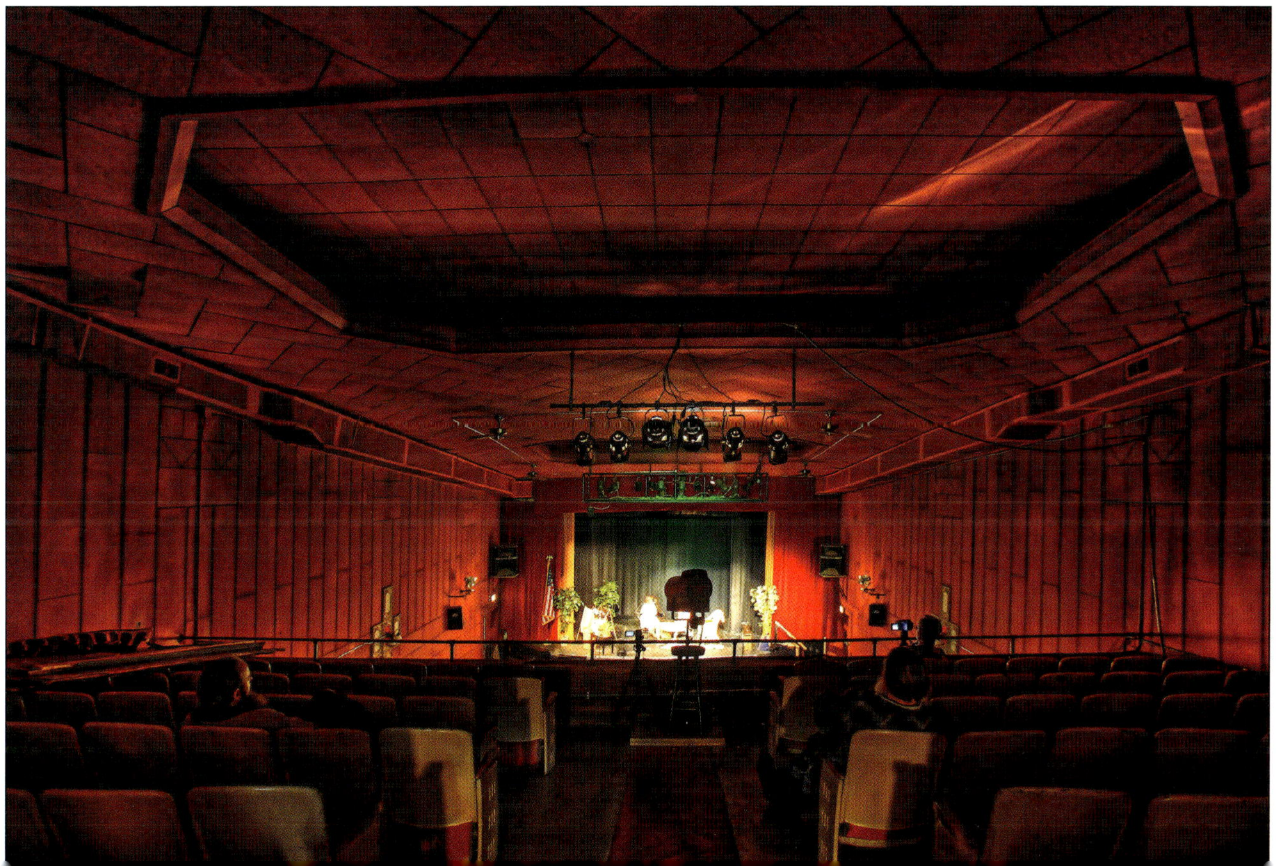

Showboat
Tony Carosella

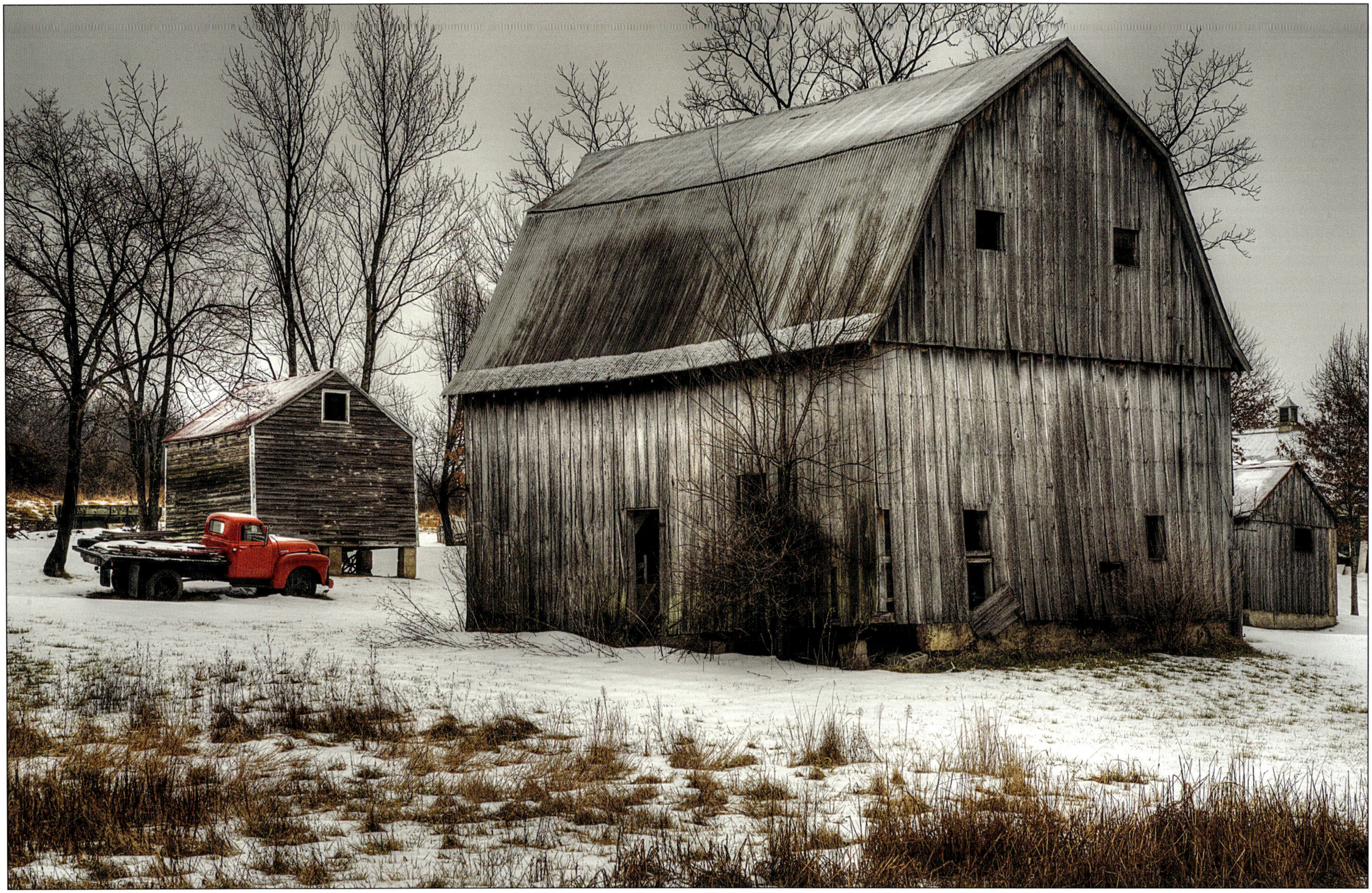

Ghosts of Farmers Give Their Blessings
William Fields

Silvery Trees Tipi
William Fields

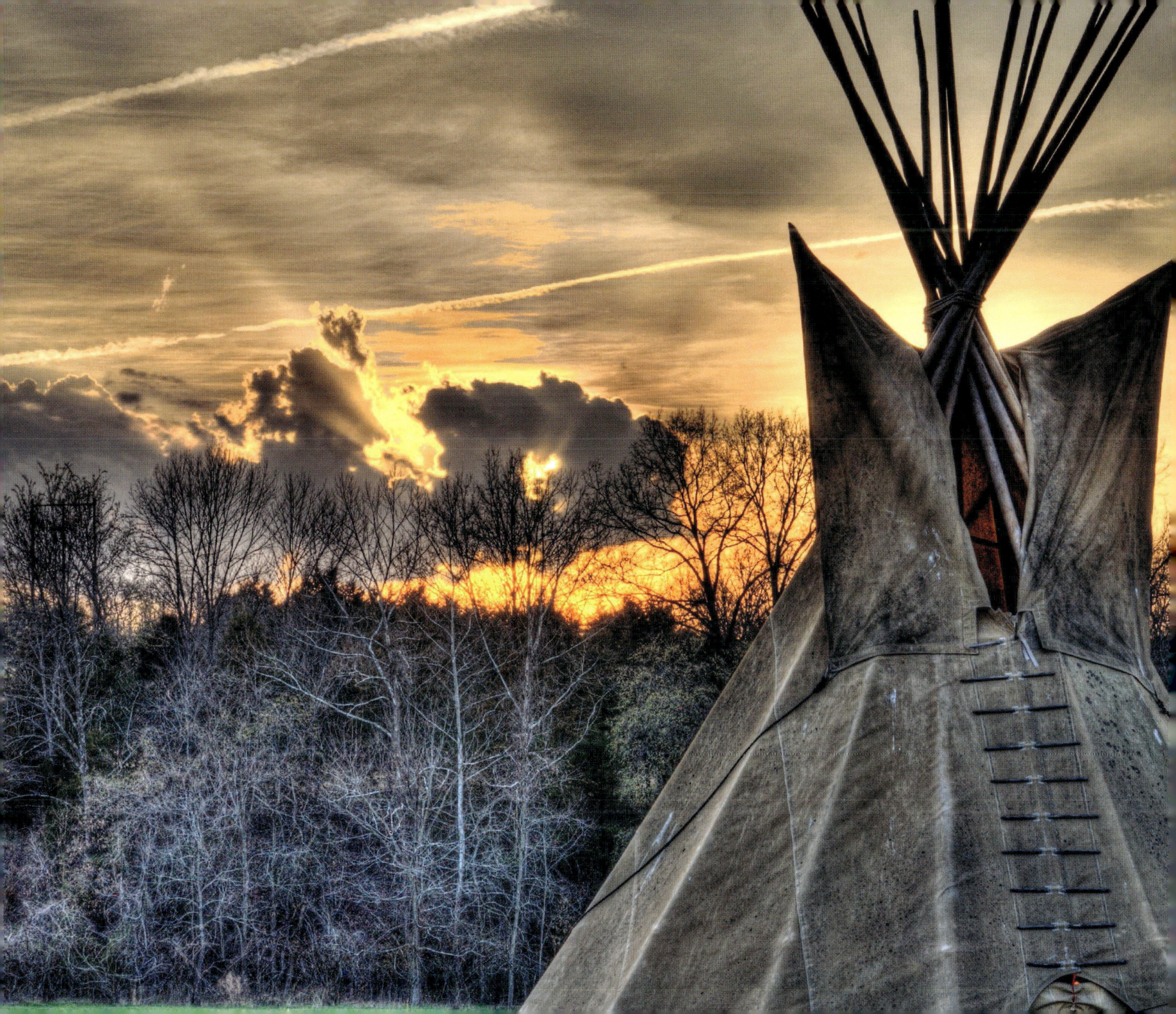

Balcony and Steeple

Tony Carosella

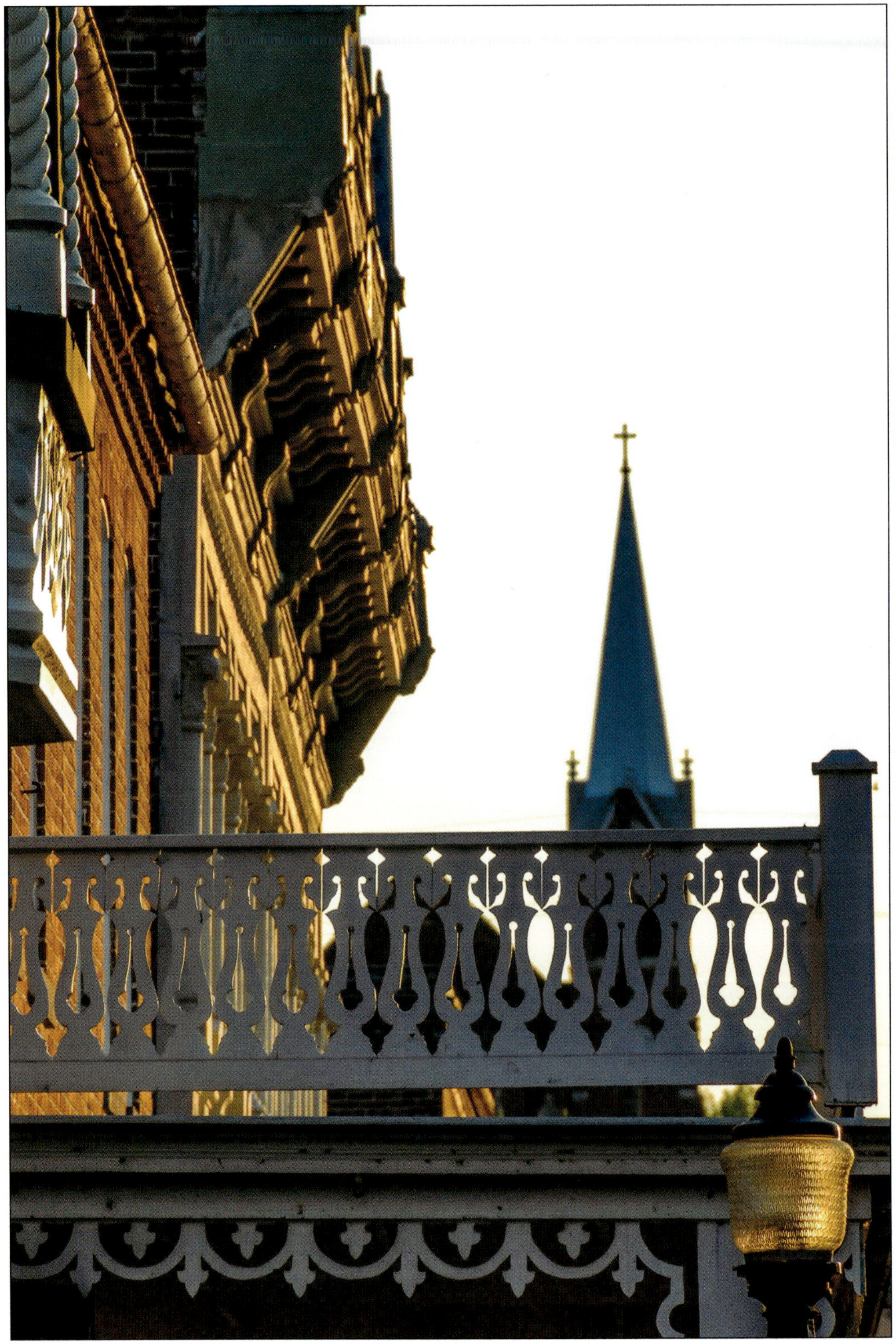

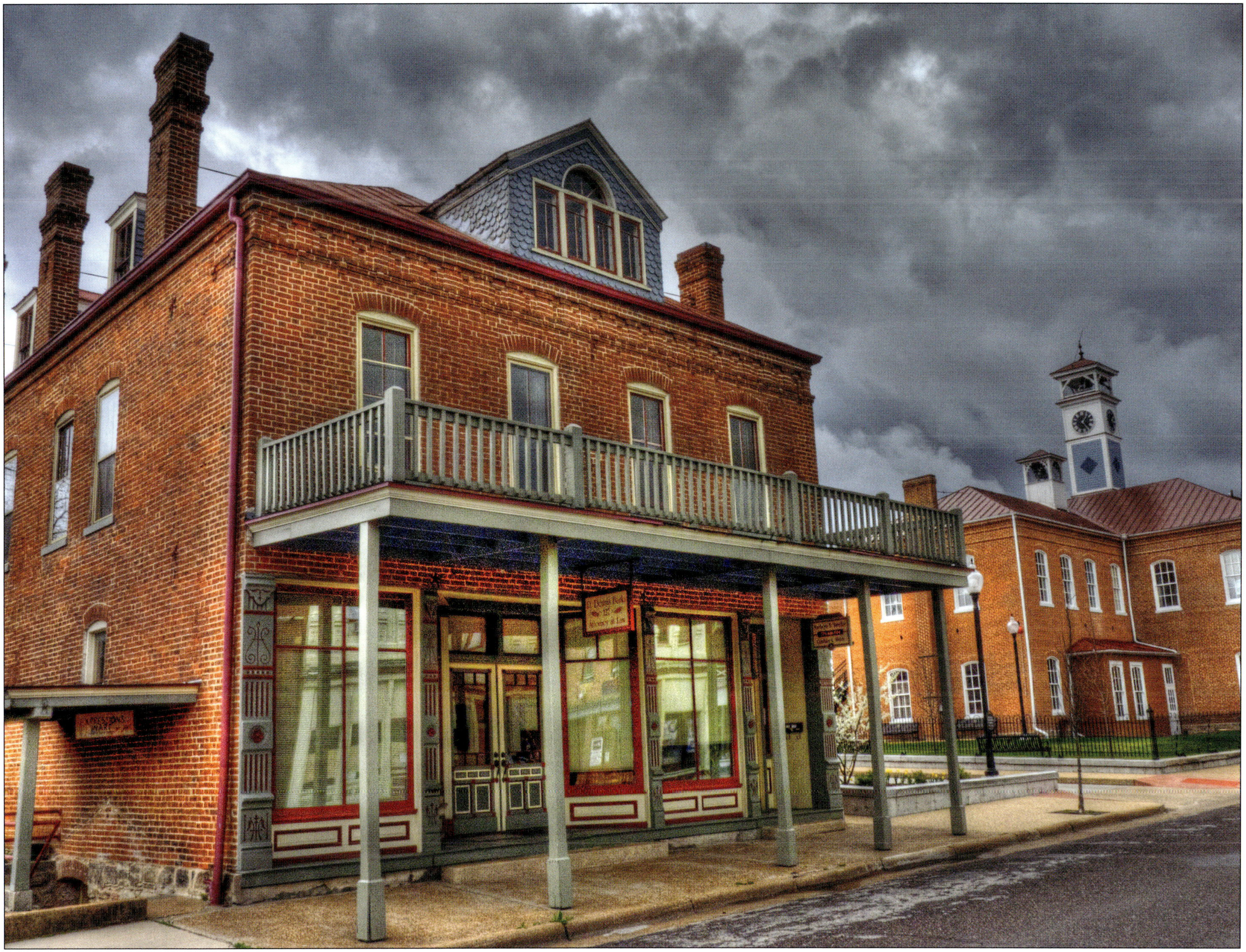

Eberlin-Strecker Building
William Fields

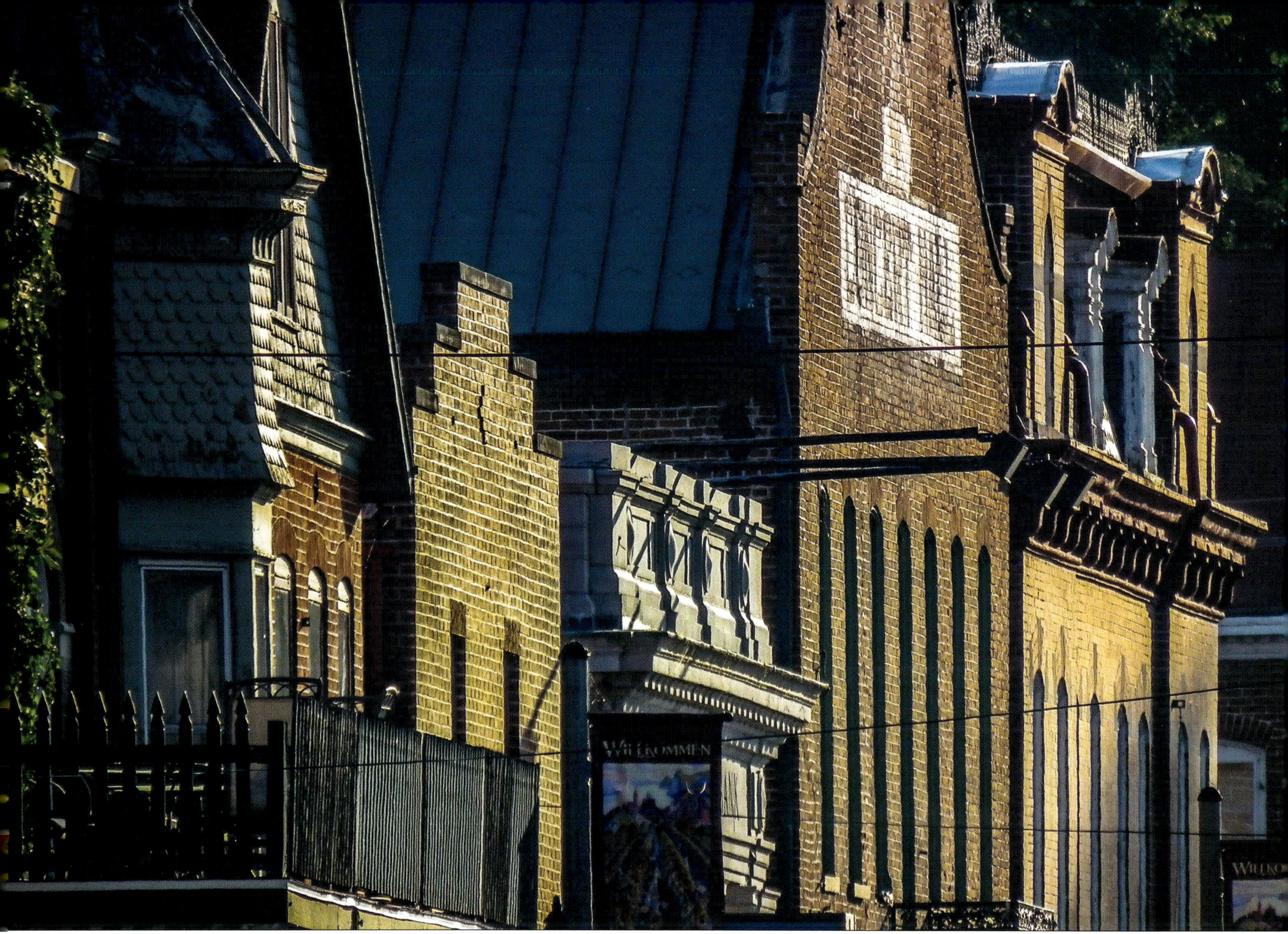

First Street Façade

Tony Carosella

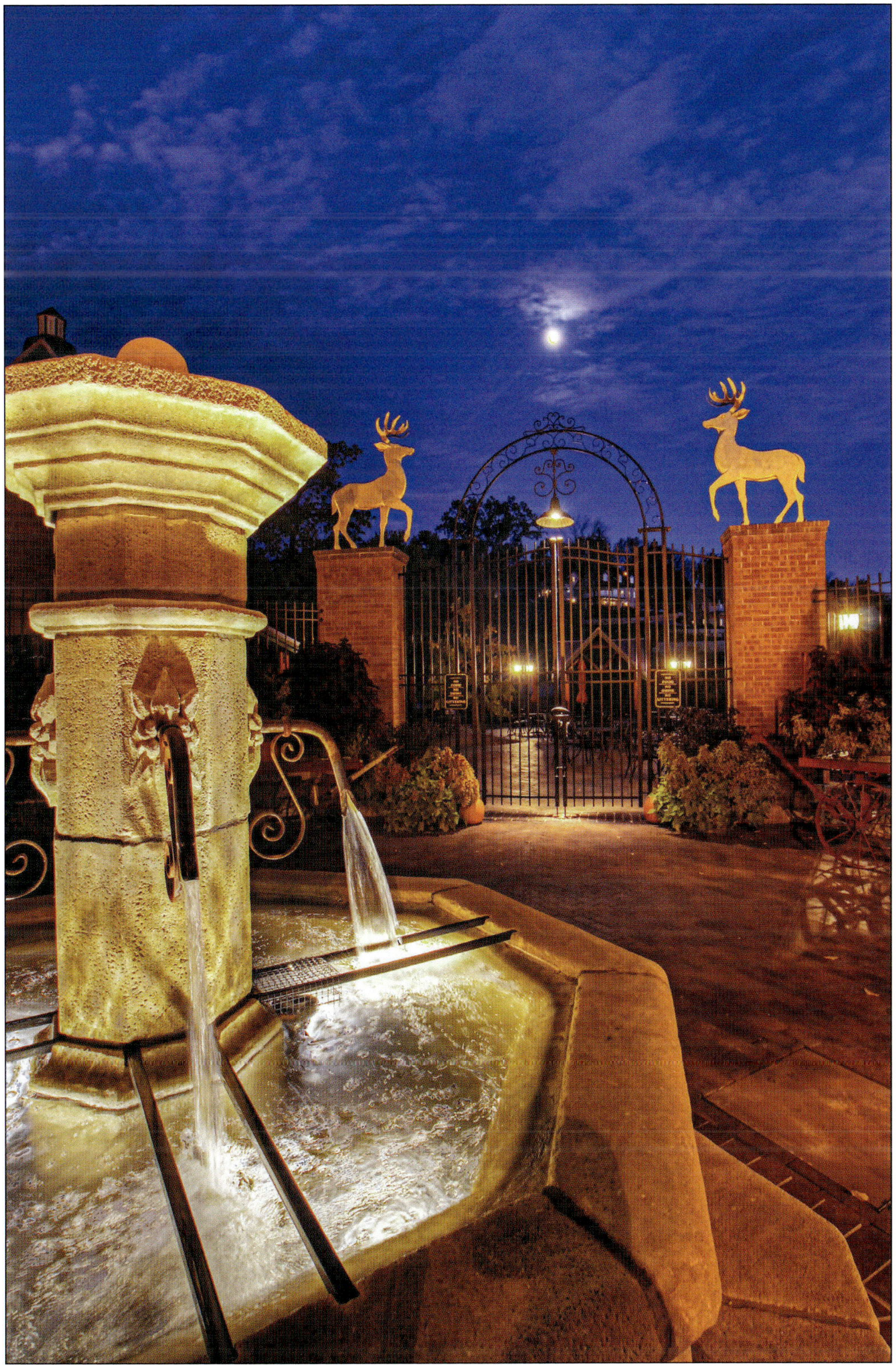

Hofgarten Fountain
Tony Carosella

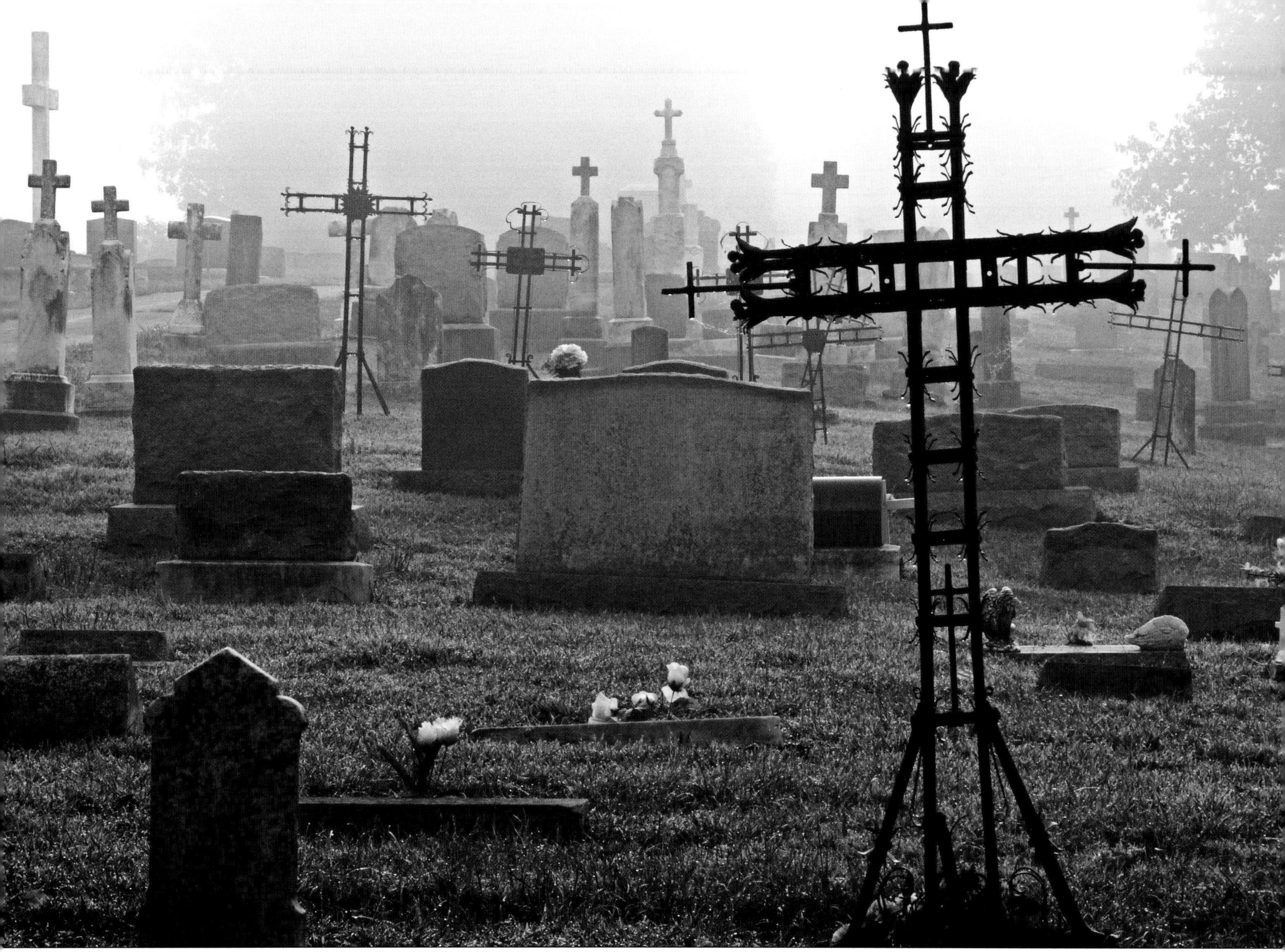

Catholic Cemetery
William Fields

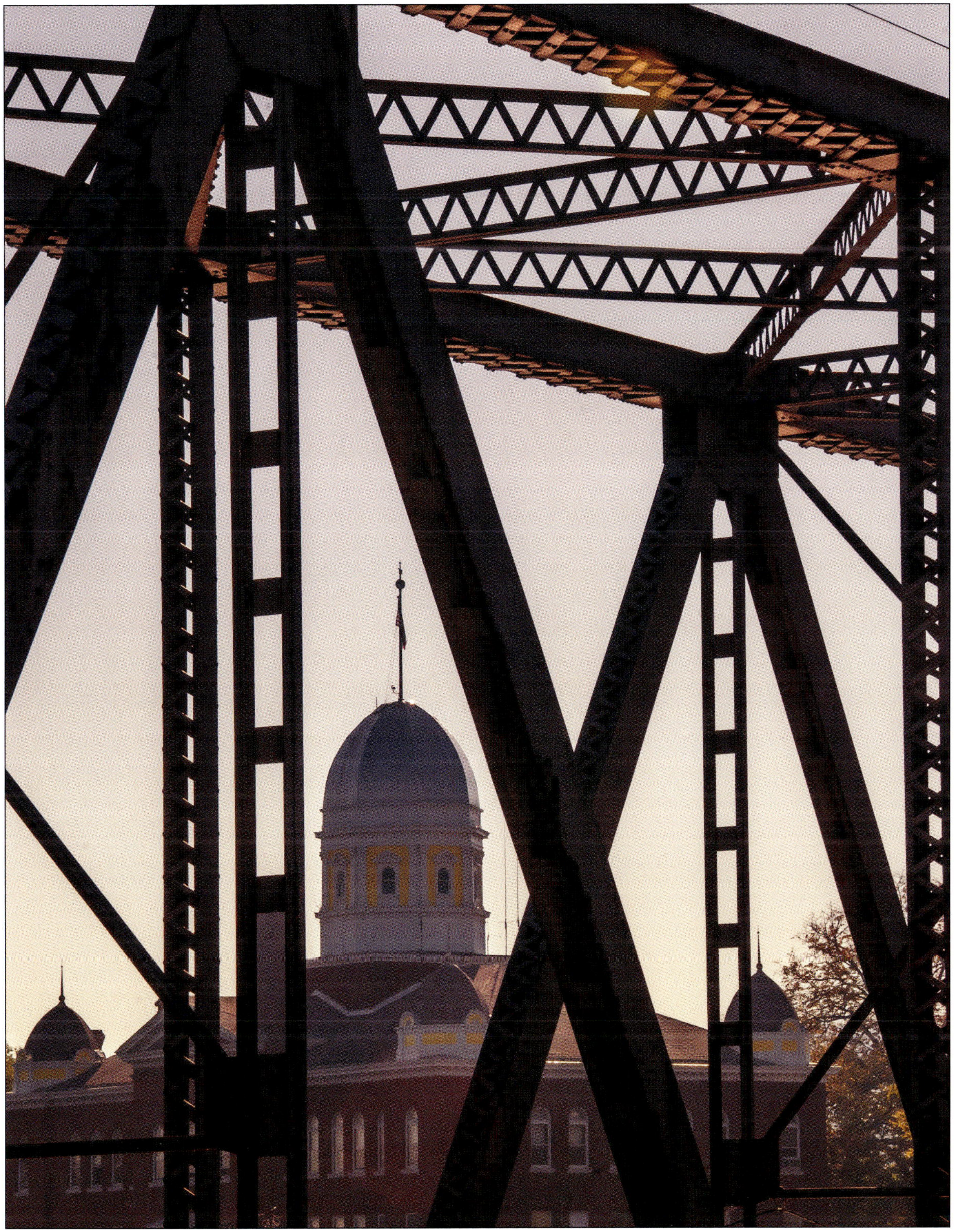

The Dome Framed

Tony Carosella

Festhalle Stag

Tony Carosella

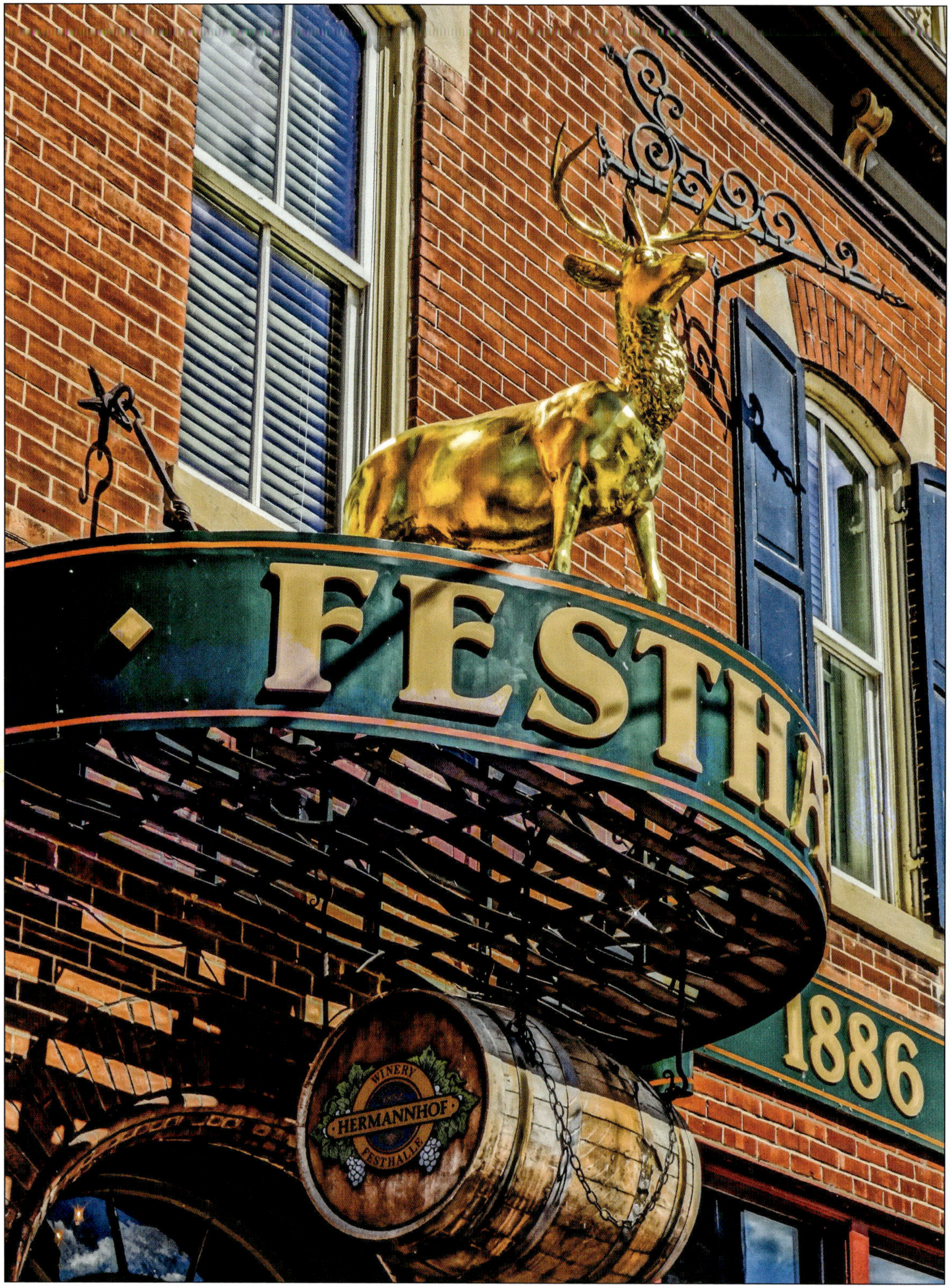

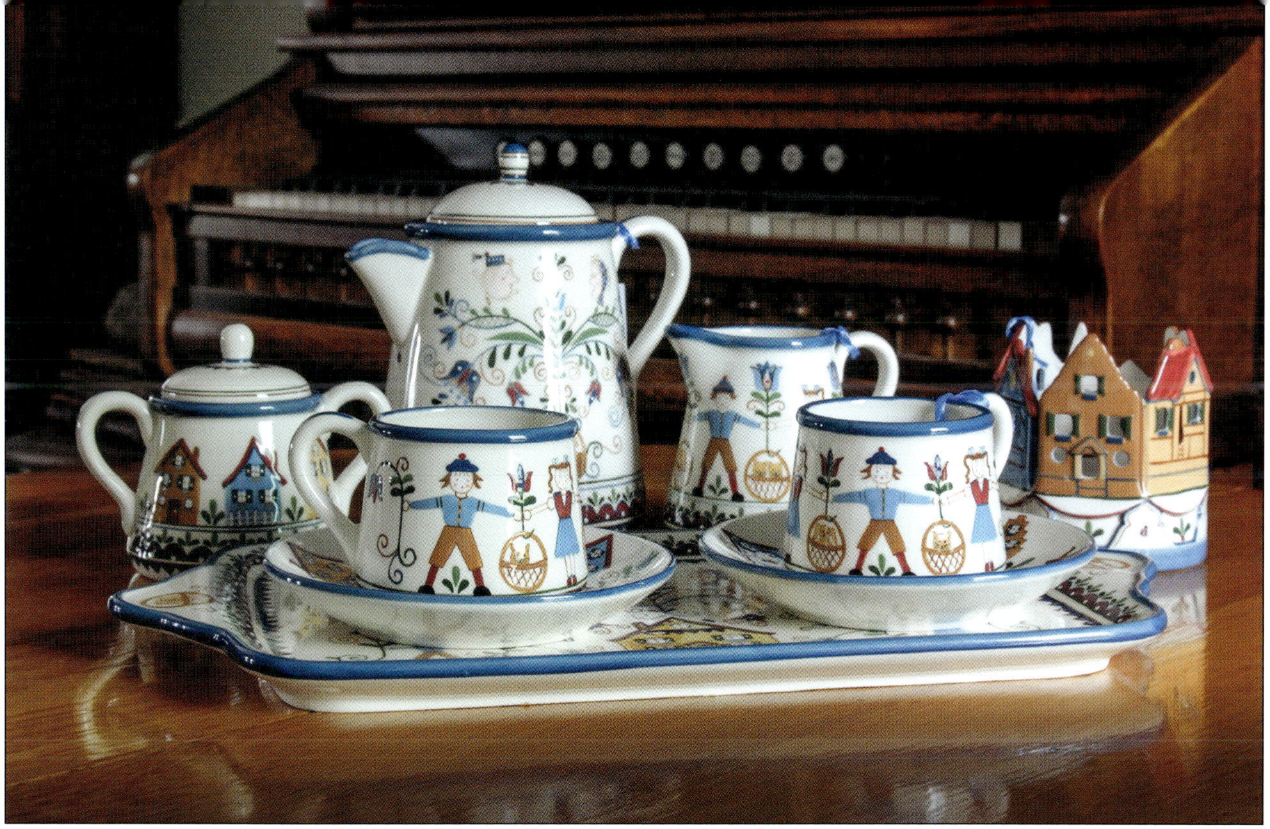

German Tea Set
Tony Carosella

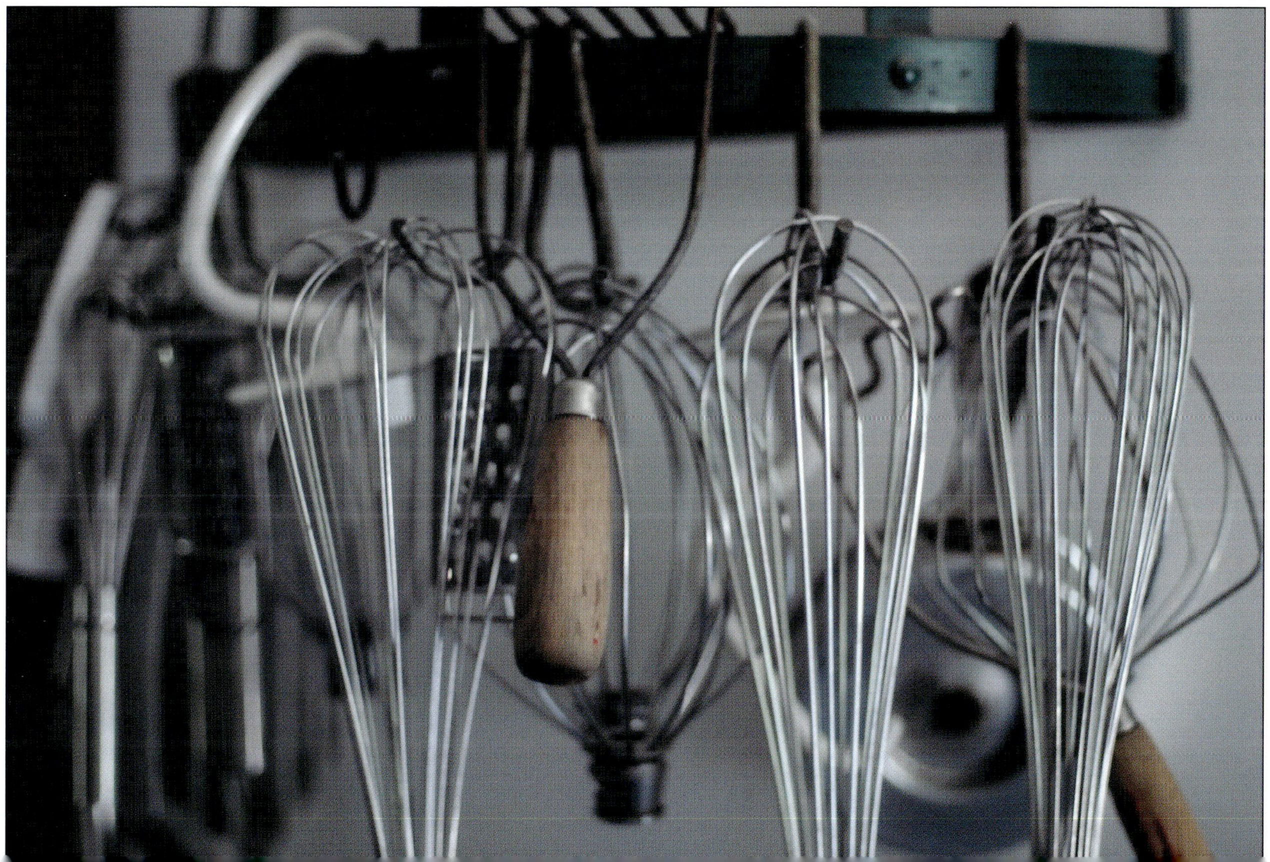

Whisks
Tony Carosella

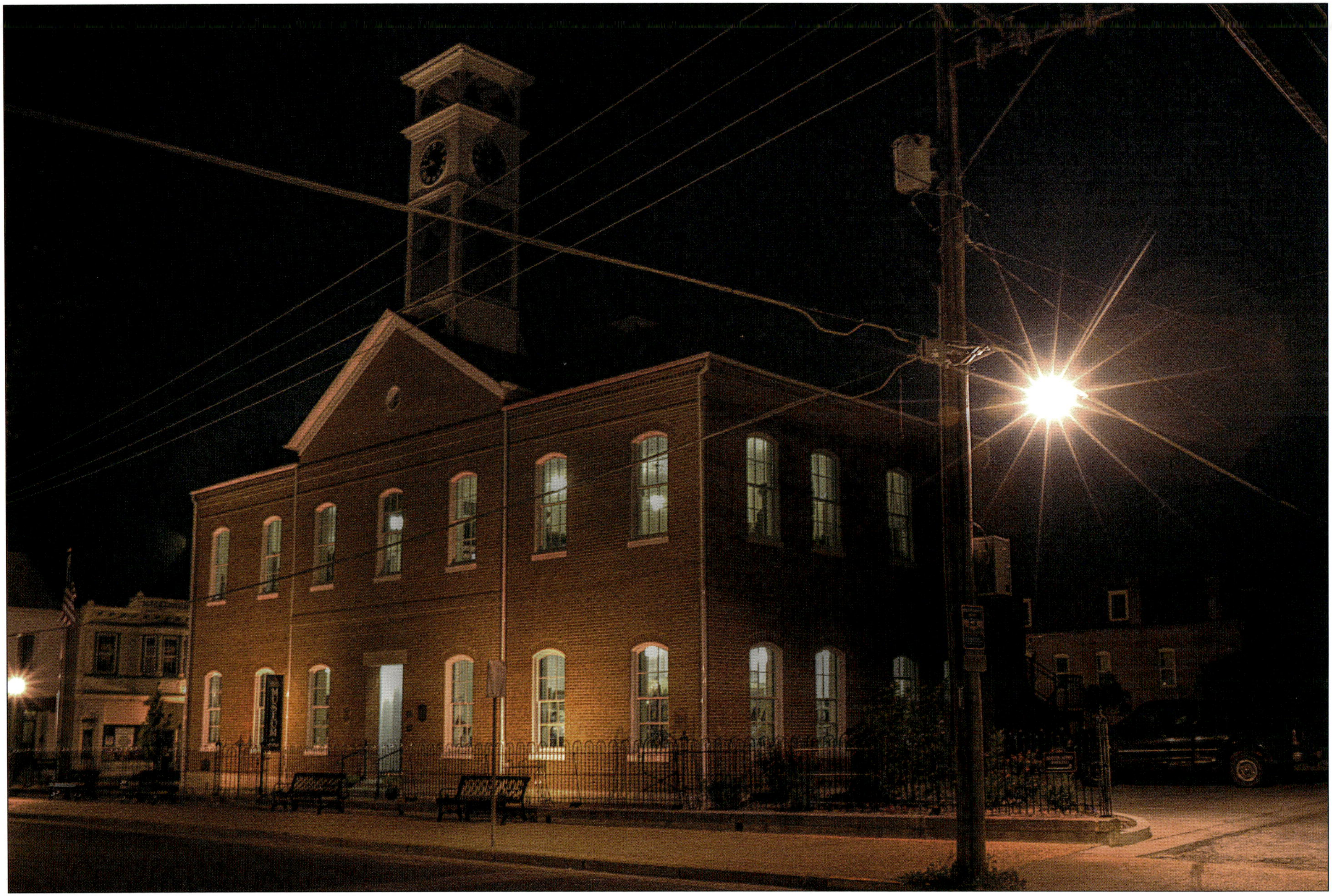

Schoolhouse Nocturne

William Fields

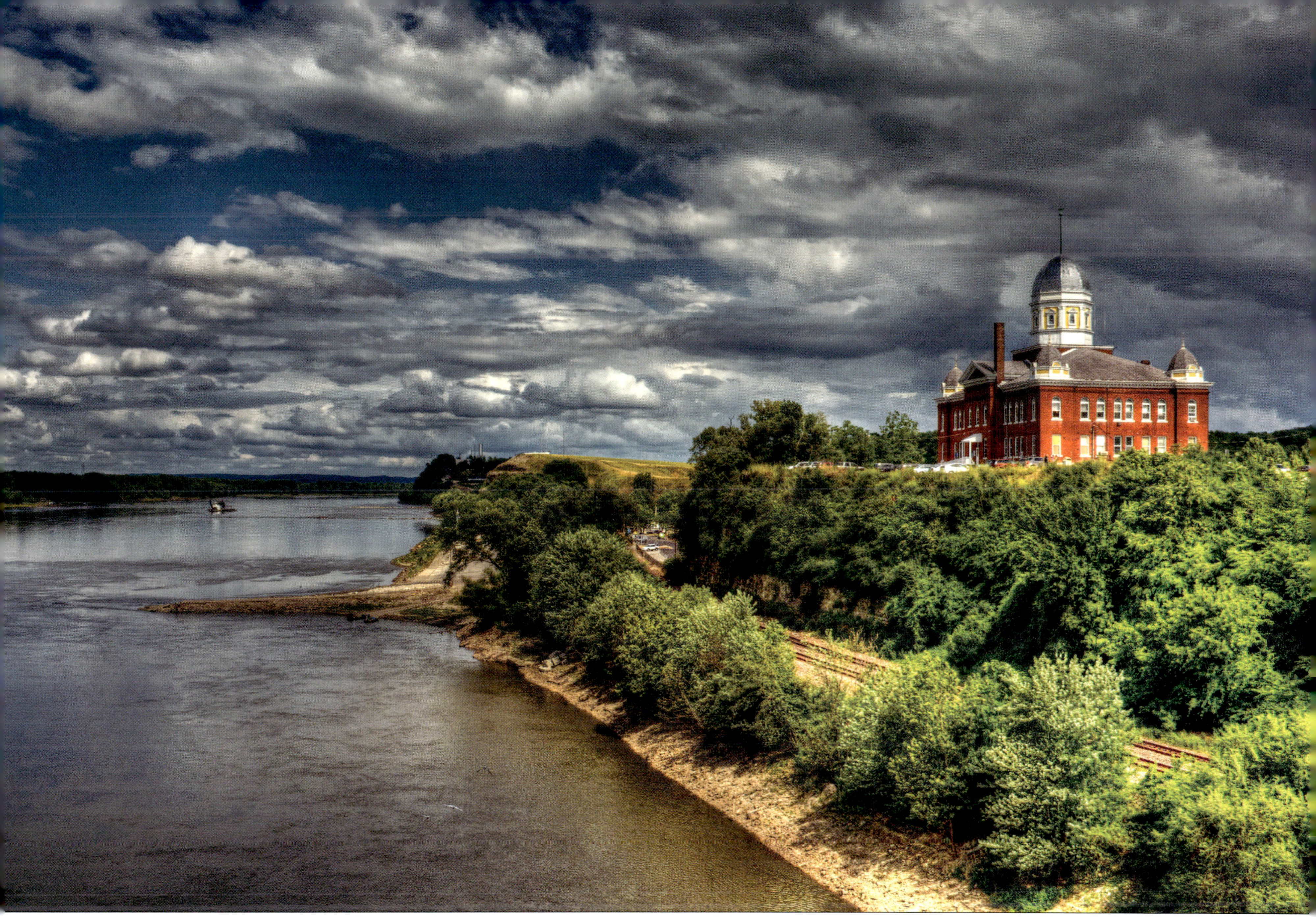

Courthouse Vista
William Fields

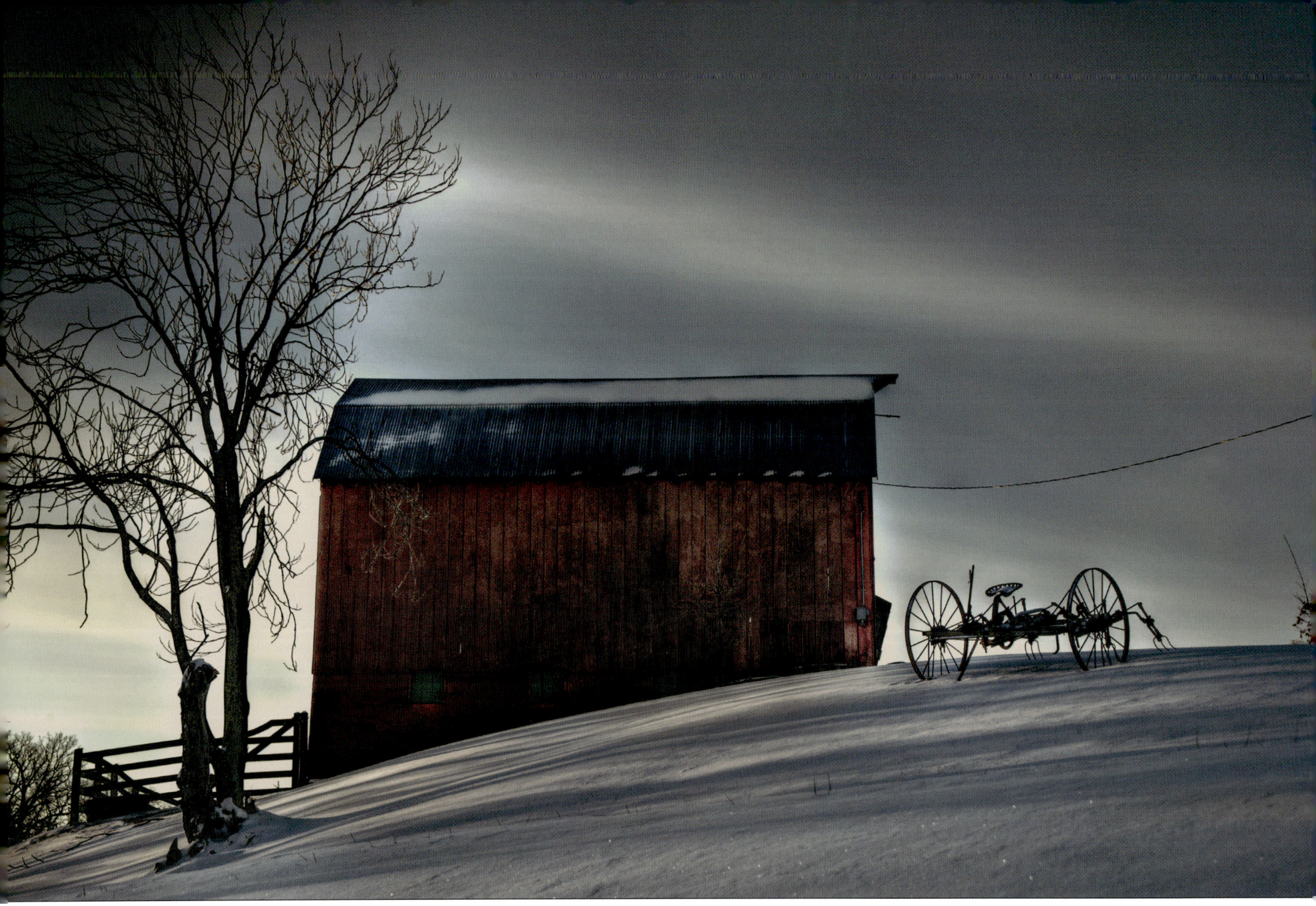

Not Used Much Anymore
William Fields

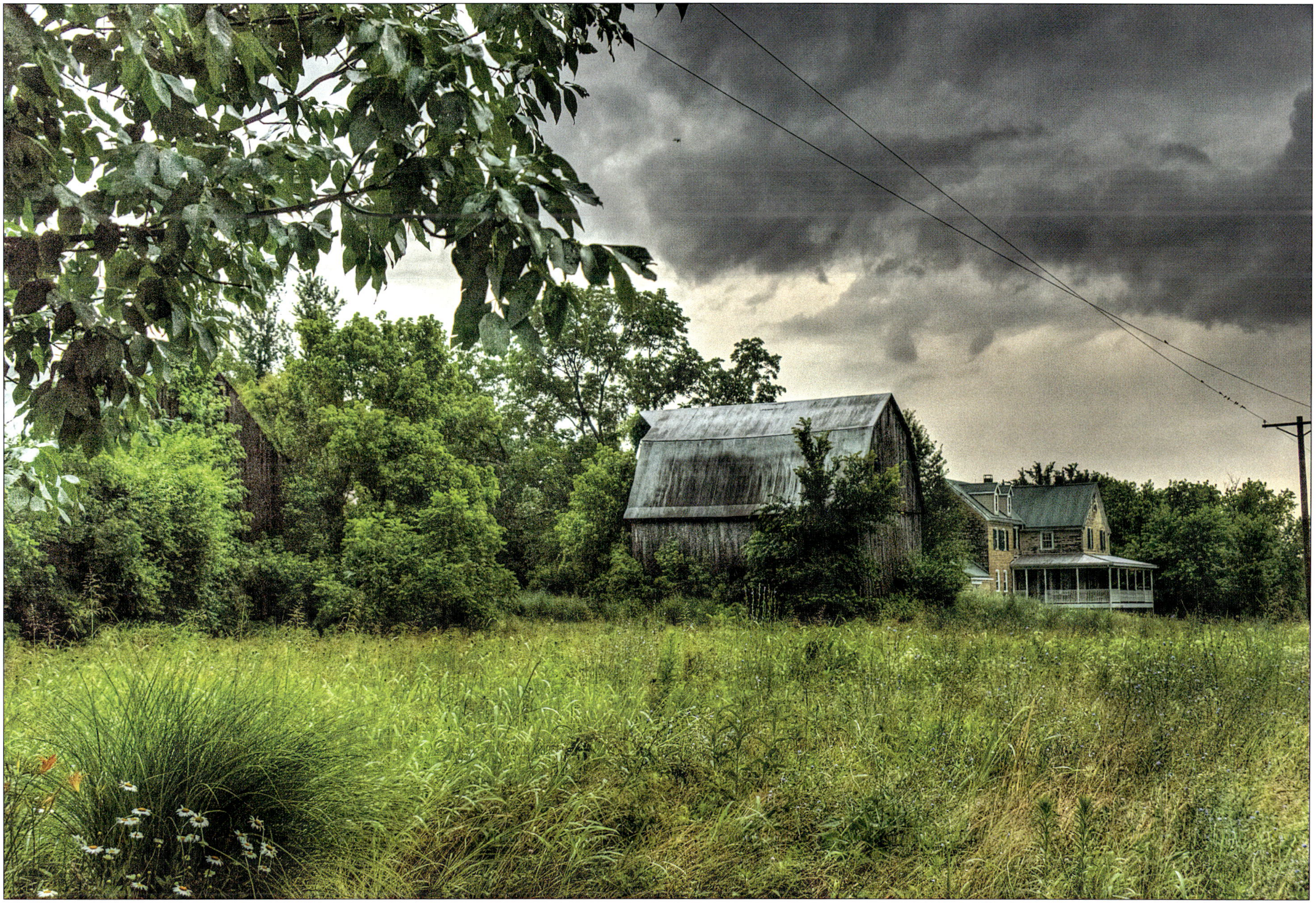

O'Toole Farm

William Fields

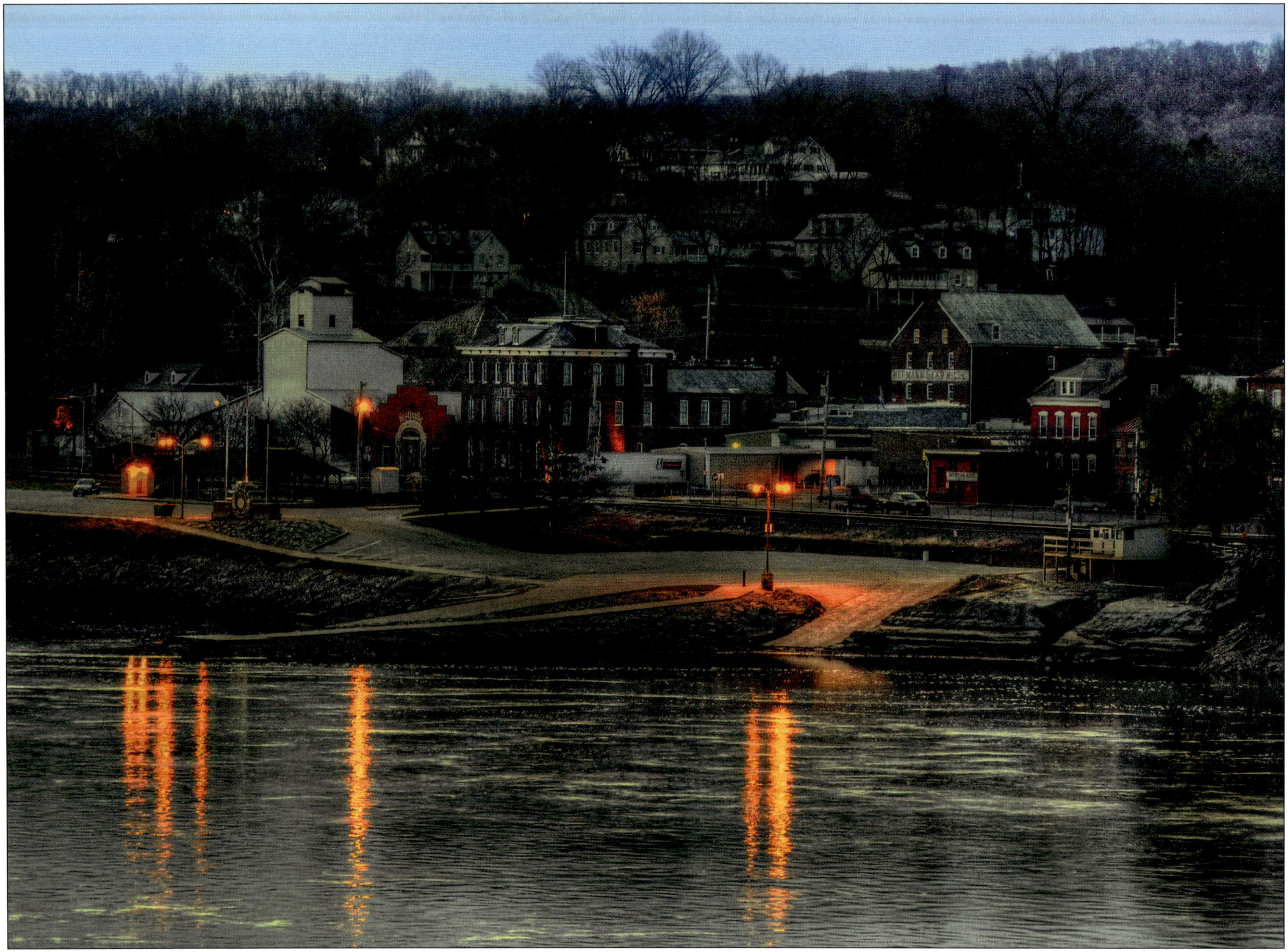

Brigadoon II
William Fields

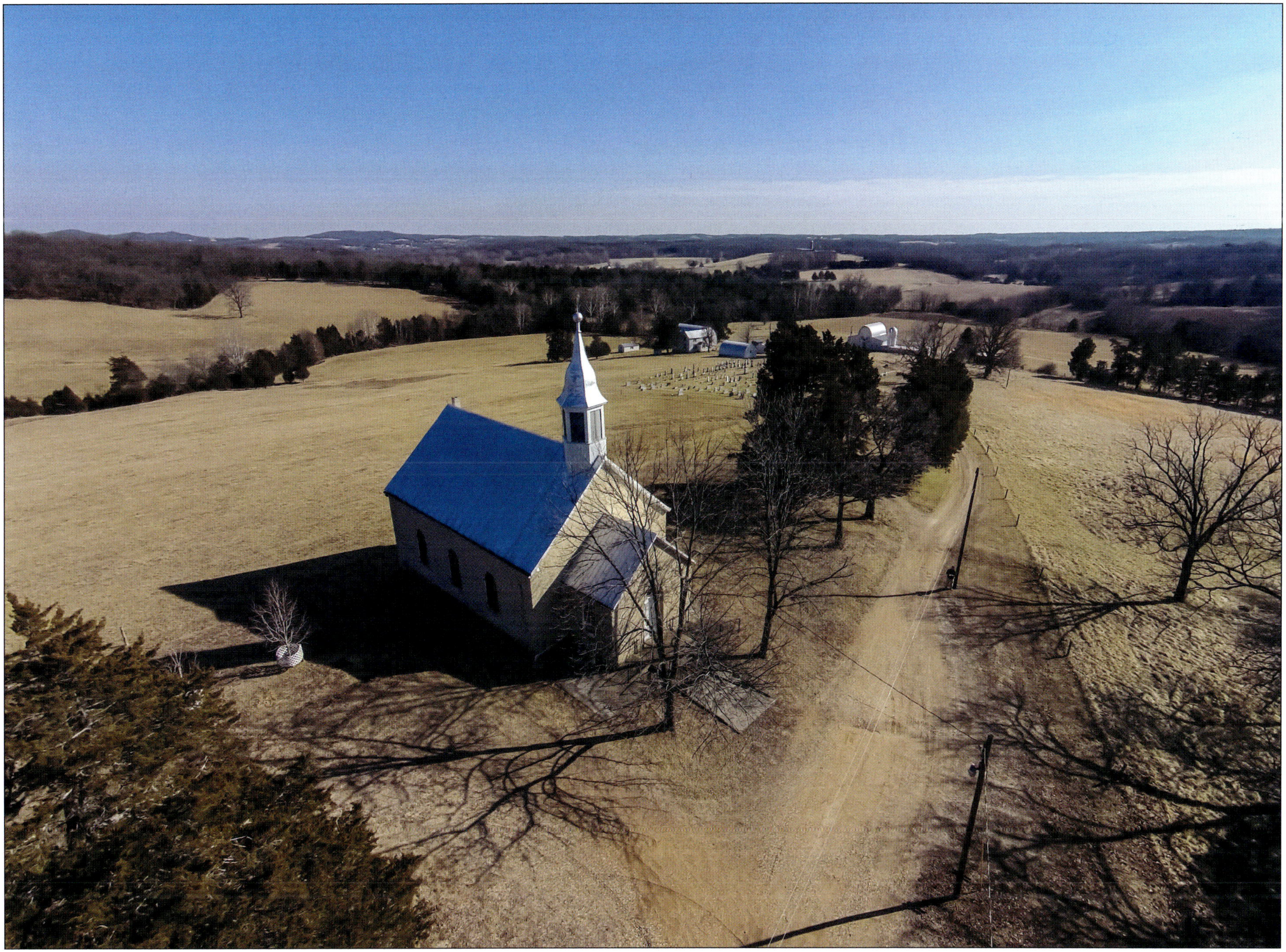

Bethel UCC
Tony Carosella

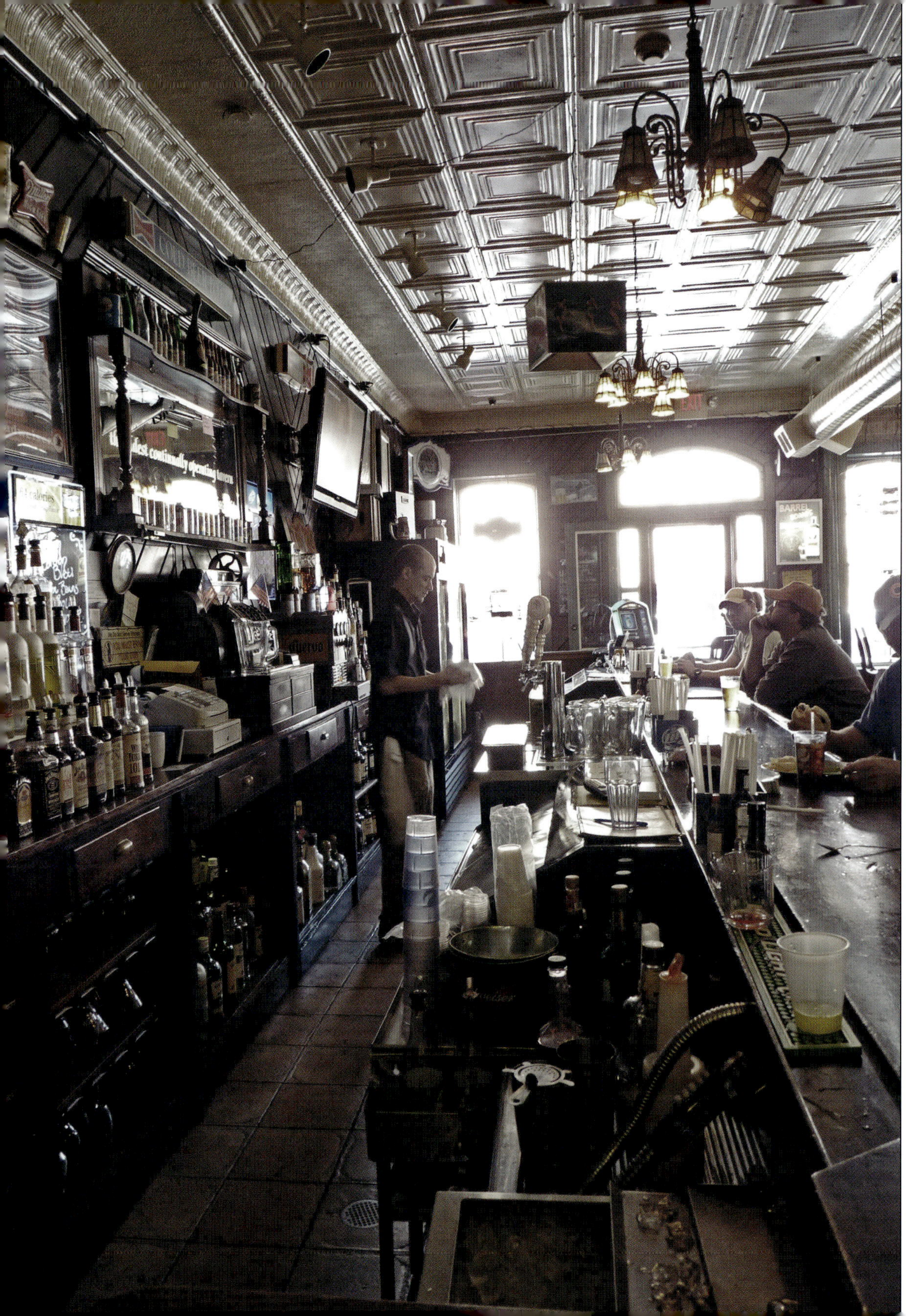

The People

This section is dedicated to our friends and neighbors who really are what our town is all about. Hermann, like any other place, is just geography until you add people into the mix. So here's to those who fix our cars and mix our drinks and make our meals and serve us and each other each and every day.

– William Fields

Belly-up to the Bar
William Fields

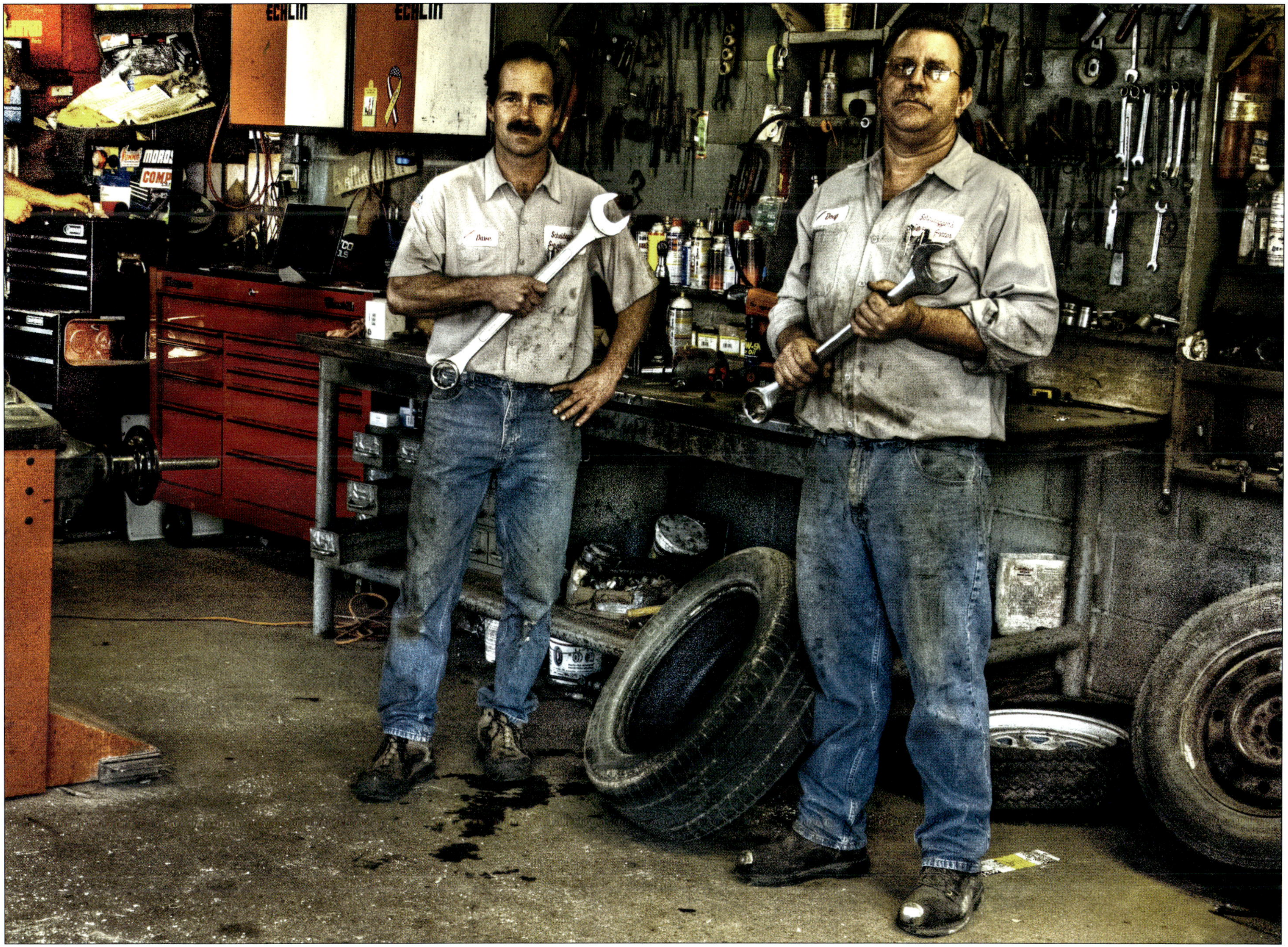

Big Wrenches
William Fields

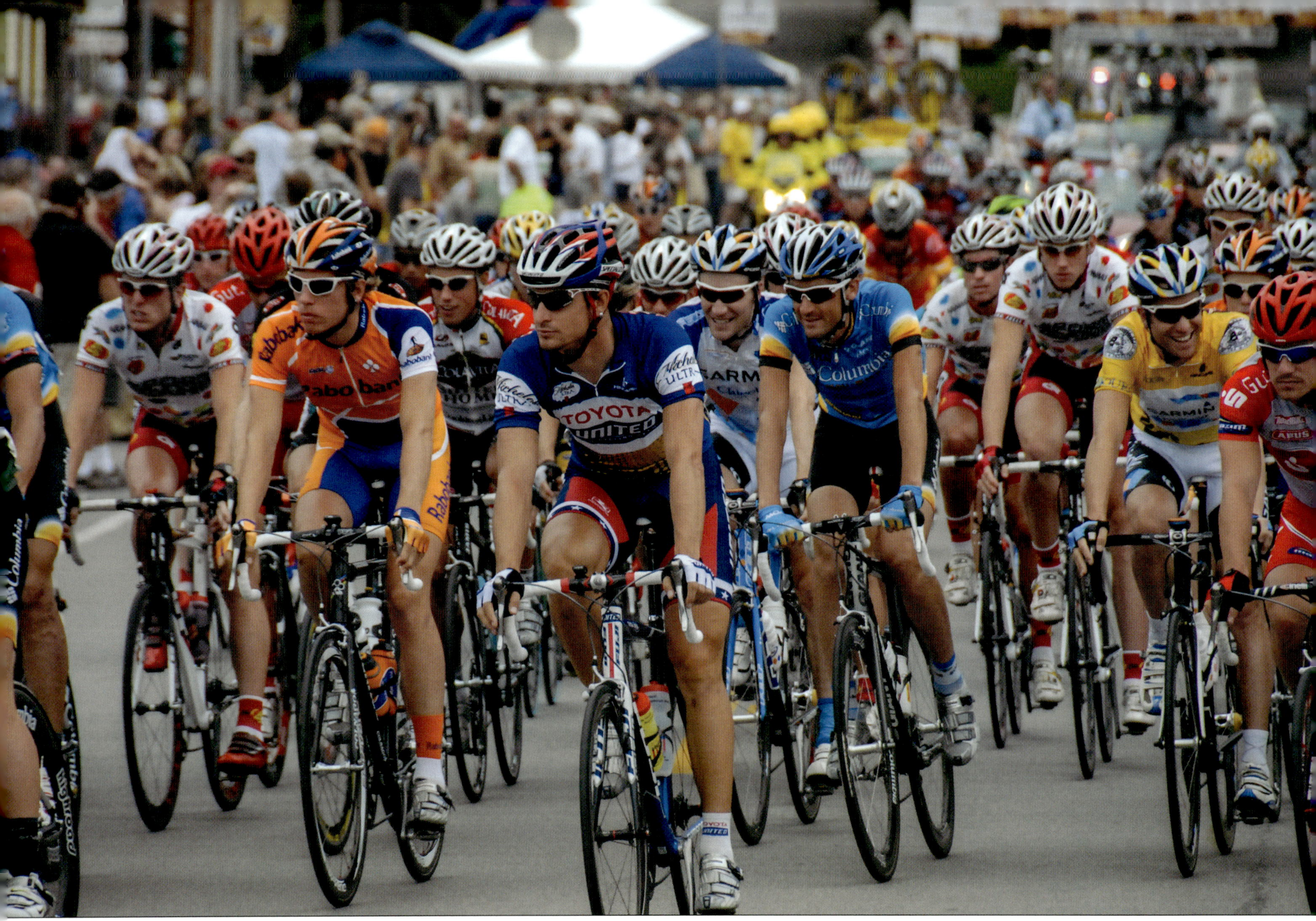

Criterion

Tony Carosella

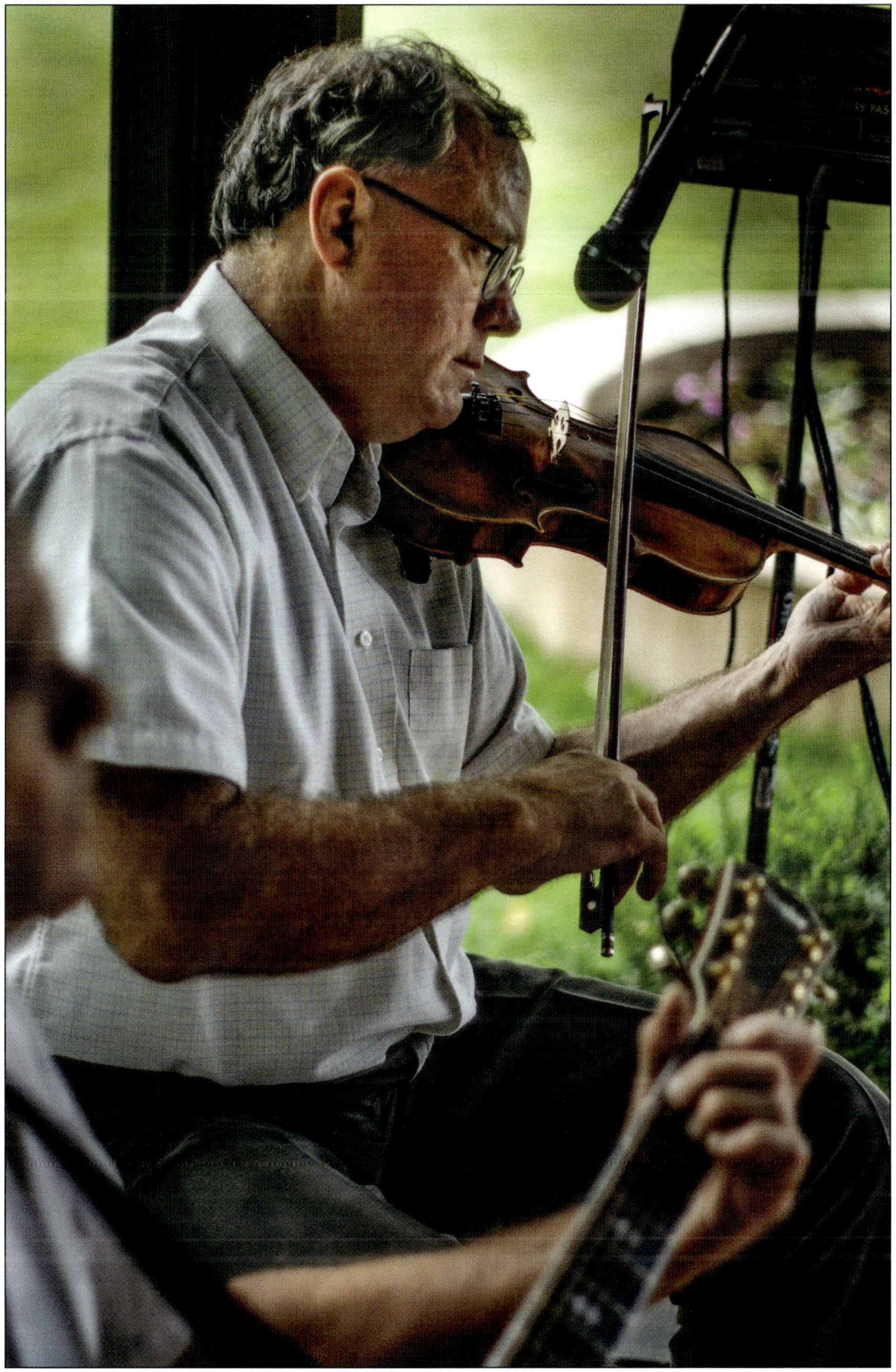

The Fiddler
Tony Carosella

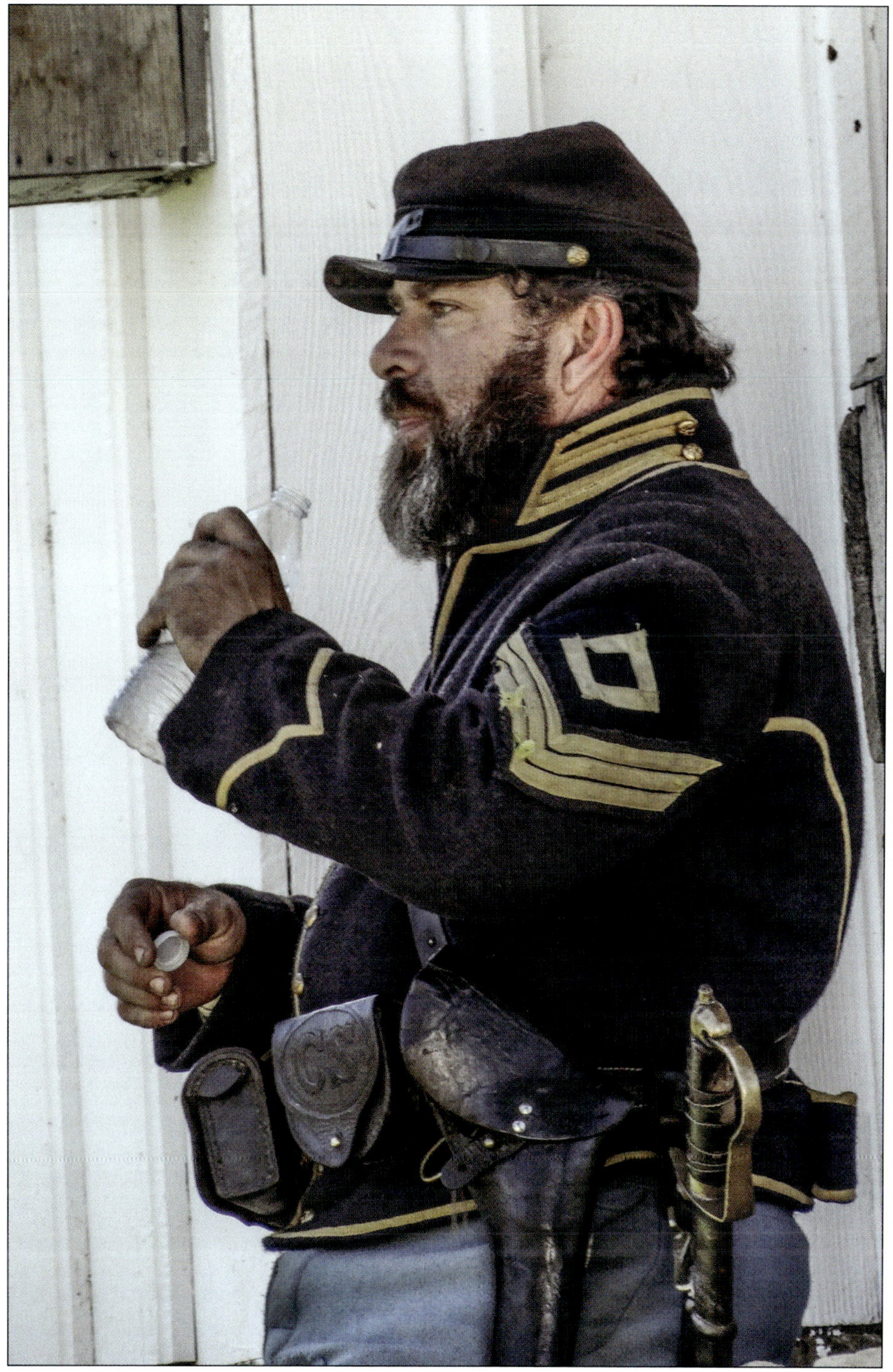

Bottled Water
Tony Carosella

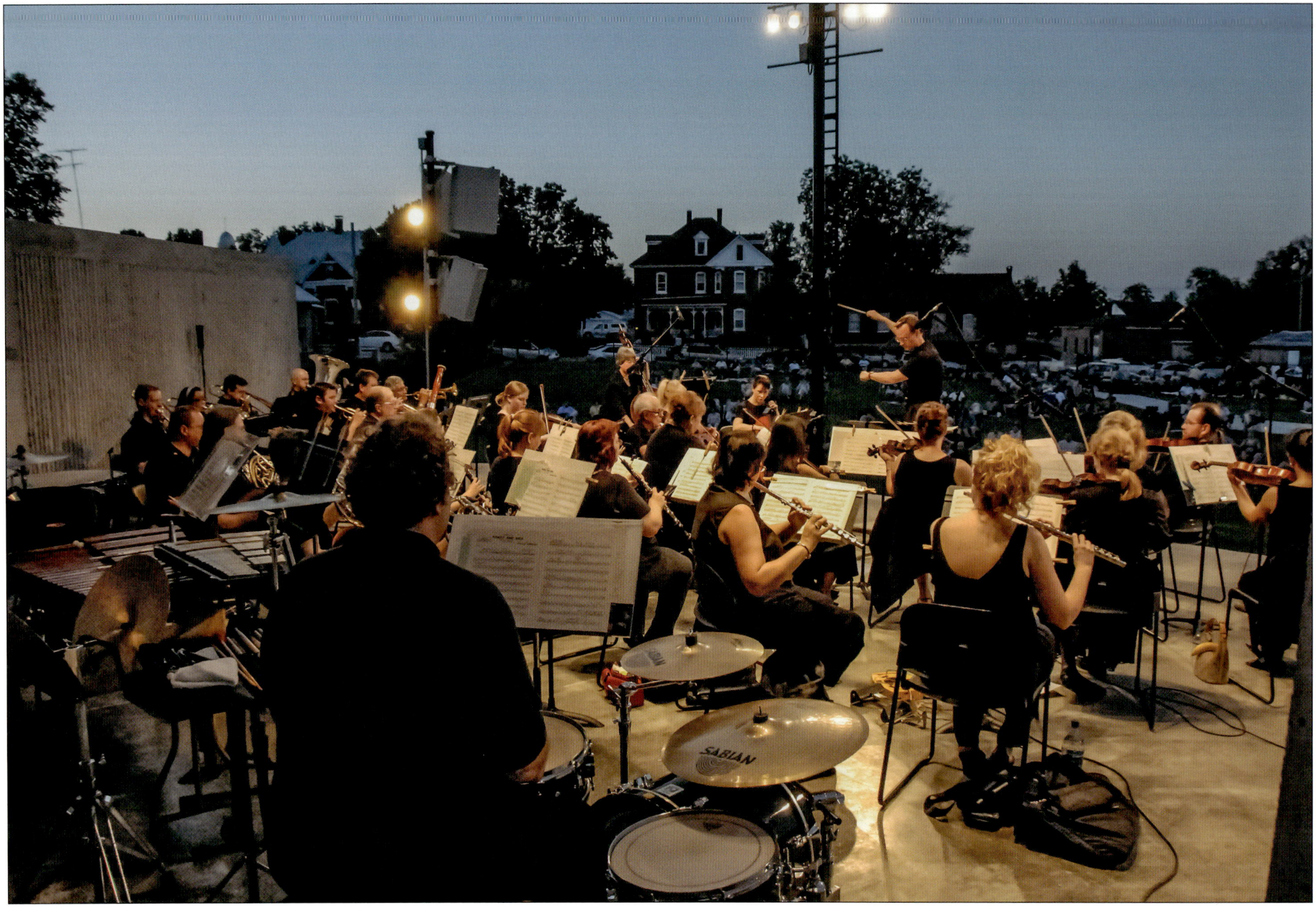

Concert at the Eitmann
Tony Carosella

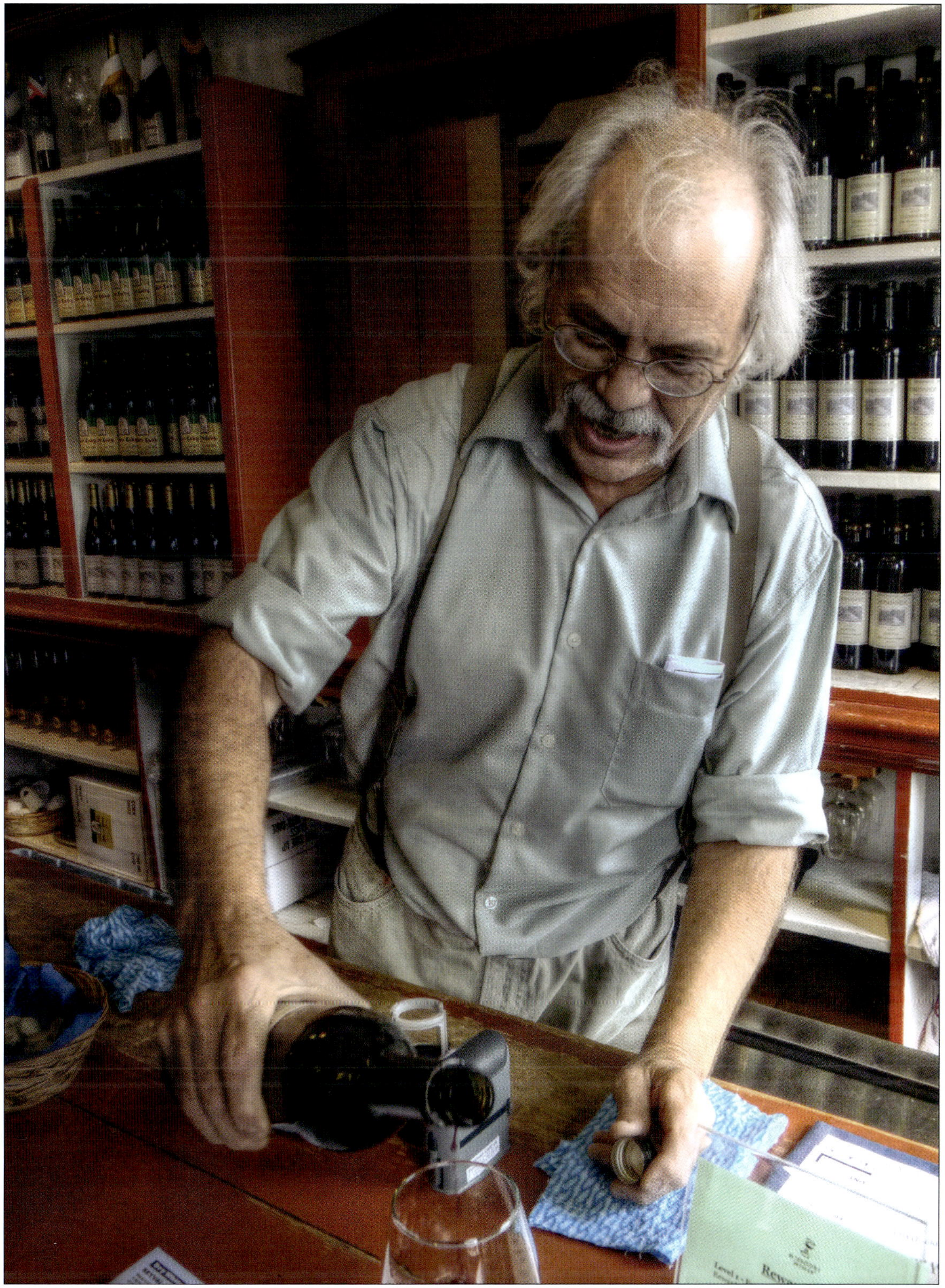

The Wine Steward

William Fields

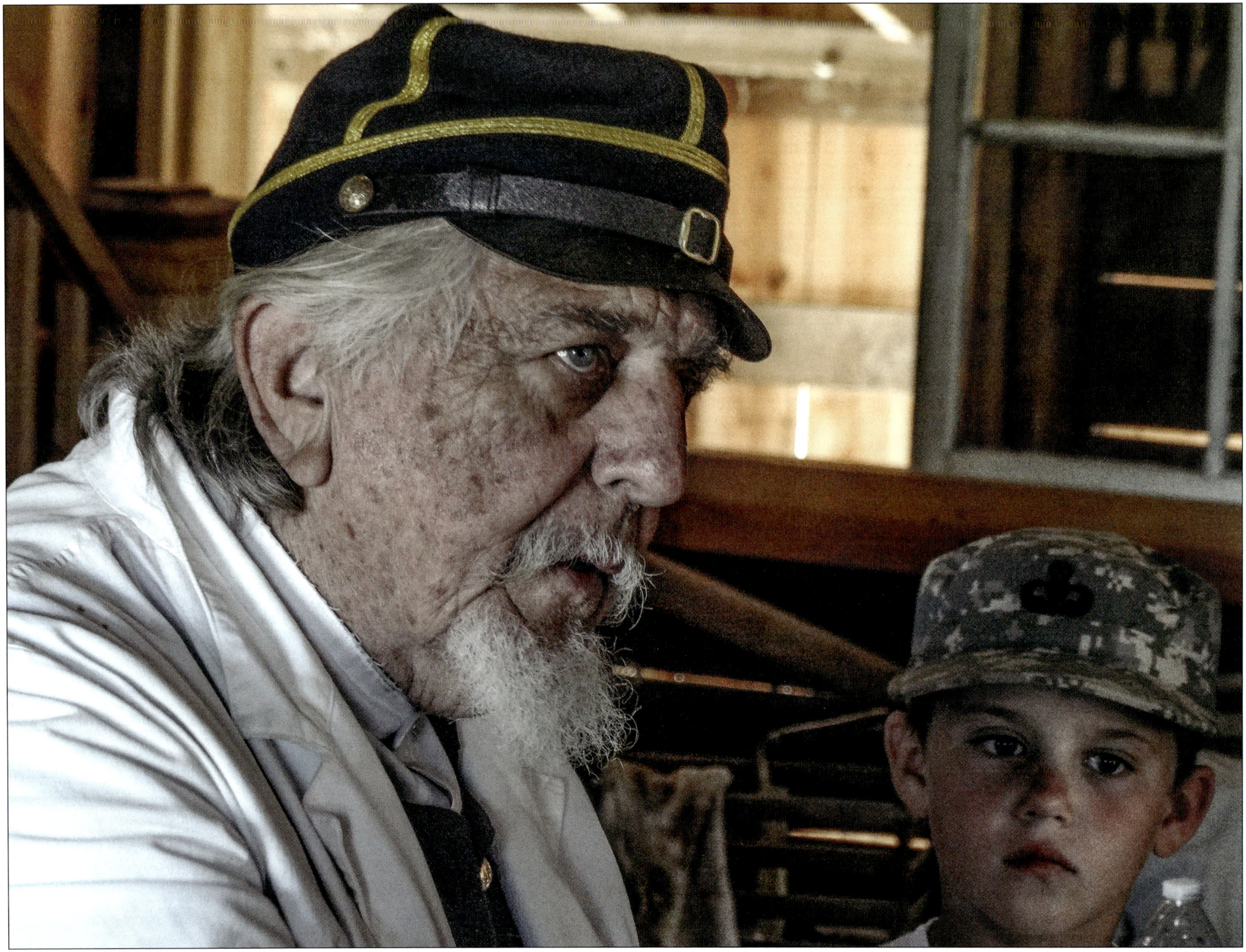

The Vet
Tony Carosella

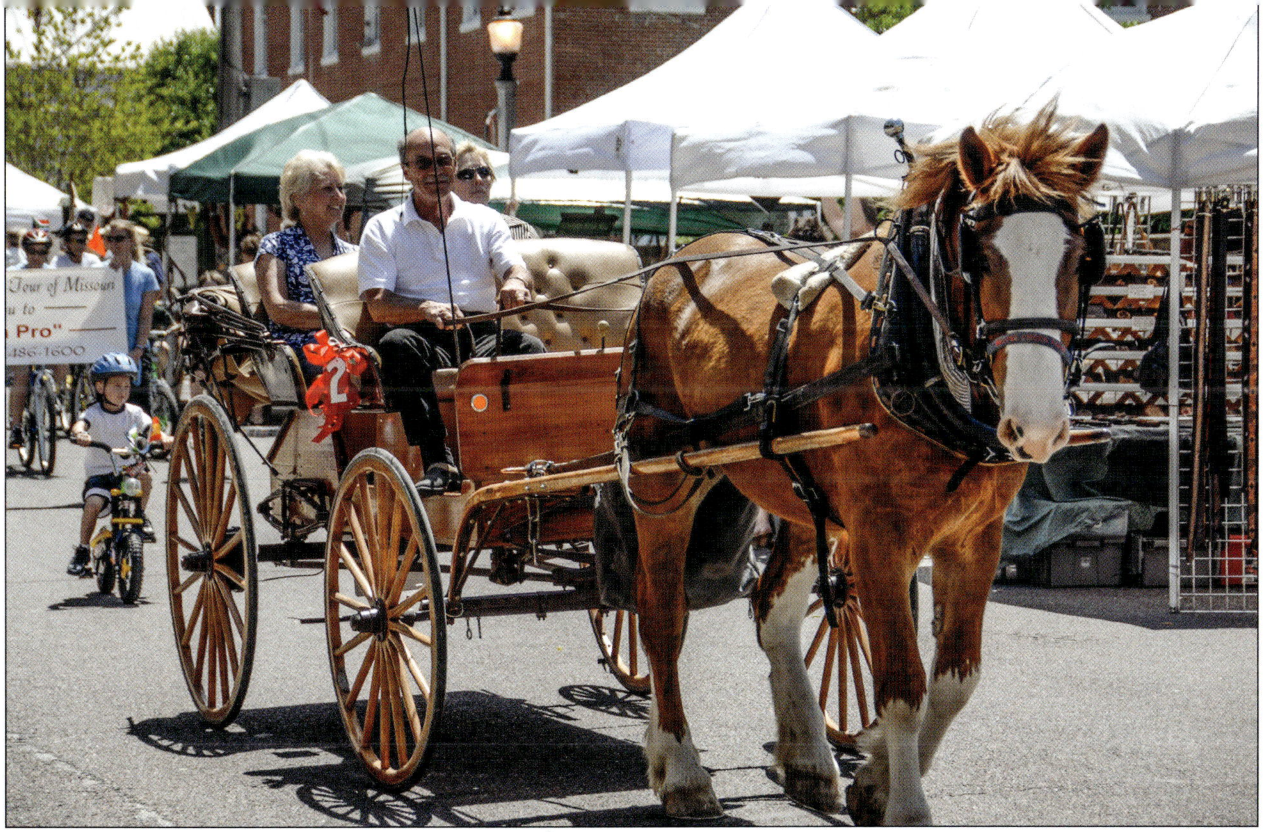

Driving a Team
Tony Carosella

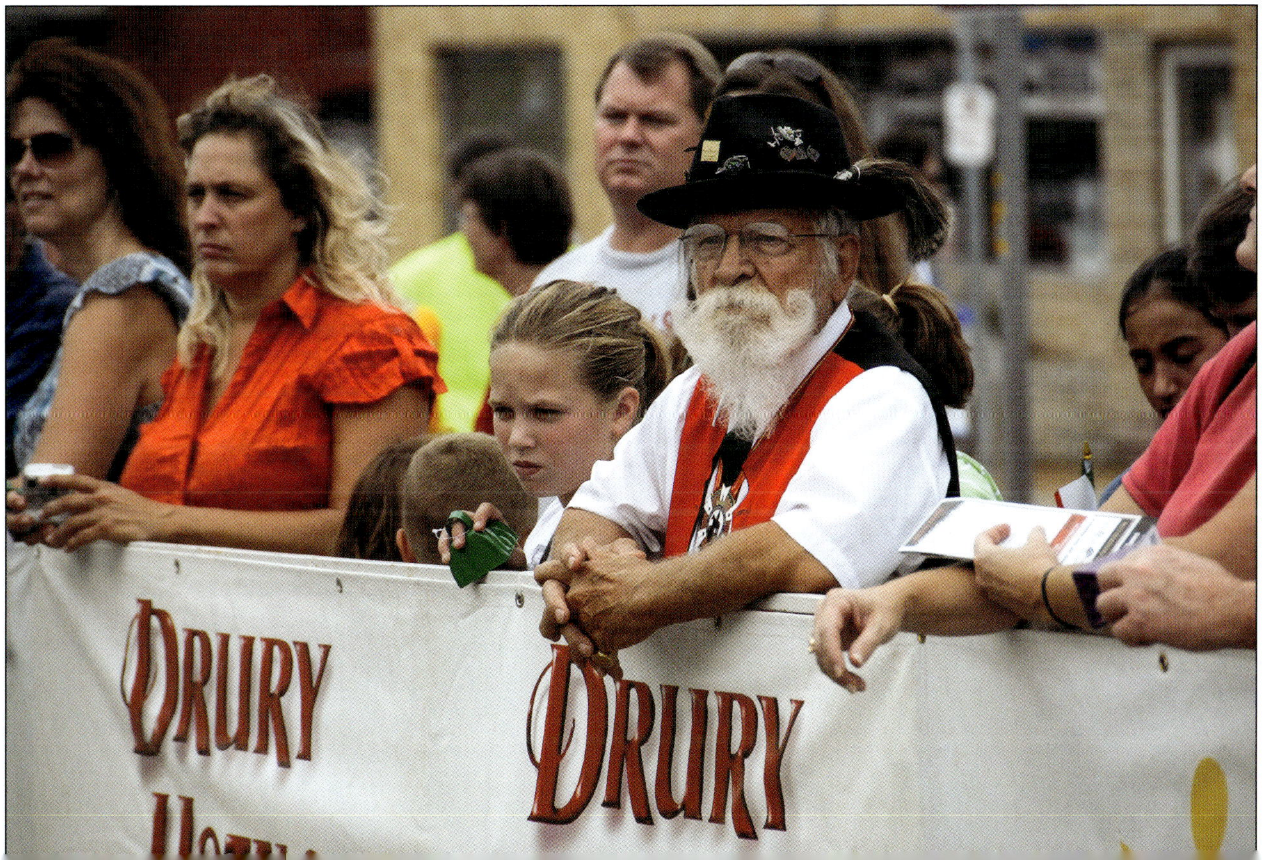

Jack
Tony Carosella

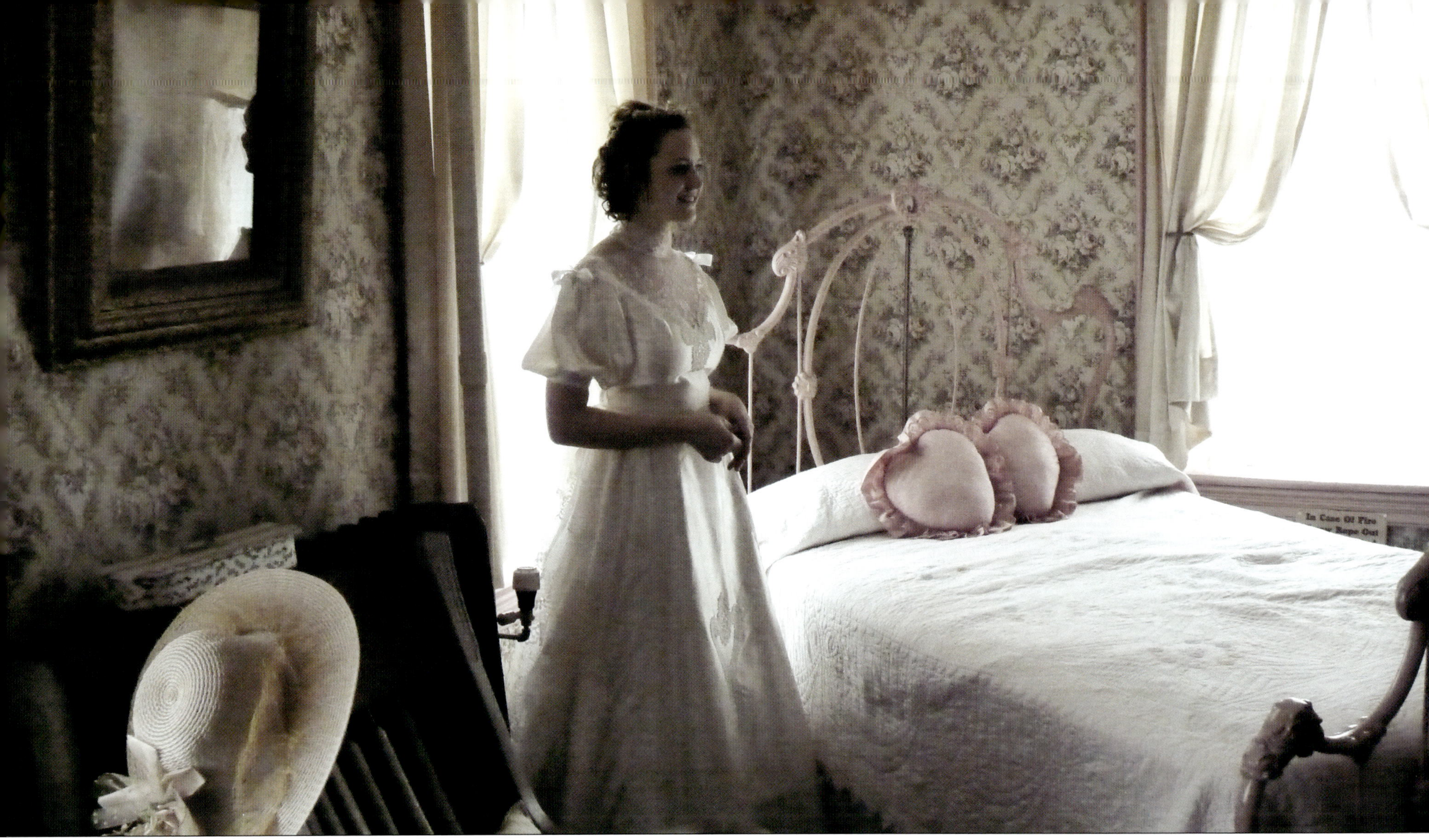

Sadie

William Fields

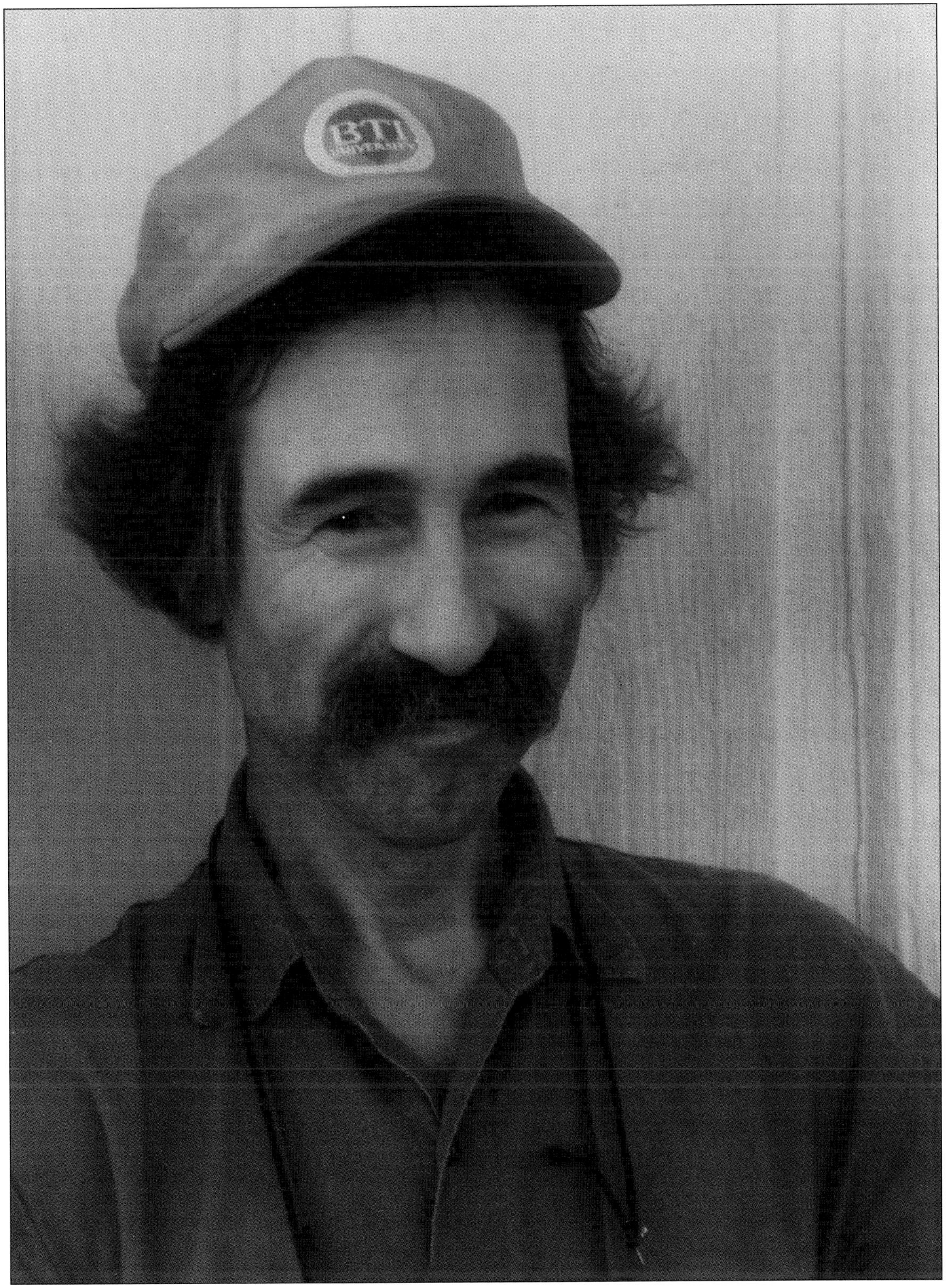

In Memoriam–Corky

William Fields

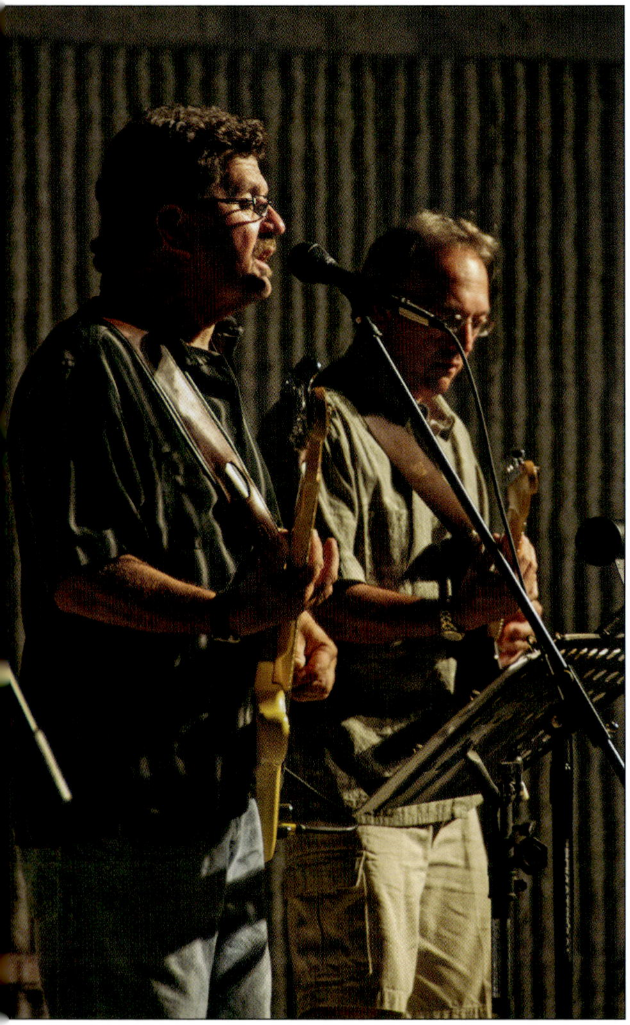

Blufftones Solo
Tony Carosella

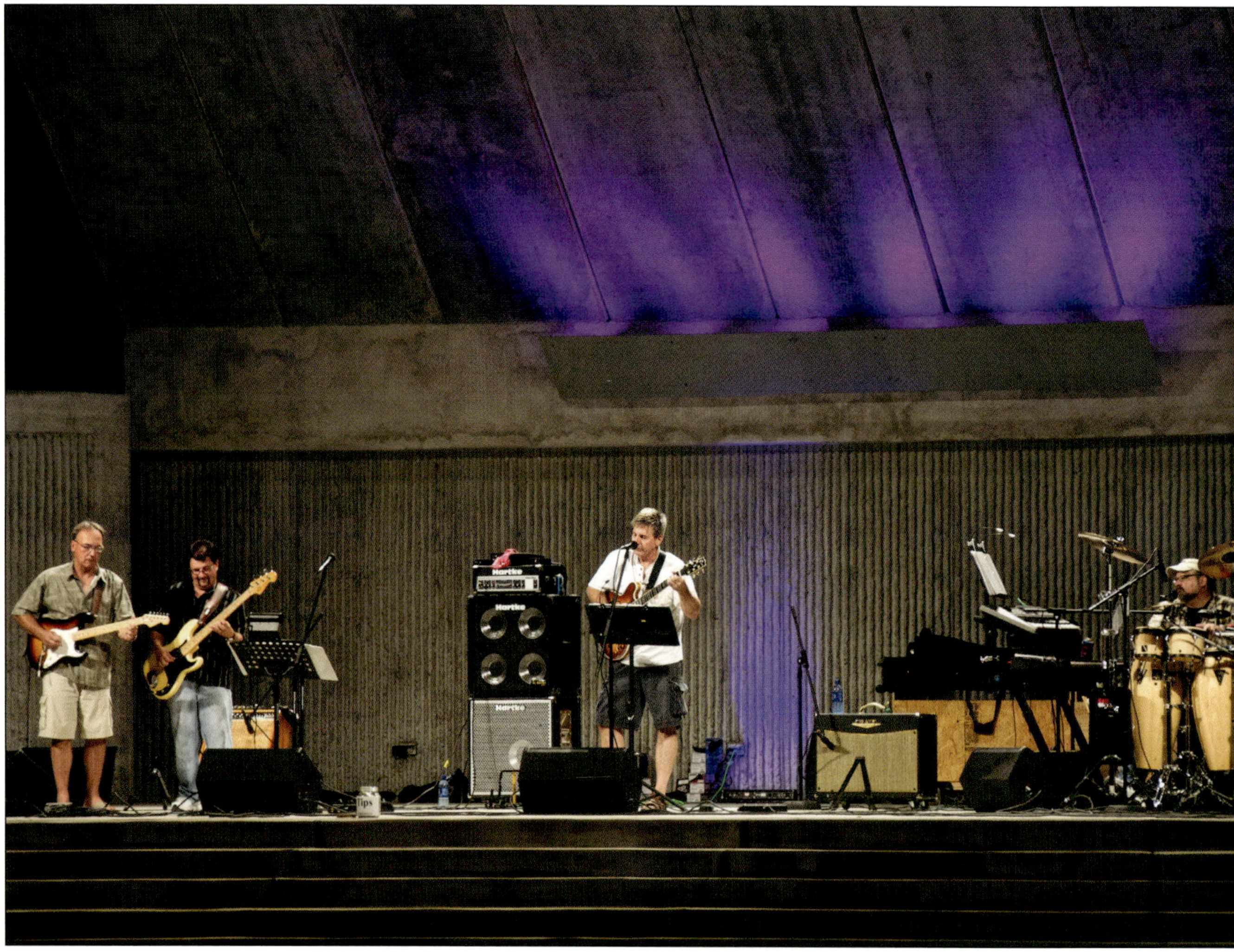

The Blufftones
Tony Carosella

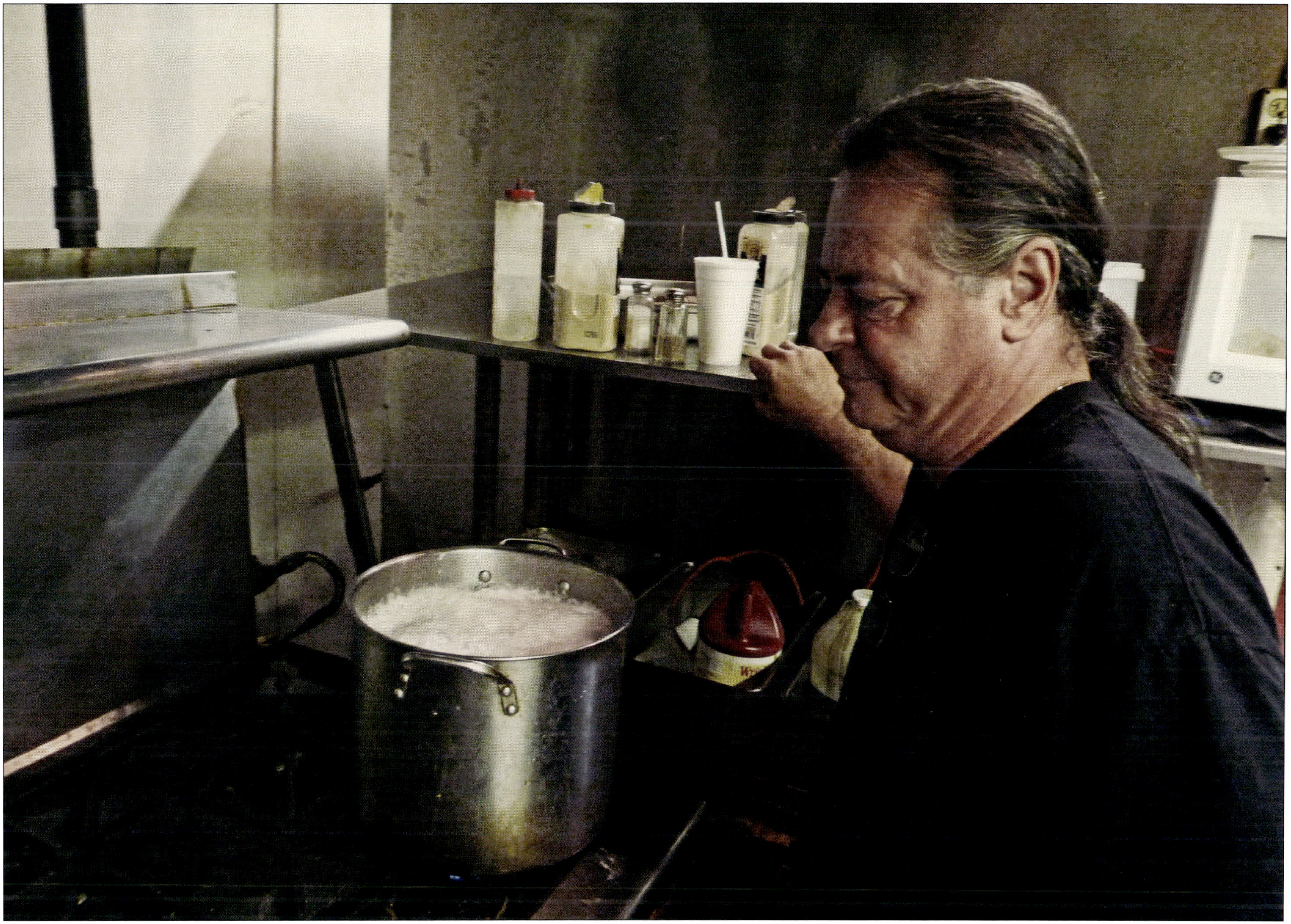

Making Gumbo
William Fields

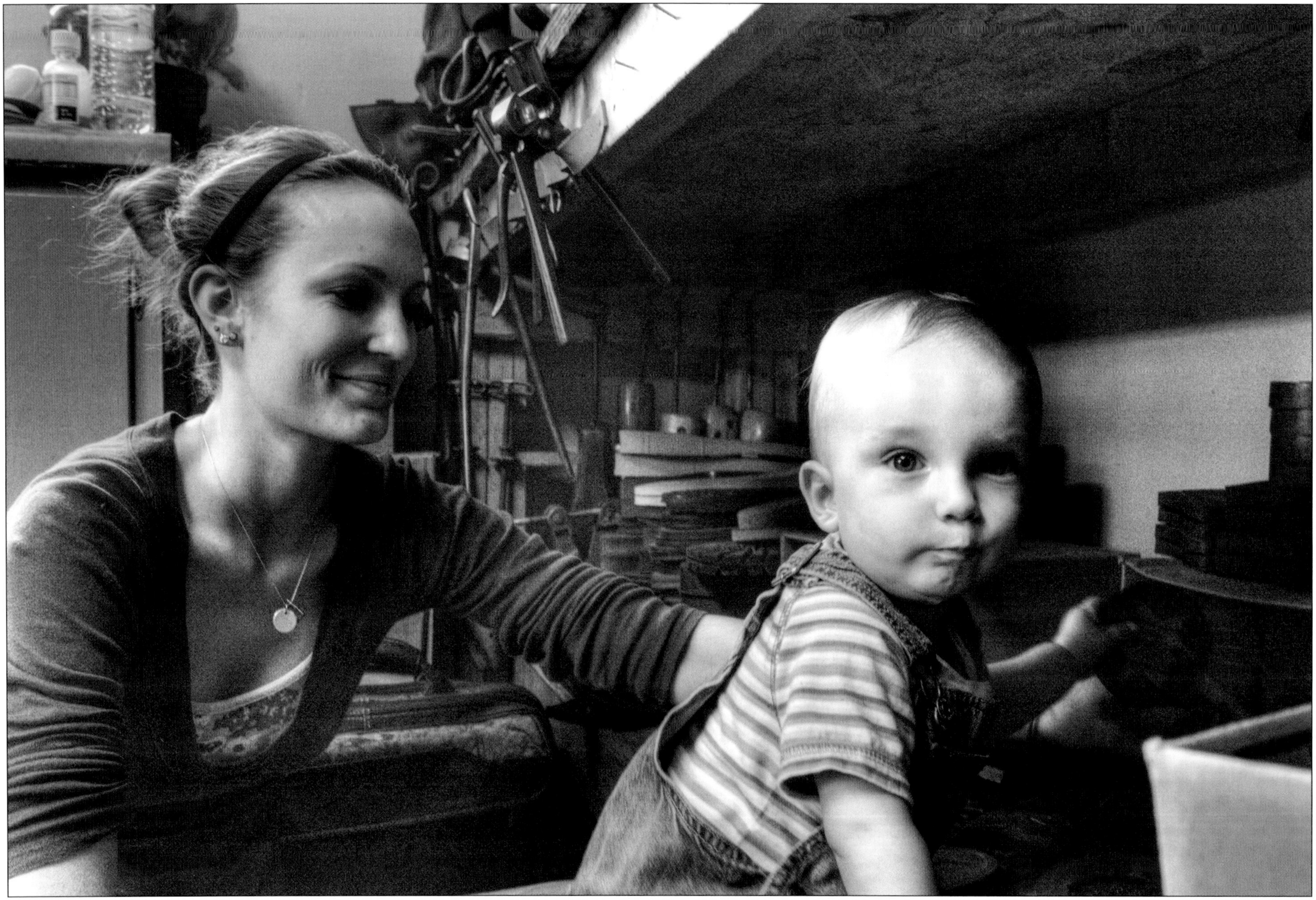

Under the Cobbler's Bench
William Fields

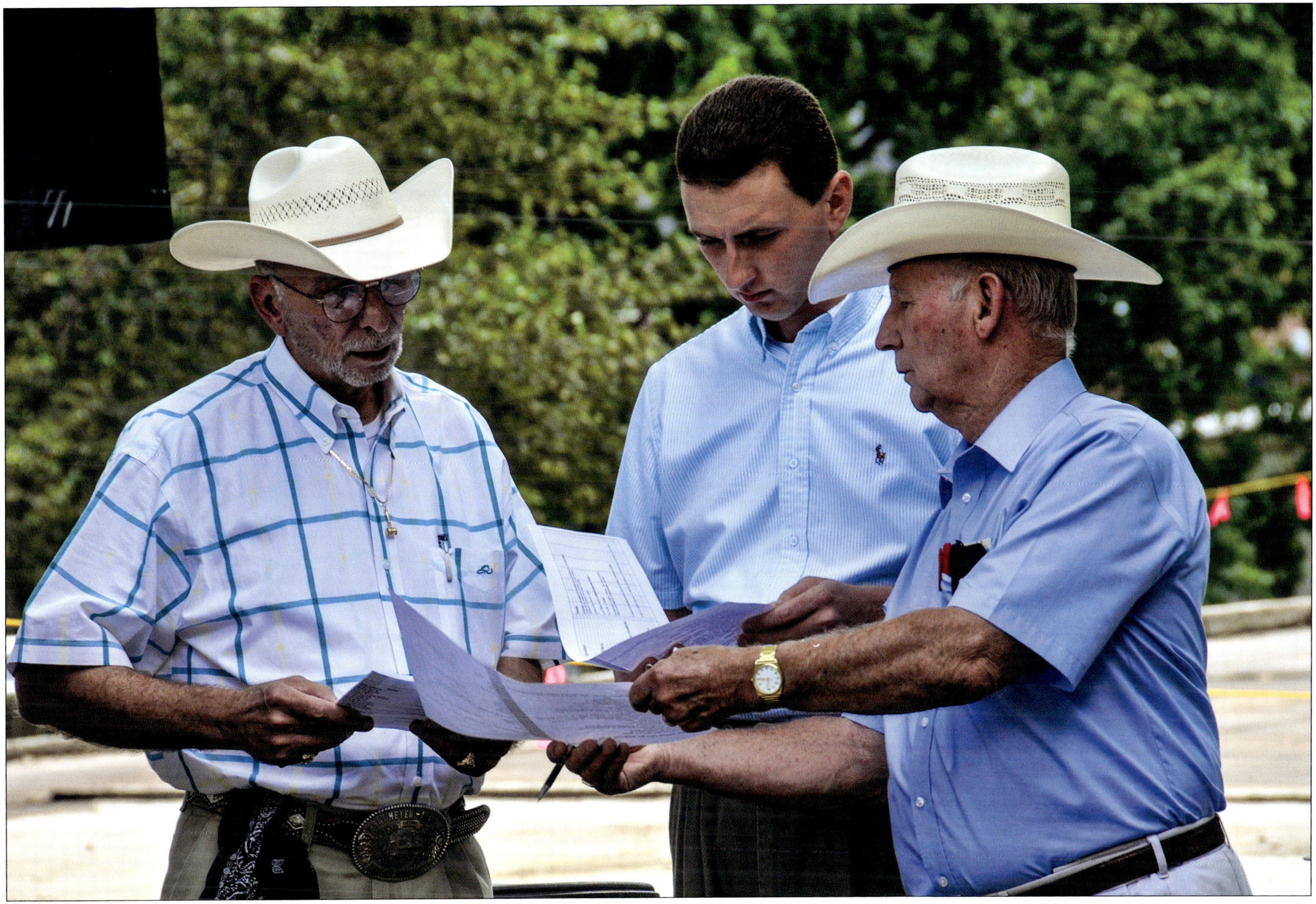

The Auctioneers
Tony Carosella

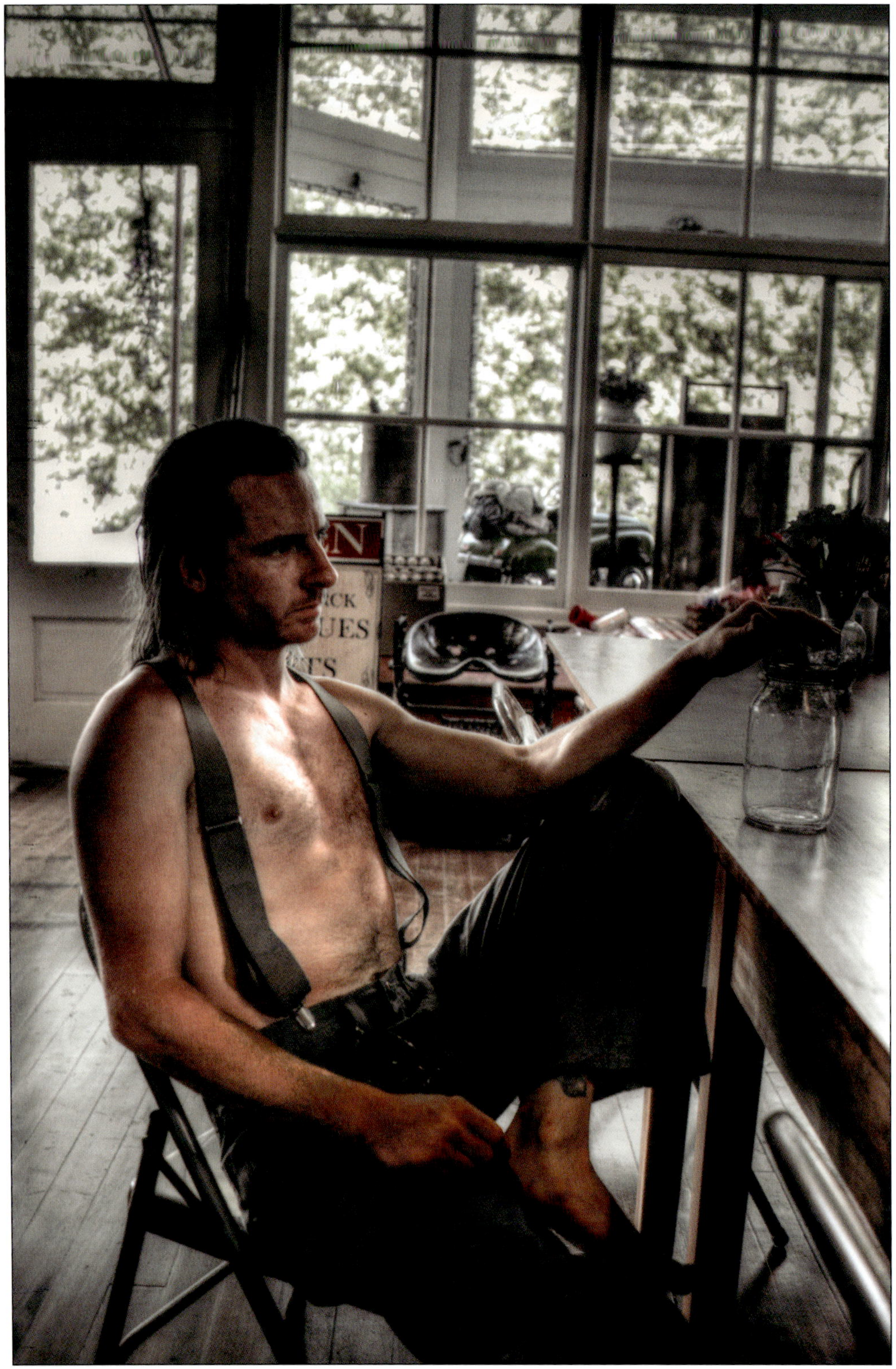

92 in the Shade

William Fields

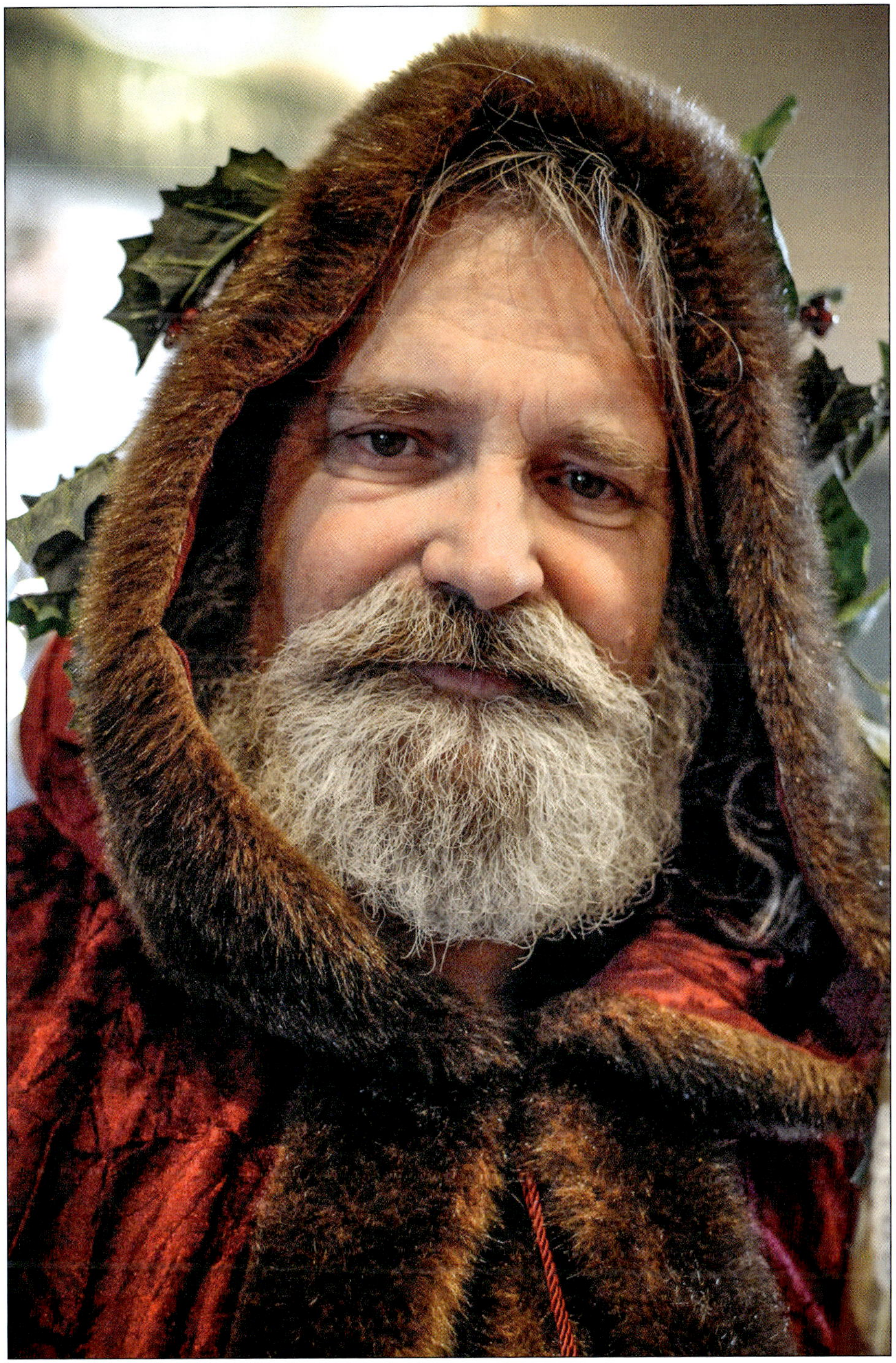

Father Christmas Terry
Tony Carosella

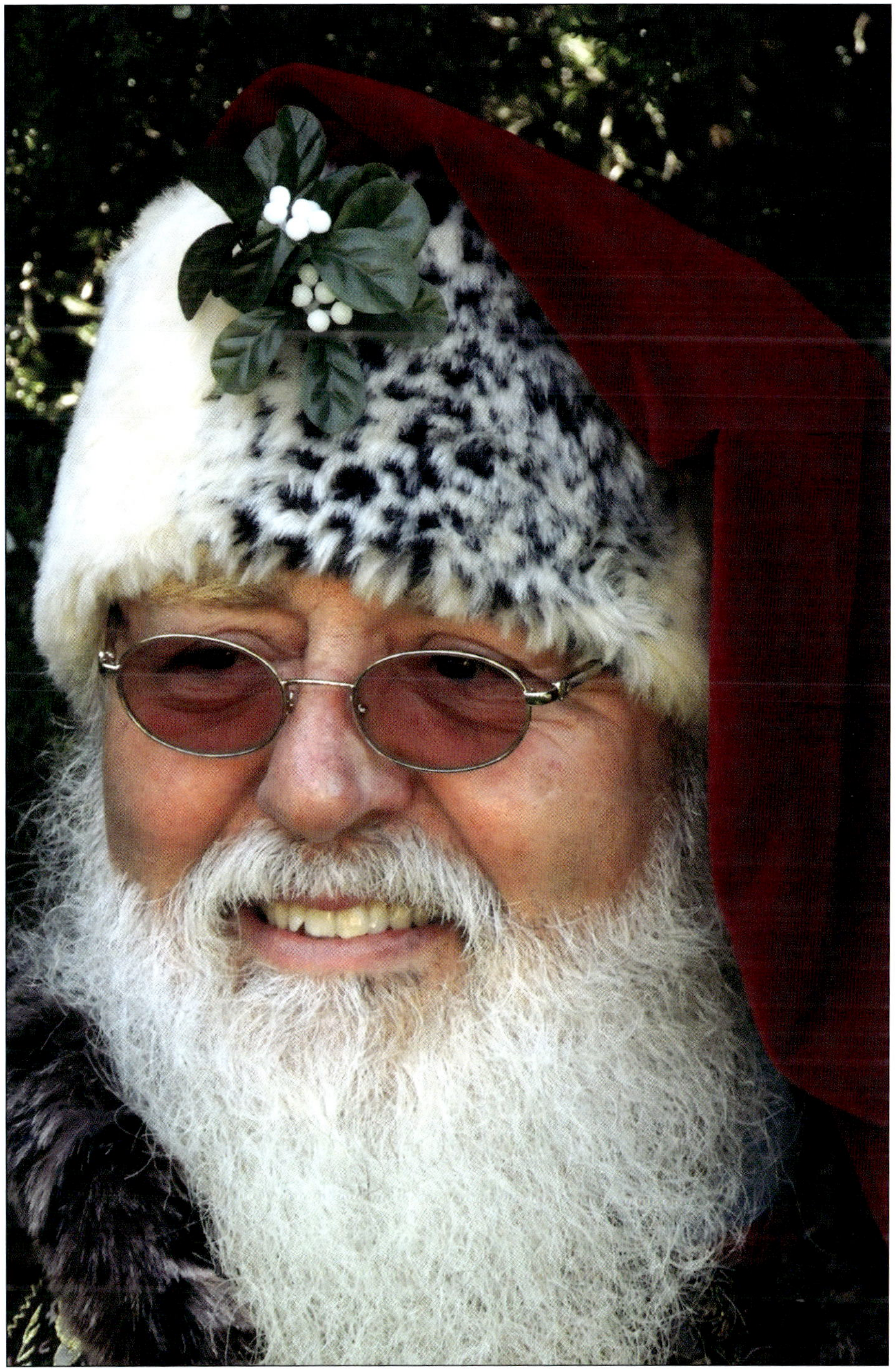

Father Christmas William
Tony Carosella

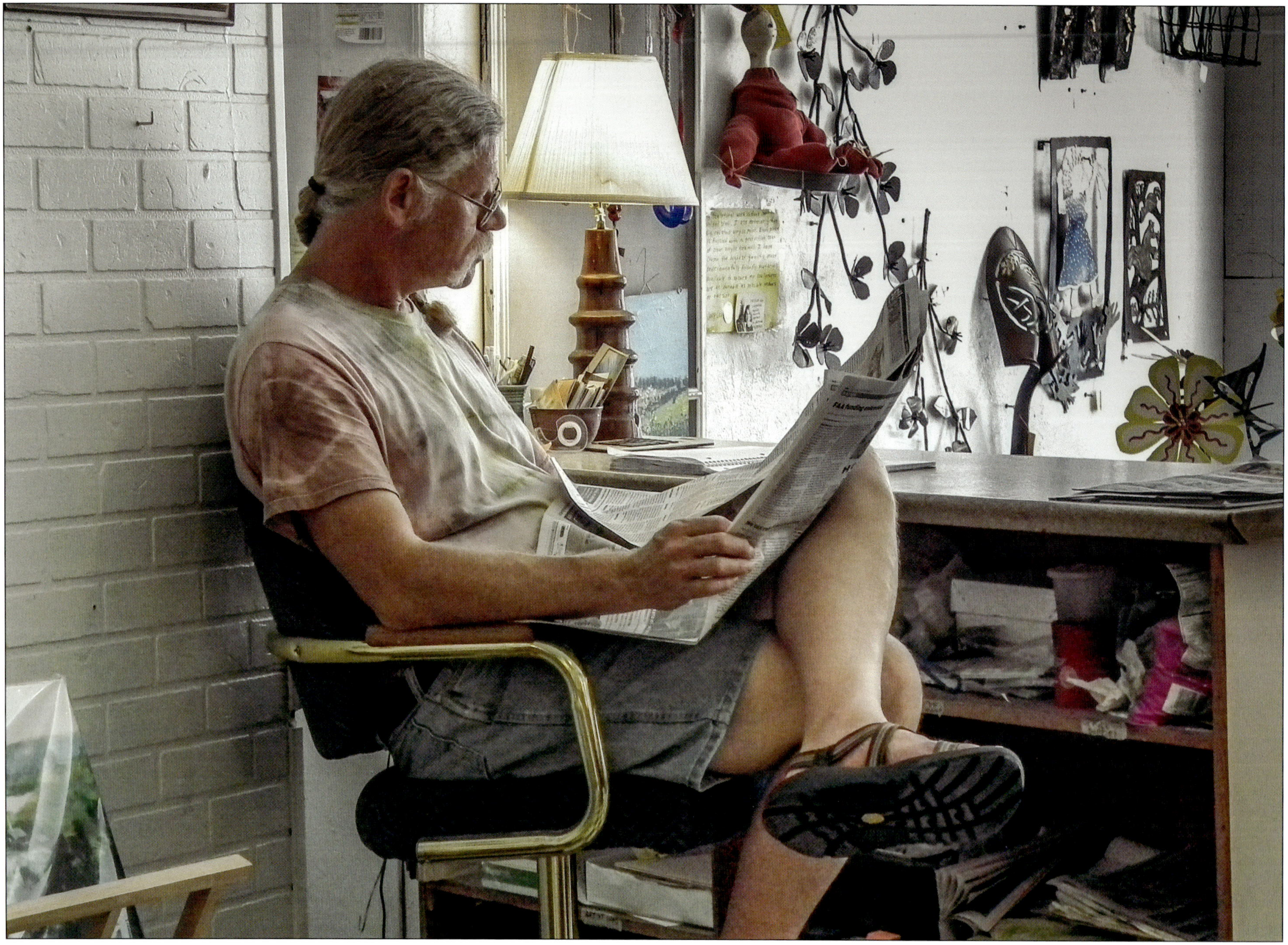

Dave at the Gallery
Tony Carosella

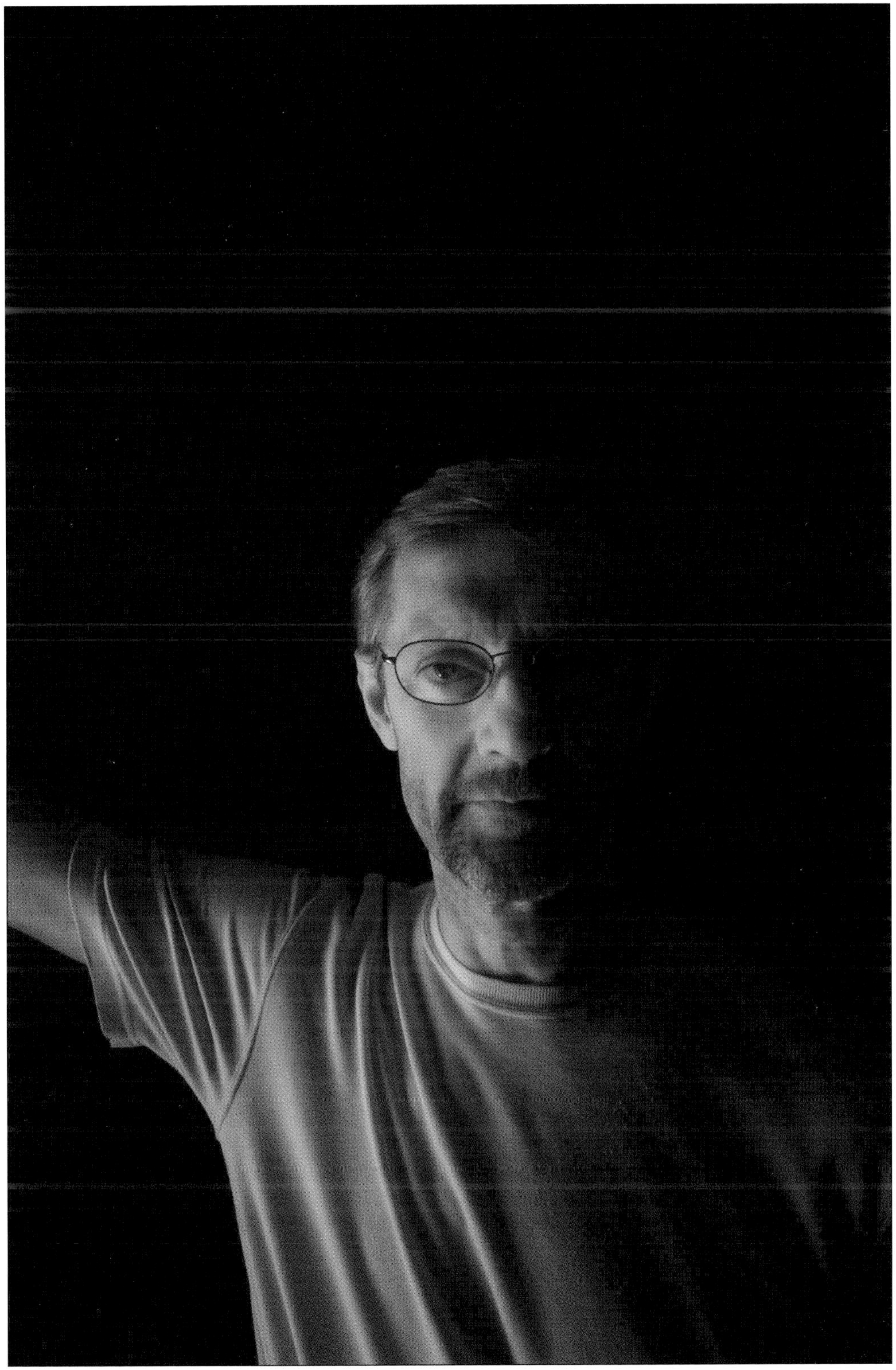

Keith
William Fields

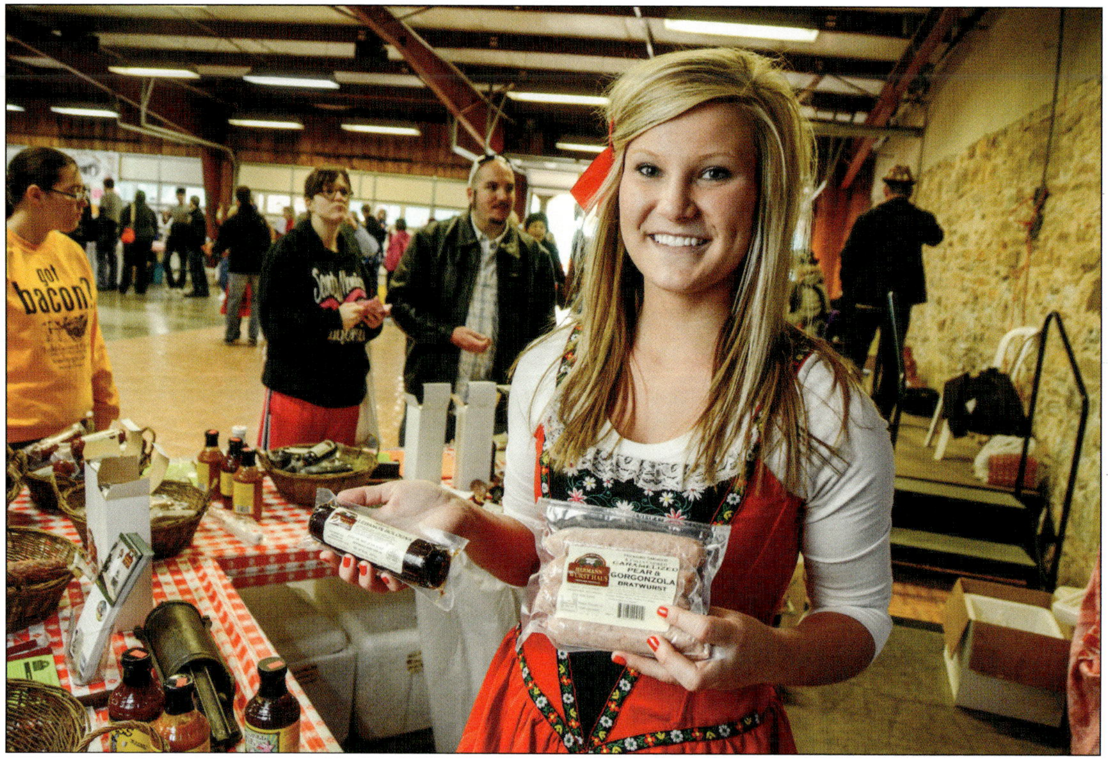

Fraulein
Tony Carosella

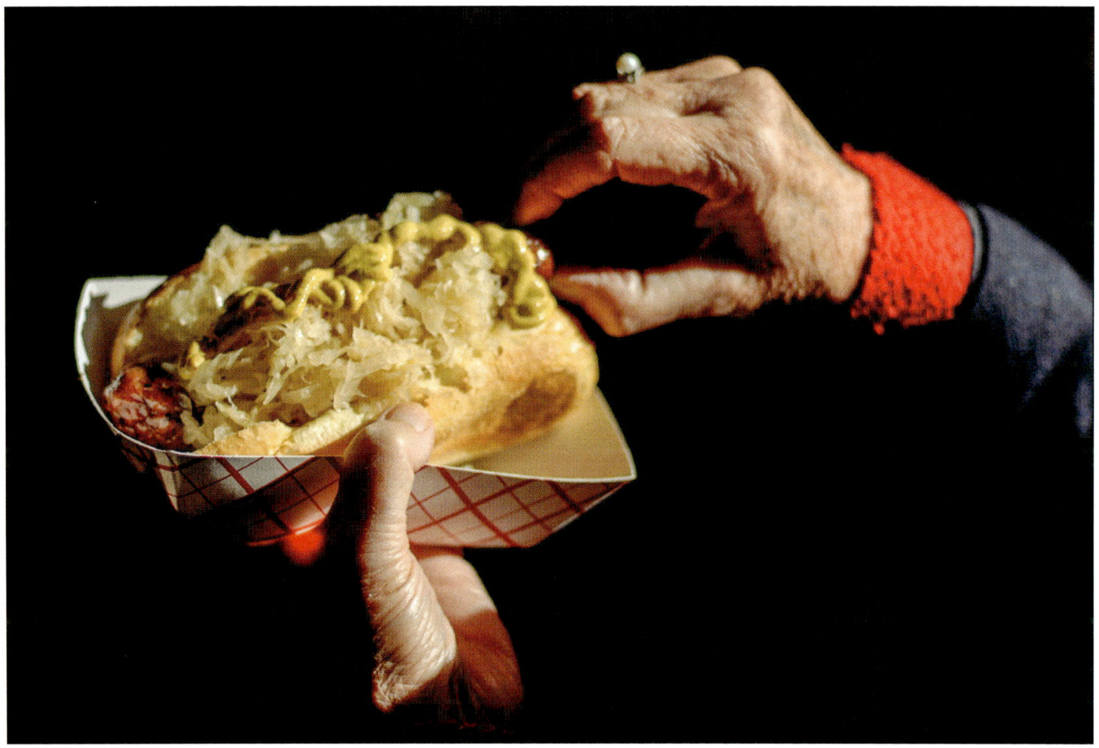

Sampling Bratwurst
Tony Carosella

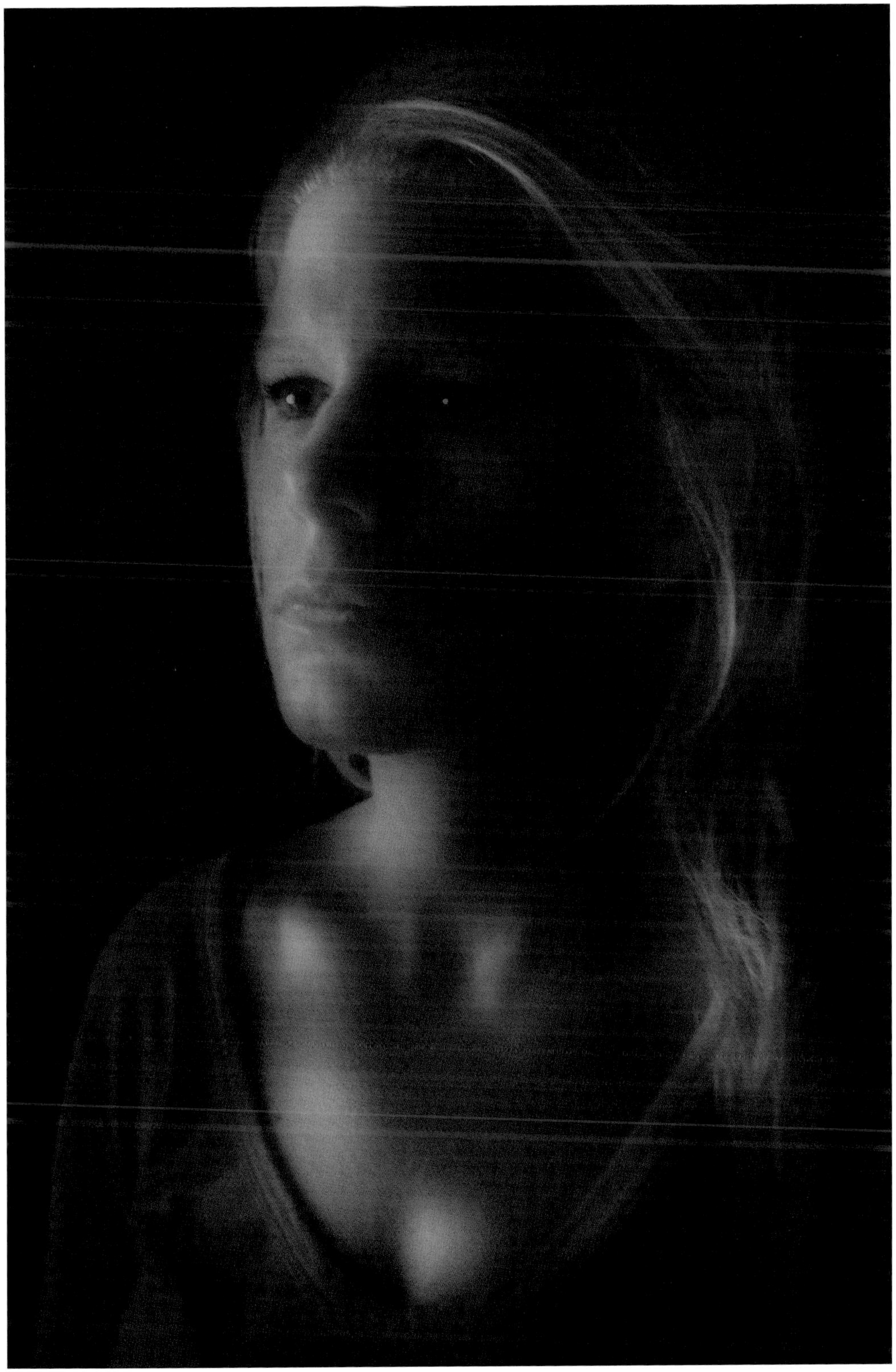

Diane

William Fields

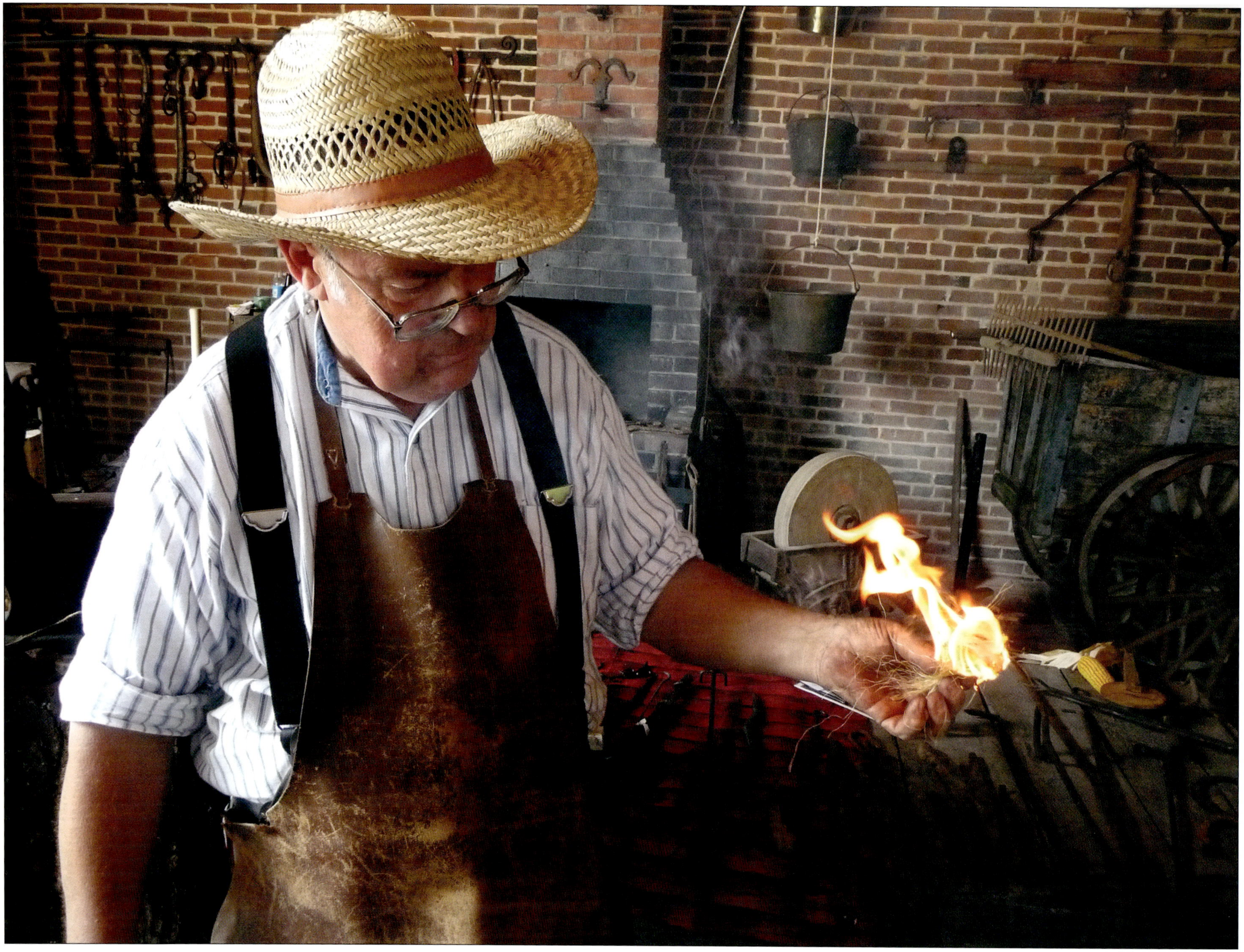

The Village Smithy Making Fire
William Fields

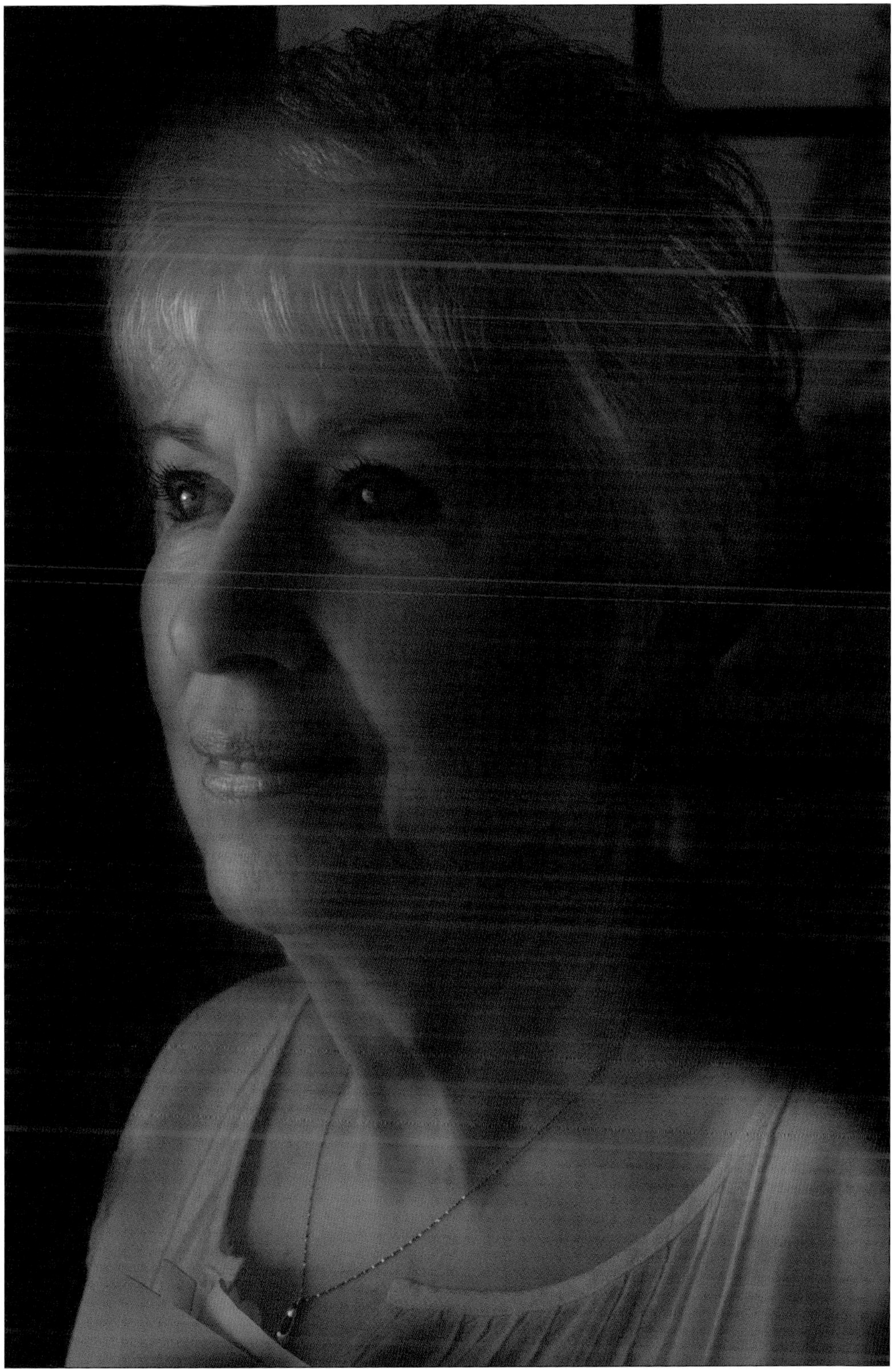

Molly
William Fields

Maifest Kids

Tony Carosella

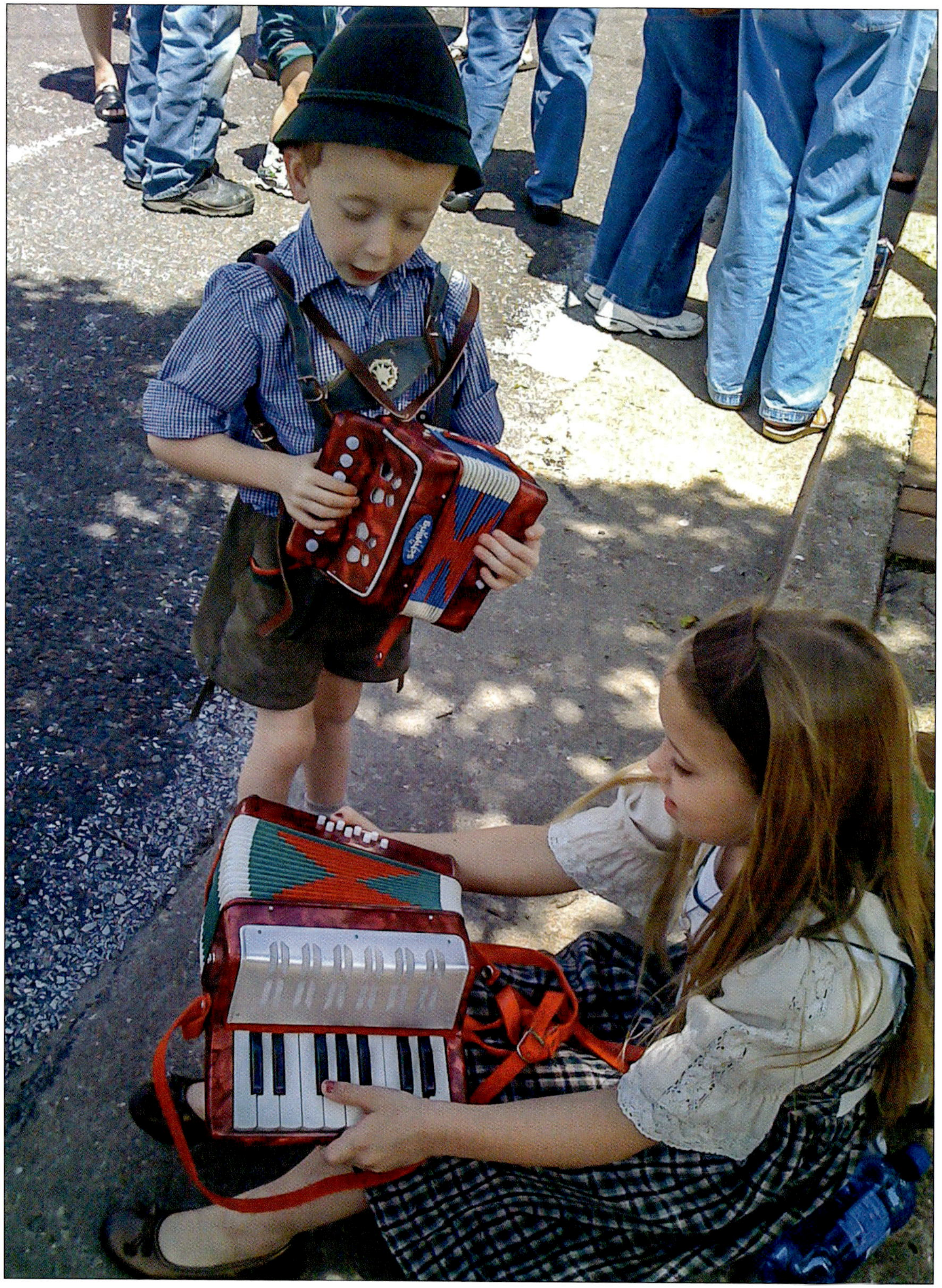

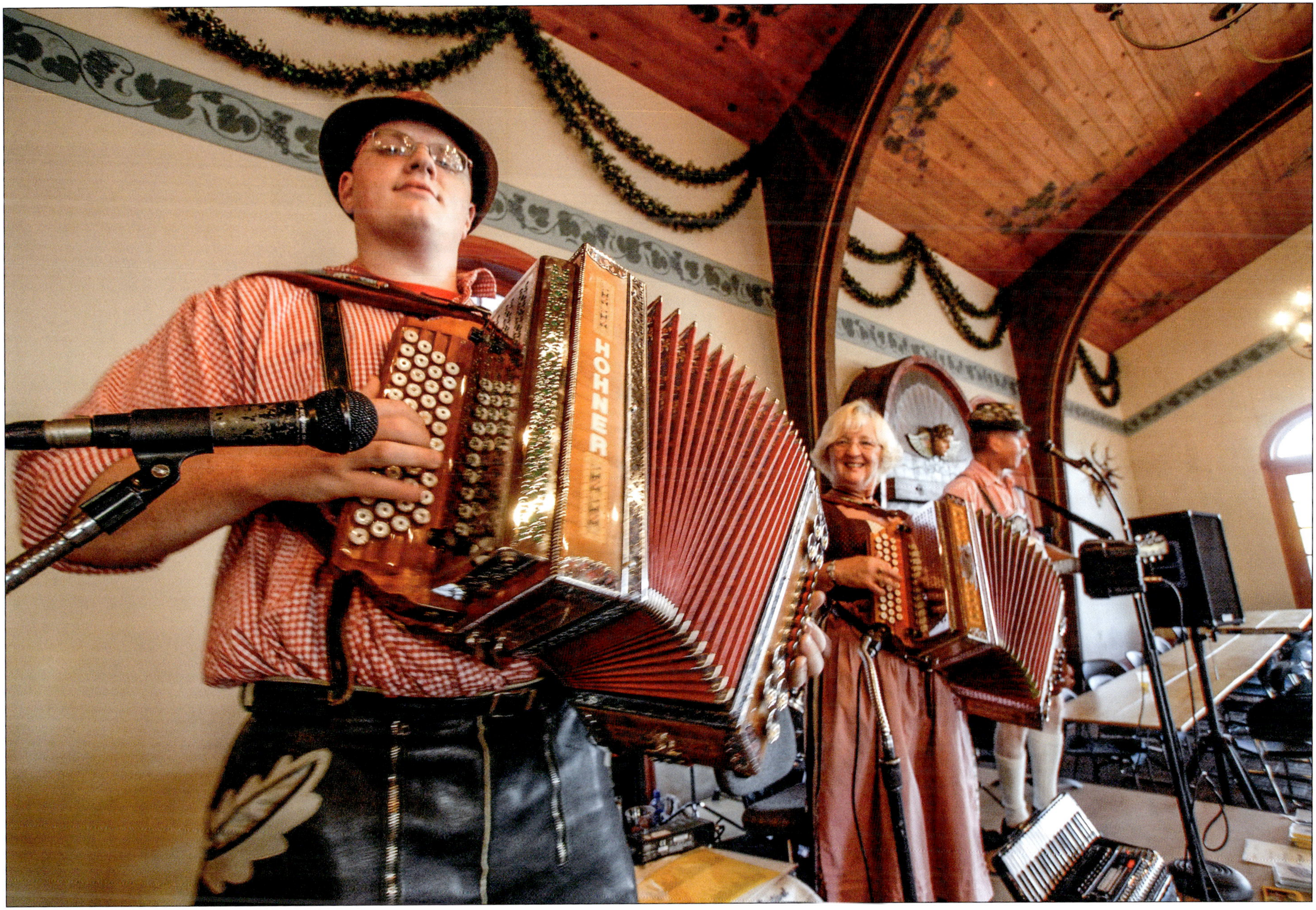

Polka Band

Tony Carosella

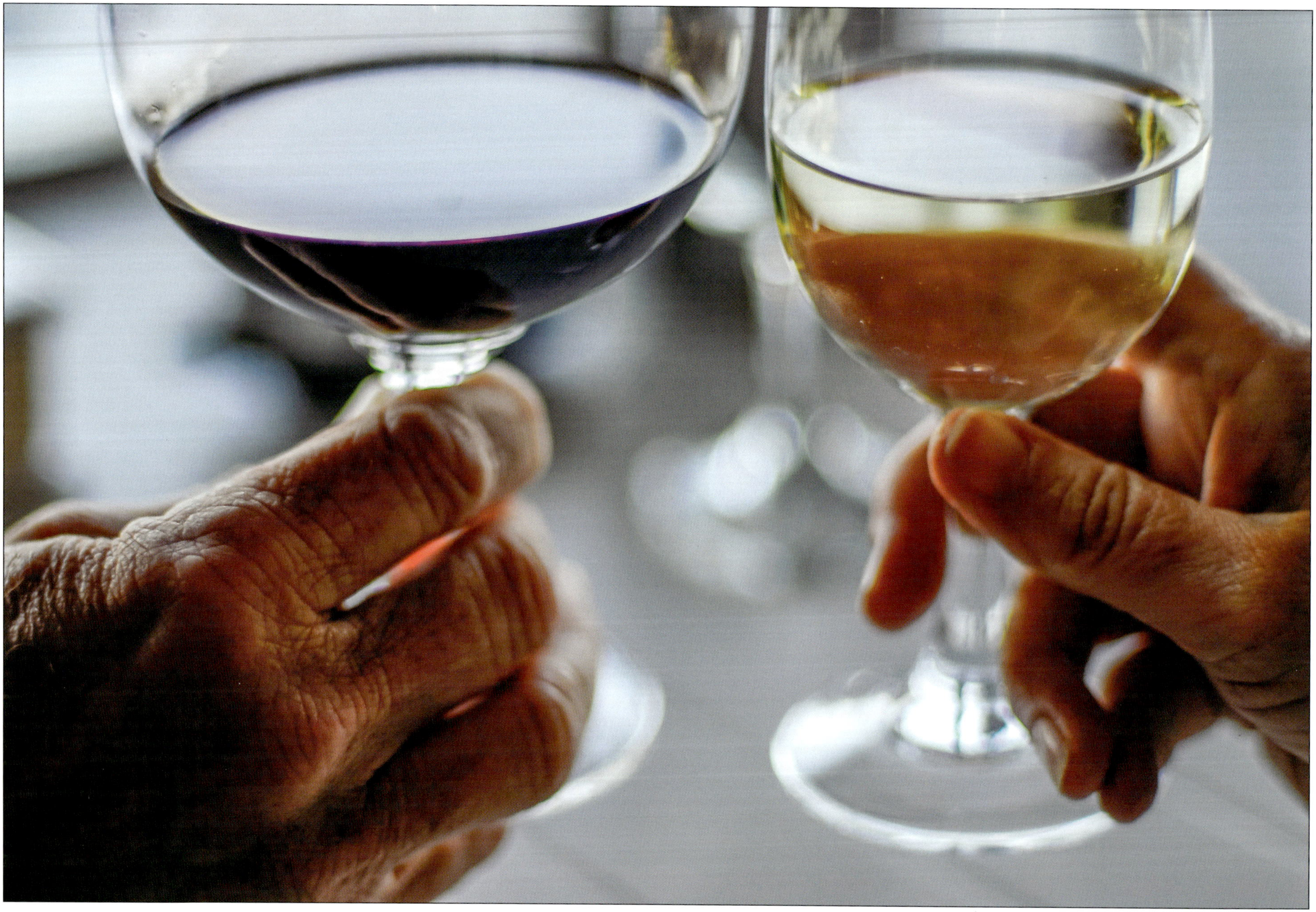

Toasting
Tony Carosella

Betty
William Fields

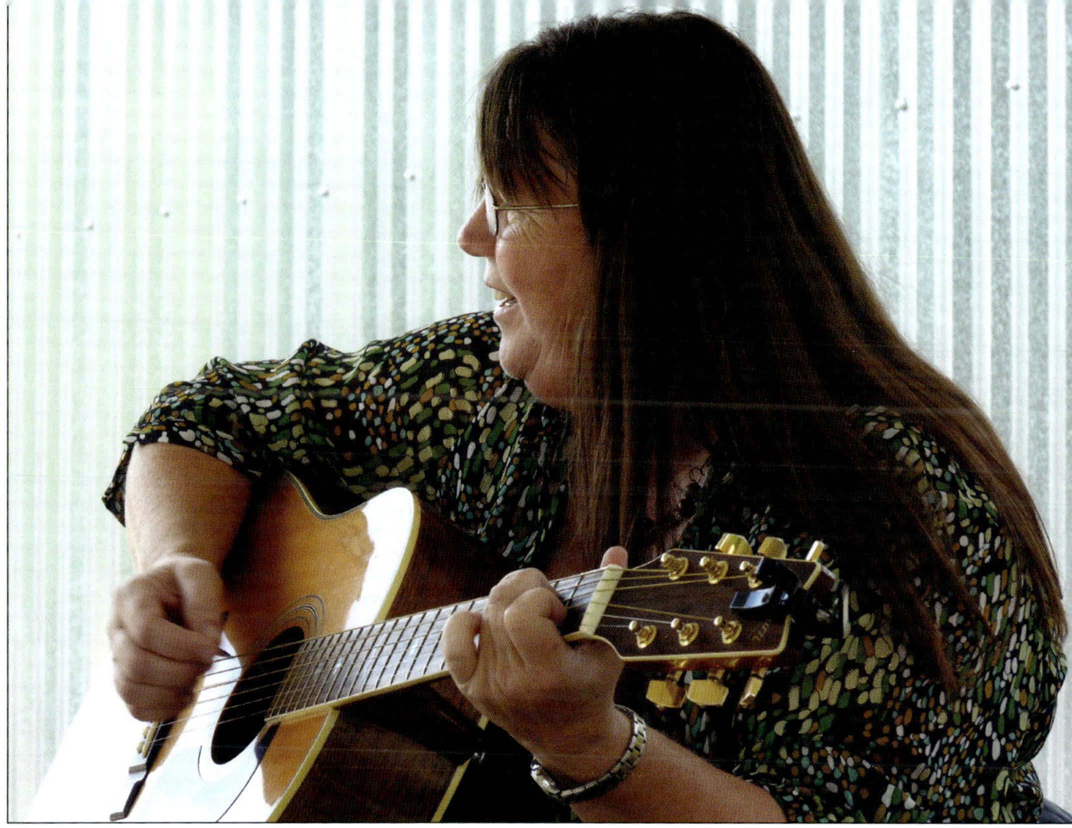

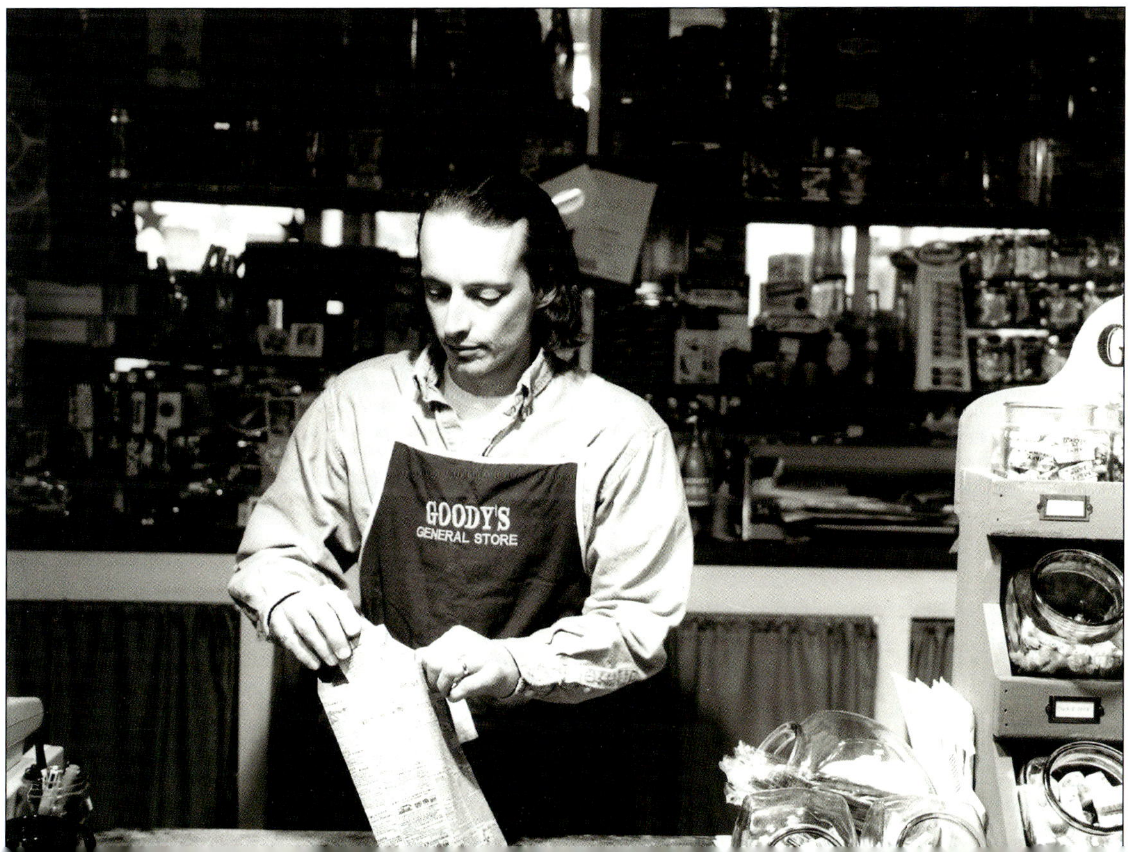

At Goody's
William Fields

Marylin

William Fields

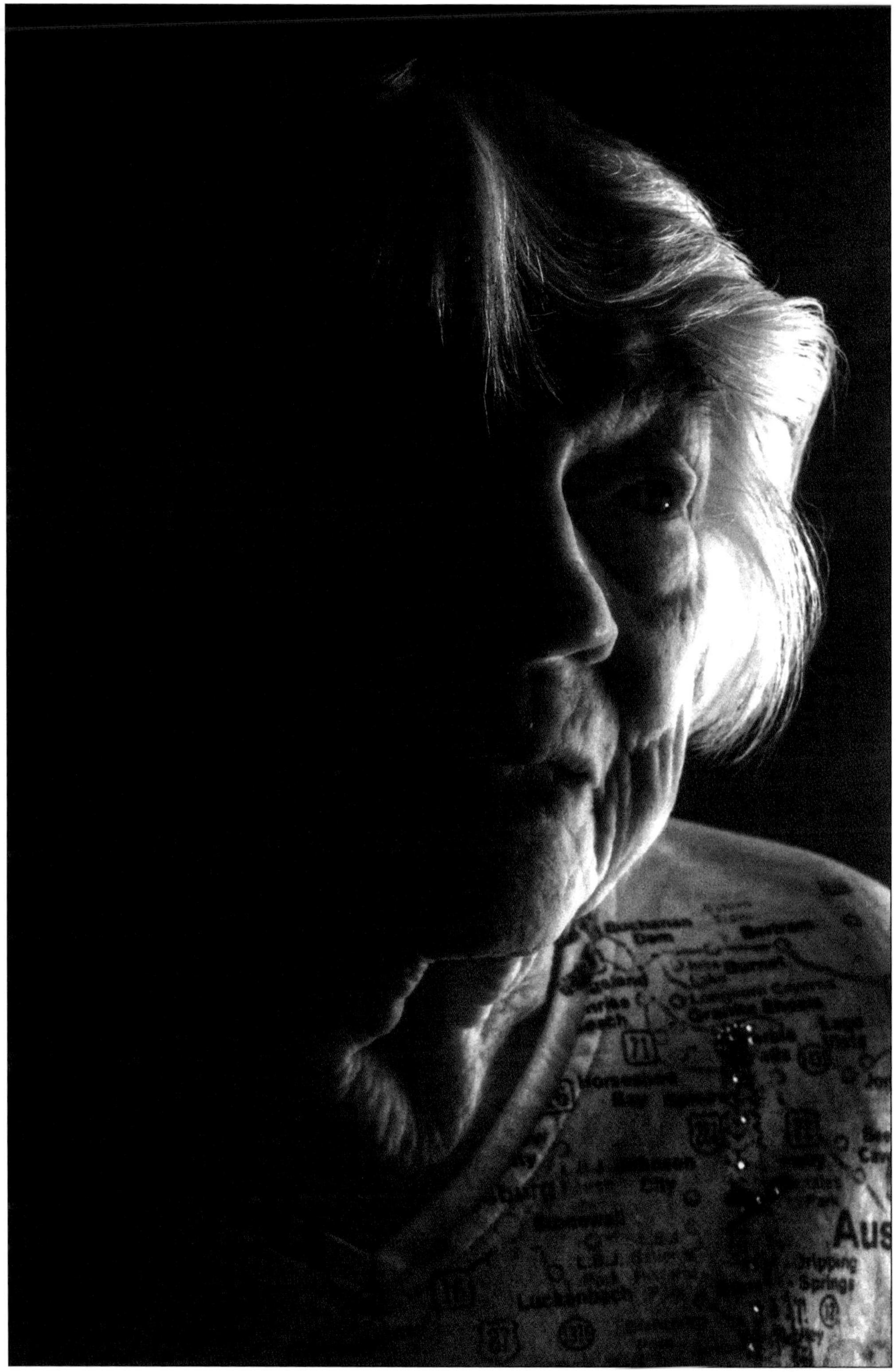

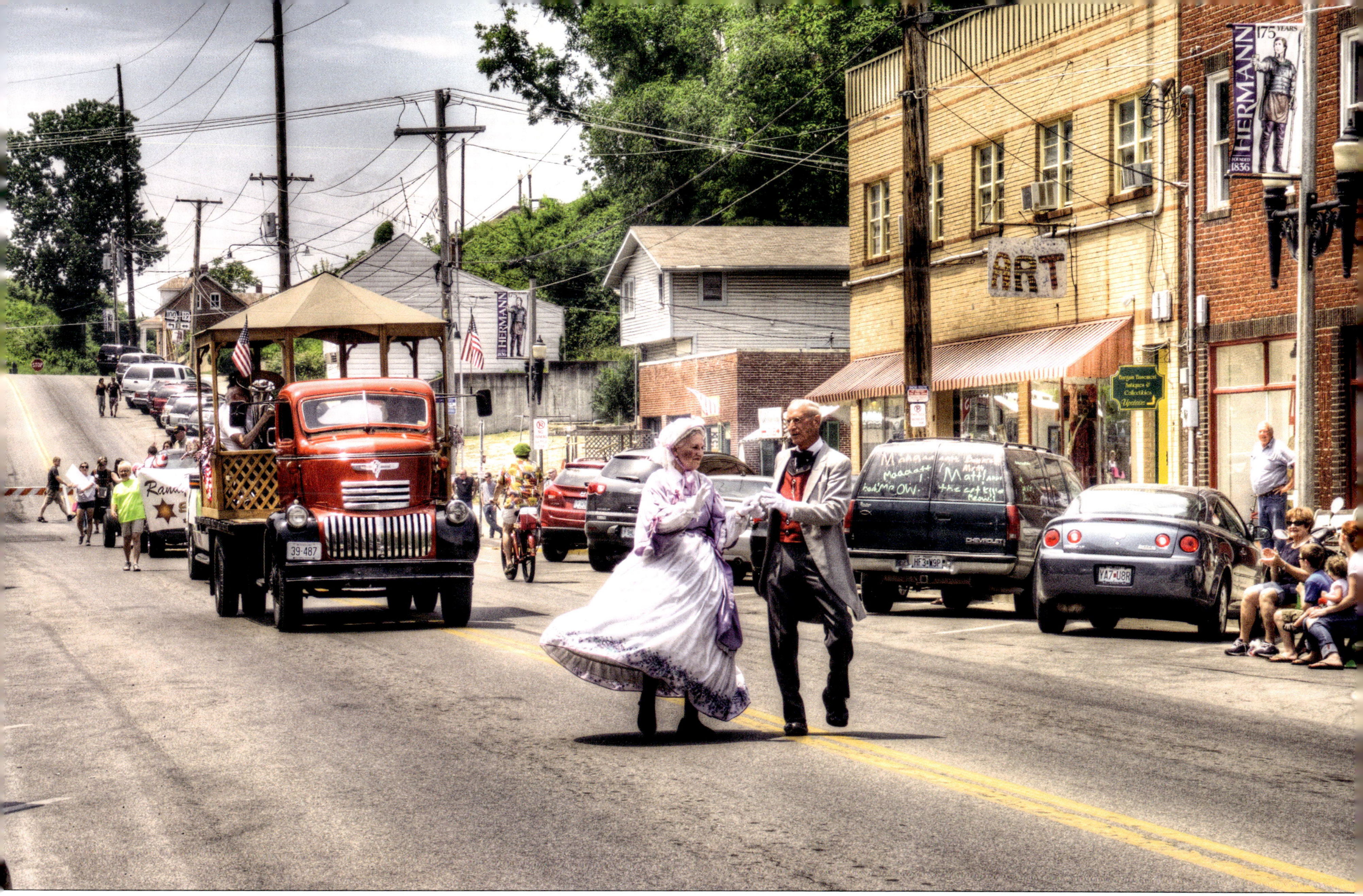

You Make Me Feel So Young

William Fields

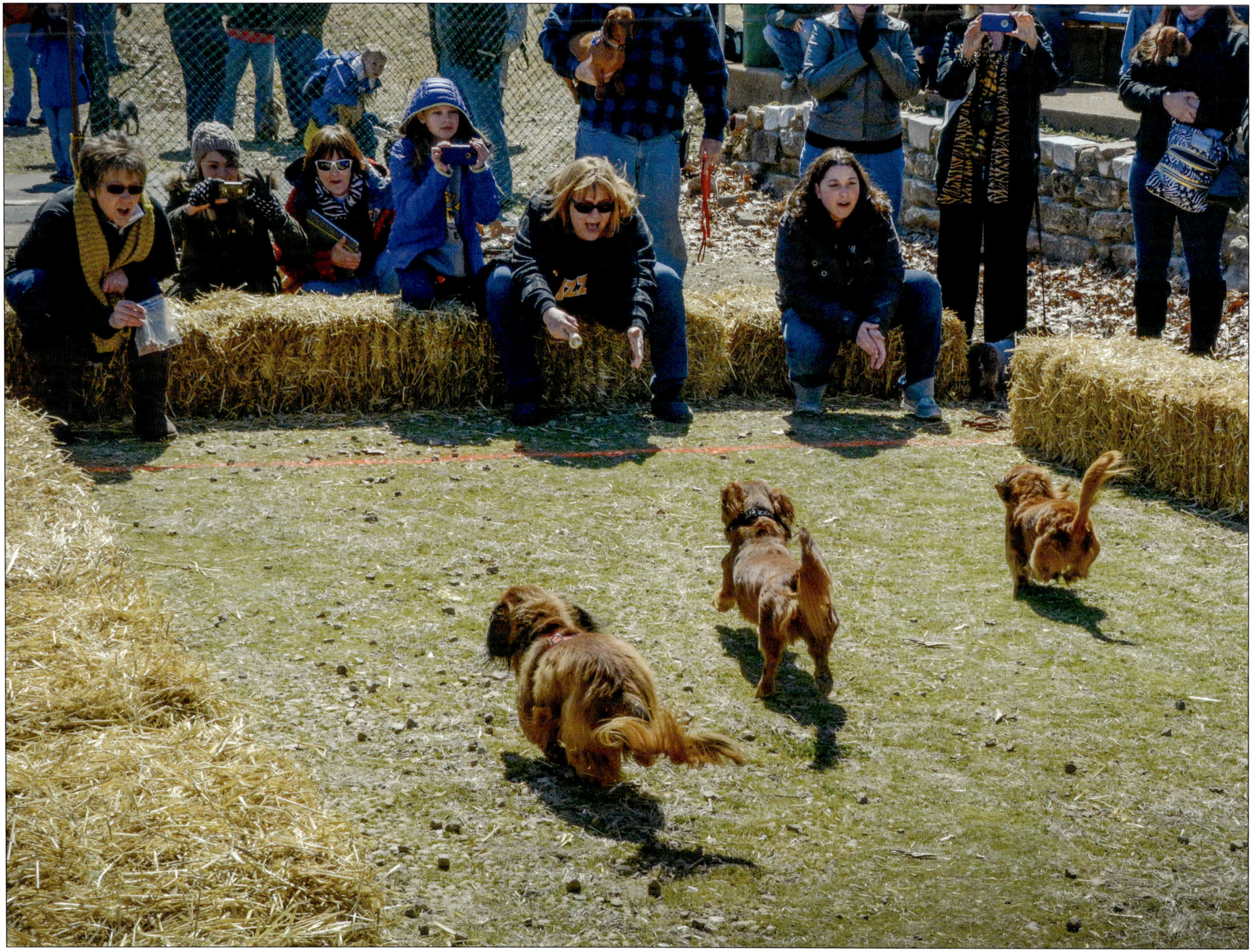

Wiener Dog Races
Tony Carosella

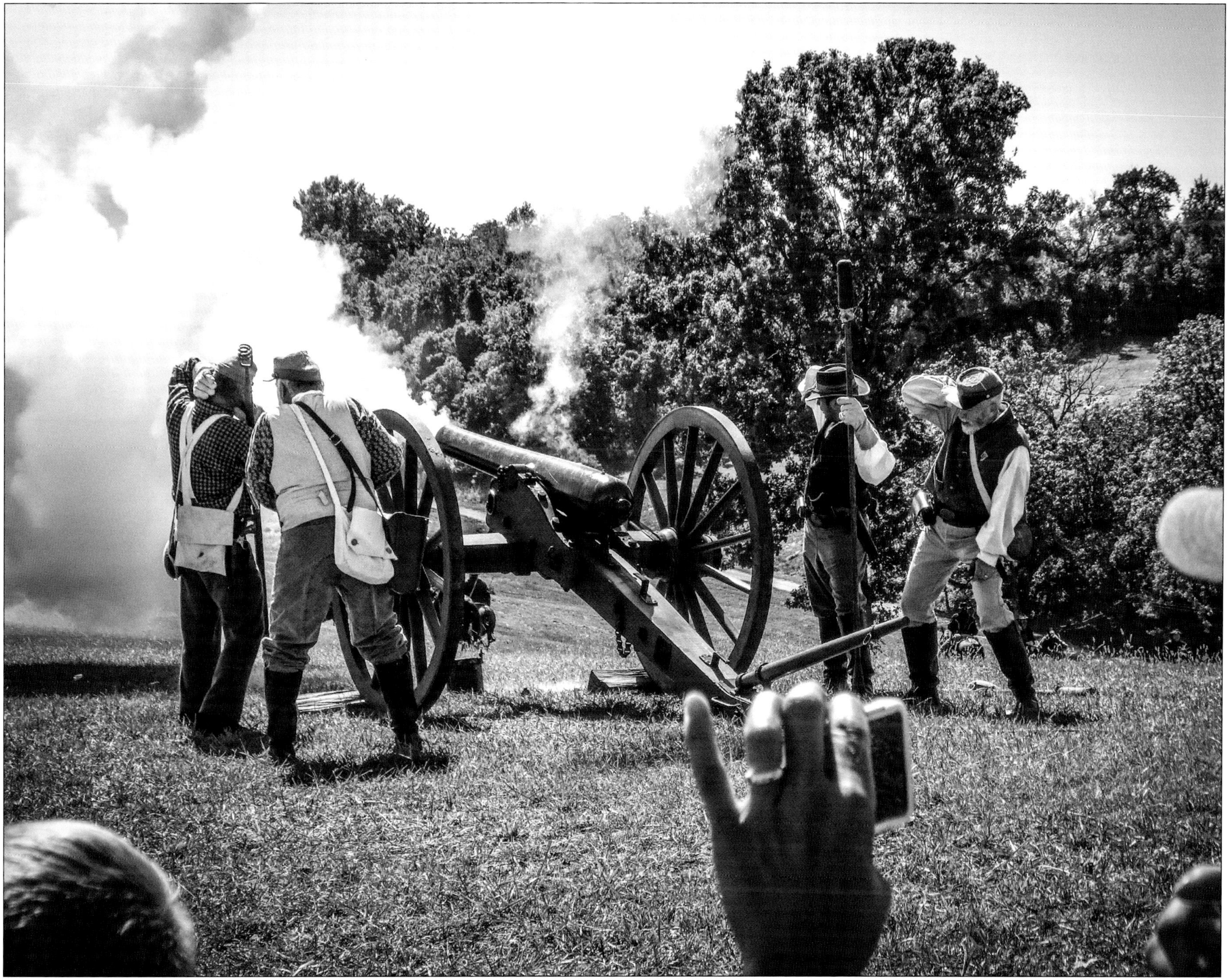

Getting the Shot
Tony Carosella

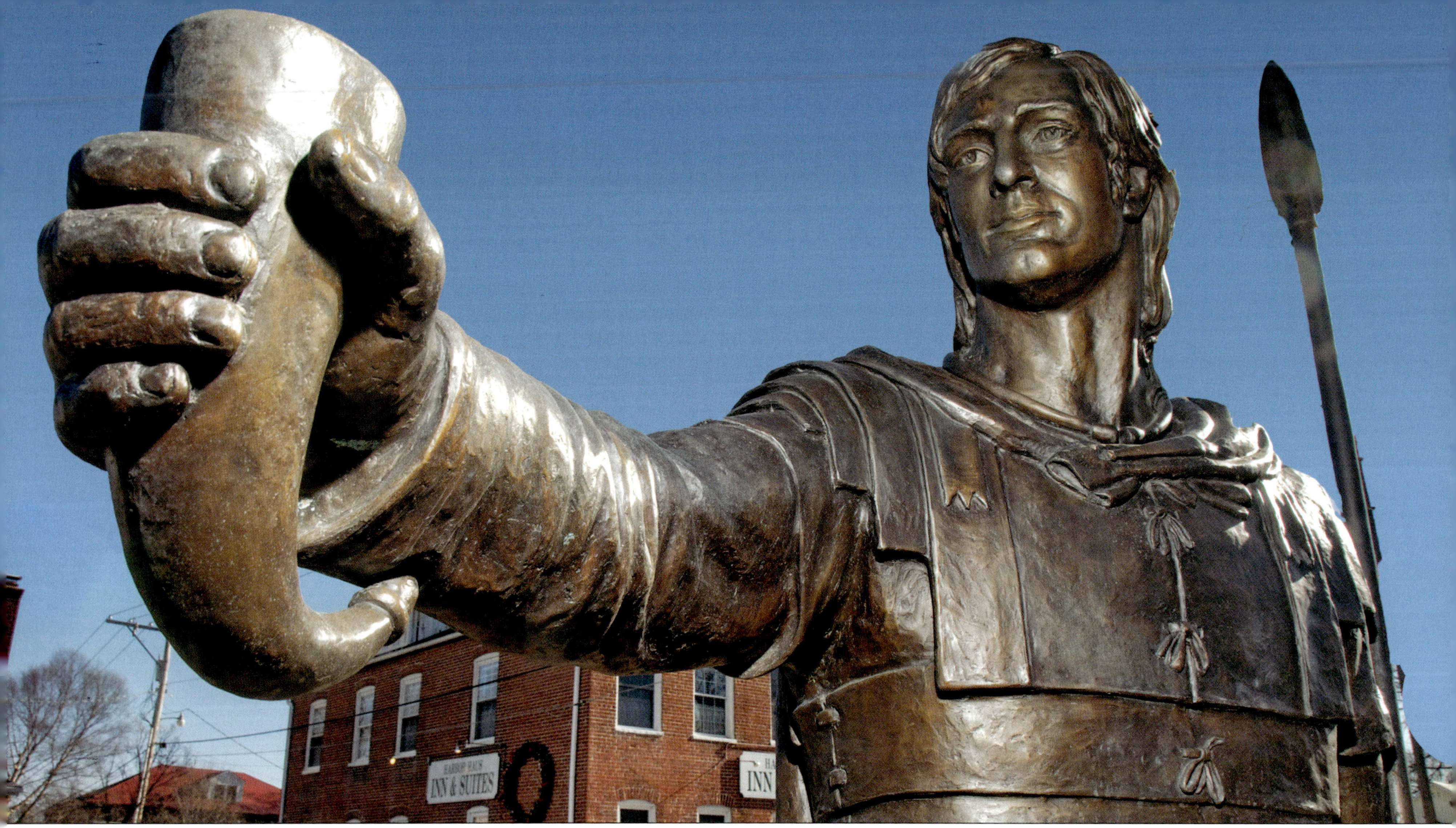

Statue of Hermann or Arminus

Tony Carosella

We questioned whether we should include this fellow in the people section because he's more of an idea than a living, breathing person, but because he's the guy the town is named for we felt we could not leave him out. Hermann, or Arminus as he was called in the first century C.E., was a Germanic tribesman who, as a scout for the Roman Army, plotted with his kinsmen to set up an ambush to run the Romans out of the territory. This statue is a fanciful interpretation that honors the German heritage of the people of Hermann and celebrates welcoming all with a cup of wine.

– William Fields

About the Artists

William Fields

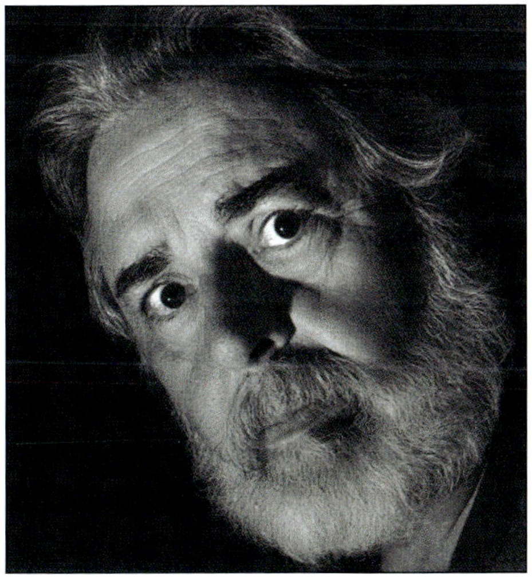

William Fields has been a visual artist throughout his entire life, creating drawings, watercolors, art prints and ultimately, fine art photographs. He became a full-time art photographer after retiring from a career in aerospace and automotive management consulting. William is devoted to and inspired by the Missouri countryside. His work has been used as set decorations on a Steven Spielberg television series and can be found in both public and private collections. He lives on a forested hilltop overlooking the Missouri River with his wife, Louise, and a dog named Smooch.

Tony Carosella

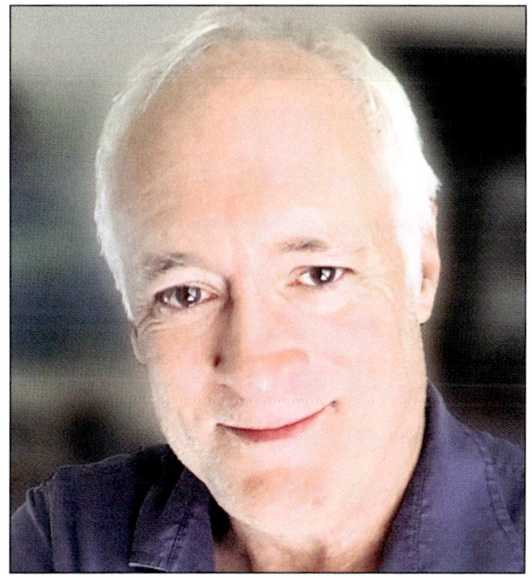

Tony Carosella began his career as a freelance photographer in St. Louis, Missouri. His clients included Industrial and Architectural firms and he traveled around documenting their projects. Tony settled in New Haven, just a little east of Hermann, and loves photographing the beauty of Missouri Wine Country.

Photograph Index